NEW EN
The most remarqueable par
by the high and mighty Pr
nowe King of great Britaine
THE PORTRAICTUER OF CAPTAYNE IOHN SMITH ADMIRALL OF NEW ENGLAND
Ætatis 37
Aº 1616
These are the Lines that shew thy Face; but those
That shew thy Grace and Glory, brighter bee:
Thy Faire-Discoueries and Fowle-Overthrowes
Of Salvages, much Civillized by thee
Best shew thy Spirit; and to it Glory Wyn;
So, thou art Brasse without, but Golde within
If so; in Brasse, (too soft Smiths Acts to beare)
I fix thy Fame, to make Brasse Steele out weare.
Thine, as thou art Virtues
John Dauies, Heref:
Schooters hill
Sandwich
Dartmouth
Ipswich
Snadoun hill
Boston
Hull
Poynt Dauies
Smith Iles
South Hampton
P. Wynthorp
Cape Anna
Bristow
Barnstable
Salem
Talbotts Bay
Fawmouth
Sangus
Charles Towne
Fraunces Ile
The River Charles
Charlton
Claiborne Ils.
P. Saltonstale
London
Oxford
Poynt Suttliff
Poynt Gorge
Cape James
NEW
Plimouth
P. Standish
GENS IN

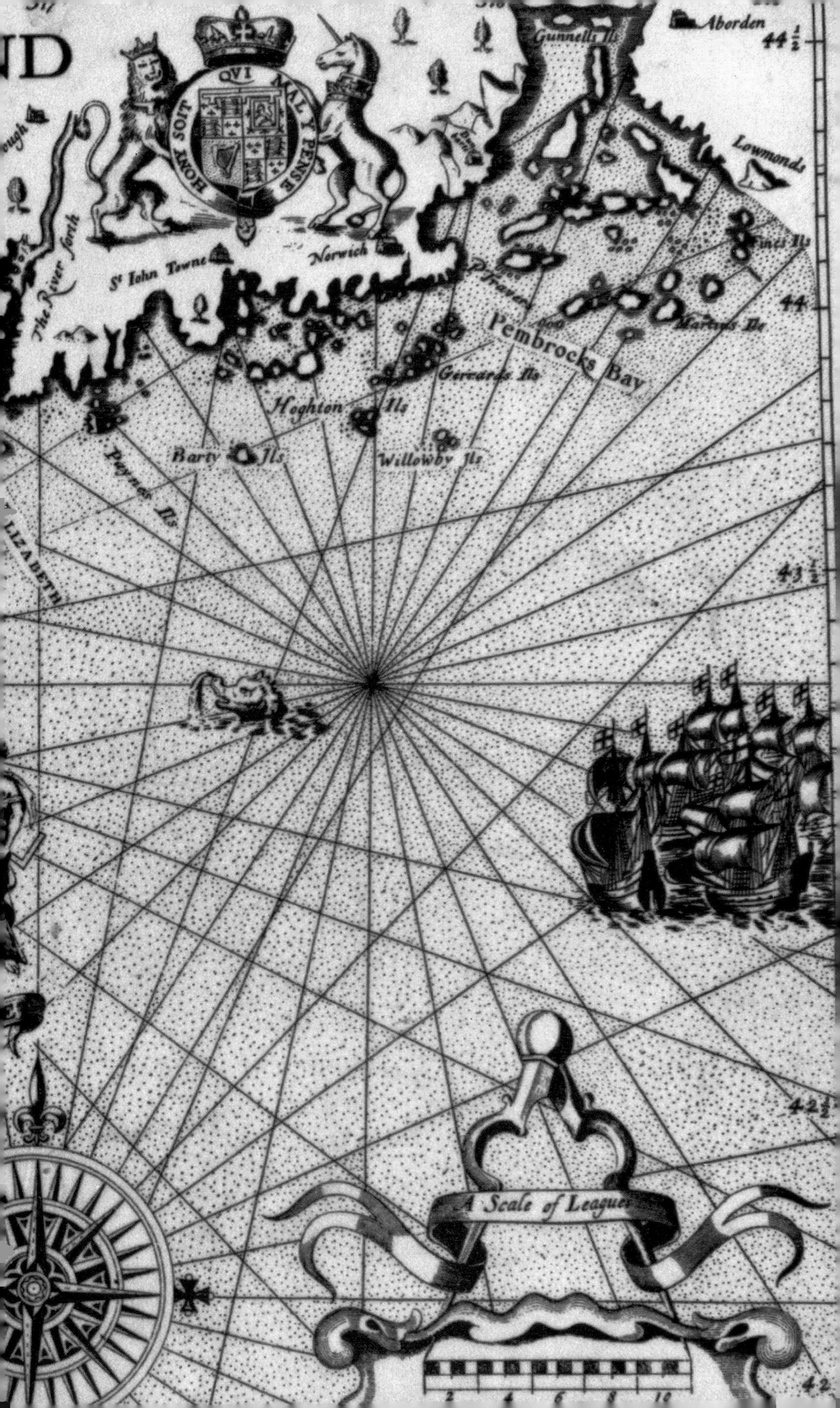
ND
QVI MALY PENSE
HONY SOIT
Gunnells Ils
Aborden
44 1/2
Lowmonds
Norwich
St Iohn Towne
The River forth
Fincs Ils
44
Pembrocks Bay
Martins Ile
Gervards Ils
Heghton Ils
Barty Ils
Willowby Ils
Paynes Ils
LIZABETH
43 1/2
42 1/2
A Scale of Leagues
2
4
6
8
10
42

Land of Lost Content

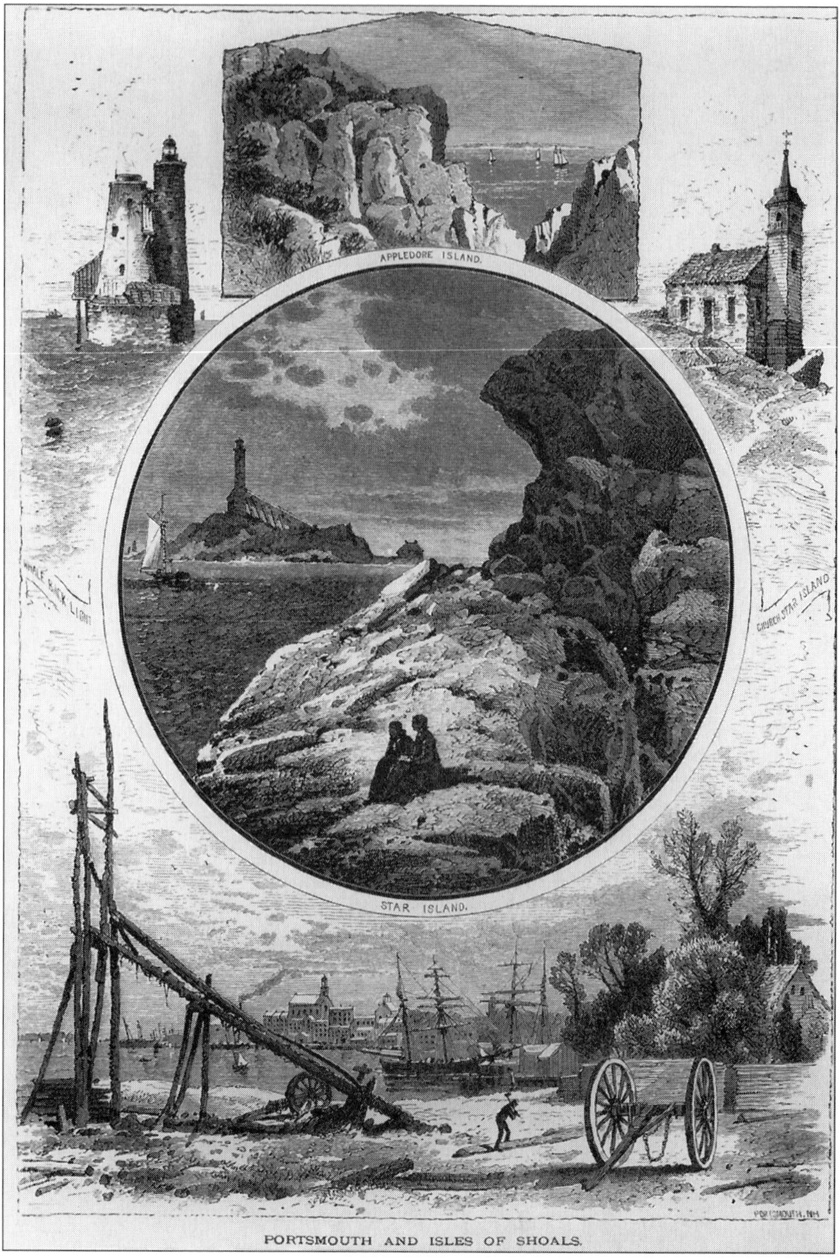

Pen and ink sketch of Piscataqua River and Isles of Shoals (New Hampshire Historical Society #4031)

LAND OF LOST CONTENT

The Piscataqua River Basin and the Isles of Shoals.
The People. Their Dreams. Their History.

ROBERT H. WHITTAKER

10 April 1995

ALAN SUTTON

First published in the United States of America in 1993 by
Alan Sutton Publishing Inc. · 83 Washington Street · Dover · NH 03820

Reprinted 1994

British Library Cataloguing-in-Publication Data
A catalogue record for this book is available from the British Library.

Library of Congress Cataloging in Publication Data applied for

ISBN 0 7509 0657 X

Typeset in 11/14 Bembo.
Typesetting and origination by
Alan Sutton Publishing Limited.
Printed in Great Britain by
Redwood Books, Trowbridge.

CONTENTS

To my father
Captain Arnold Whittaker
25 August 1917–3 October 1990

That is the land of lost content,
  I see it shining plain,
The happy highways where I went
  And cannot come again.

A Shropshire Lad, xl, Alfred Edward Housman

ACKNOWLEDGEMENTS

First of all, to my wife, Robin Lee, who was there every step of the way over the last four years as the book became our third child, while she was giving birth to Eliza Lee and Adam Arnold. I am grateful not only for her patience and support, but also for her critique, along with that of her friend Janet Stump, of the original manuscript.

To my mother, Jean Whittaker, the consummate reader and supporter, whose keen eye helped with the first reading. To my sister, Lynn Turner, and my cousin, John Hunnewell; without their help with my personal and business life, I could not have taken the time to write this book. And to my aunt, Leonice Mercer, who has seen both ends of this century and whose intellect and support and clear look on life kept the drive to finish the book alive.

To Dr. Faith Harrington, who has been conducting significant research of seventeenth-century Isles of Shoals history through endless hours of archeological "digs" at the Shoals. Dr. Faith's critique and professional help with the manuscript was invaluable to me.

To Greg and Valerie Filias, who helped immensely with the first reading, for their gifted eye in design work.

To Prudy Randall, whose lifetime living summers at the Isles of Shoals has been so unselfishly shared with me through hours of reminiscing while visiting her at Lunging Island. The bigness of her heart is matched only by the vastness of the sea she so loves.

To an old Shoals friend, Reverend Bev (Brookfield) Kinraide, whose demanding editorial critique made me see that I would need to turn my grammatical sleeves up one more roll.

To Wilbur F. LaPage, director of New Hampshire's Division of Parks and Recreation, whose dream of a residents' program at the Isles of Shoals on White Island gave me time to work on my book in the November quiet of the Shoals. Also, to Rich McCleod, who is in charge of New Hampshire's seacoast parks, for his support and assistance.

To Ray Brighton, historian *extraordinaire*, whose books on the region's history proved an invaluable resource, and his timely tidbits sent to me now and then, copied from old news accounts of nineteenth-century

Portsmouth. To all local historians, who have chronicled the life and times of the region, and to Peter E. Randall, editor, publisher, writer, and photographer, who has given those historians a means to bring their research to light through the incomparable Portsmouth Maritime Society book series. To George Sylvester, who, in his own quiet way, has amassed a Shoals photographic history of recent times which has few equals.

To Tony Codding, Oceanic Hotel manager, Star Island Corporation, and The Isles of Shoals Association for their assistance and use of rare island photos and permission to use their library and privately published books on the Shoals. To Dave and Edith Pierson, Isles of Shoals' only year-round residents, for sharing photos and stories of life on Star. To Torry Sciacca for the rare documents he supplied on the early conference era. To Dr. J. B. Heiser, Paul Littlefield & Co. from Shoals Marine Laboratory, whose unselfish assistance with the White Island project made all the difference. To John M. Kingsbury, SML founder and his providing access to Celia's garden print. To Dan and Lou Bartley, whose engineering help at my company allowed me the time needed to complete my book.

To Jim Dolph, curator of the Portsmouth Naval Shipyard Museum, who assisted me with the yard history. And to the work crew of the United States Coast Guard, who made my stay at White Island Light Station all the more enjoyable.

To Ron Titus for providing a photo of Celia's garden. To photographers Rob Karosis and Bob Billargeon. To Gary and Nancy of York Harbor Inn.

To Peter Burr, whose invaluable editorial genius helped turn my dream and my manuscript into a book. And to Alan Sutton of Stroud, England, who had the courage to gamble on this first-time writer.

And finally, to Bob Tuttle, who for the last two years has been a friend and confidant, a co-lover of the Shoals mystique, a reader of the first manuscript, and supplier of photos; to him I am forever indebted. To all of those people who over the years have kindly offered their family stories concerning the region, and the memorabilia, and the rare books they donated so willingly. To Portsmouth, without the support of its city fathers and its people I would not have been a part of its waterfront history. To the State of New Hampshire and its port authority, without their support over the last twenty years, my ferry service would not have survived the way it has. To those who have been left out through my oversight, I thank you.

ROBERT H. WHITTAKER

INTRODUCTION

In writing this book I have answered the requests of the many people who for years have listened to my stories. Four years ago I decided to write them down. I thought I would need only a weekend at most to finish my personal account of the history of the Piscataqua River Basin and the Isles of Shoals.

Soon I discovered not two, or three, or even a dozen weekends would be enough time. The difficulty, at first, was where to start; how much of this history should I include; how detailed should I be? I knew that the lie of the land was what I loved most about this region, with its knobby granite Isles, the deep swift waters of the Piscataqua River, and the rich fertile valley that borders it. The lie of the land it was that attracted life to the region thousands of years ago. So, with this fundamental understanding, I found my starting point: to describe the land.

I wrote in chronological order, highlighting the major events that have made this region stand out in American history. However, something was missing. I found that I was simply repeating in time-line fashion what had been written many times over the past 150 years. I began to sense that there was far more to this particular history than I had originally thought. What was it that made this region's history stand out from the rest?

Eventually the pieces began falling into place. The picture that lay before me was the picture of America on a small scale. A picture emerged showing great people who possessed great dreams, and the courage, the vision, and good fortune to realize their goals and fulfill those dreams. The picture also revealed a region that at times, when it lacked those certain people of vision and leadership, became diminished in its quality and importance.

The dynamic people of the region were not those who followed popular trends. This became evident during my reading about the first English immigrants to central New England. Men and woman who became known as "the Shoalers" left us a rich heritage of self-reliance, a self-reliance that lately seems diminished in our land. Though the revolutionaries fought for and gained their freedom, they were their father's children. Their own descendants would become a mirror which reflected the same image of repressive control once so feared and hated by the colonists.

The names John Paul Jones, Samuel Adams, Paul Revere, and George Washington are familiar to all Americans; they all played a part in Portsmouth's history. David Thomson, William Badger, Thomas Laighton, Celia Thaxter, Thomas Elliott, and John Kingsbury, are names less likely to be widely known, yet each of them has affected American history with their own vision and dreams.

This is not only a book about great people who accomplished great feats, but also about how this land and its people failed at times to hold on to that greatness. Because of my love of this land, I found myself searching the natural world for a similar history. I found it in the history of the Colorado River. As you read on through the book you, too, may see the similarity. In the beginning the river was only a trickle running down from the snow fields but fresh, clear, full of vitality and eager to move on down the mountain. Because of that eagerness the river attracted other mountain waters, as it turned into a powerful force that cut the land into a deep and grand canyon, a tribute to its relentless determination and freedom. Once history was made the river waters were trapped and tamed by dams and aqueducts, which dictated when and how they would flow, until all vitality was drawn off, save for a trickle that found its way to the Gulf of California. This is an ending which has not yet been written for the river Piscataqua and the Isles of Shoals and which can therefore be avoided. If area leaders are willing to look beyond hopeless attempts to legislate a perfect world and are compelled to do what instinct tells them is right, there is hope. If they possess the courage required to guide the region forward into the twenty-first century and a vision coming not from the intellect but rising from gut feelings, as it did for those people who left their mark upon the land, we hope a different fate may be written.

There will be those readers who wish I had dedicated more time to one part of this history or another. To them I respectfully recommend they turn to the bibliography for a list of fine history books on the region. It was tempting to wander from the book's theme and lose myself and the reader in the process. For those scholars and historians who are more versed in the details of the local history than I am, who might find this book too thin to do the region's history justice, I can only say that the book's course was set in such a way as to best avoid the reefs and sandbars and false channels upon which similar books have occasionally been wrecked. Finally, by spending my entire life on the waters of the region and being a part of its history, my personal bias cannot but touch the book throughout; thus I disqualify myself from being an impartial historian.

Of the many fine histories that have been written about the Piscataqua River basin and the Isles of Shoals, few attempt to give the reader a broad view showing how this particular history ties in with that of New England and the rest of the country. There is a common thread drawn from the land of the "Drowned Valley," through New England, and through all of America, a thread which links our rich and wonderful past with the present, a thread which I hope will someday be woven into the fabric of the future my children will inherit.

We never know how high we are
Till we are called to rise
And then, if we are true to plan
Our statures touch the skies.

No. 1176, st. 1, Emily Dickinson

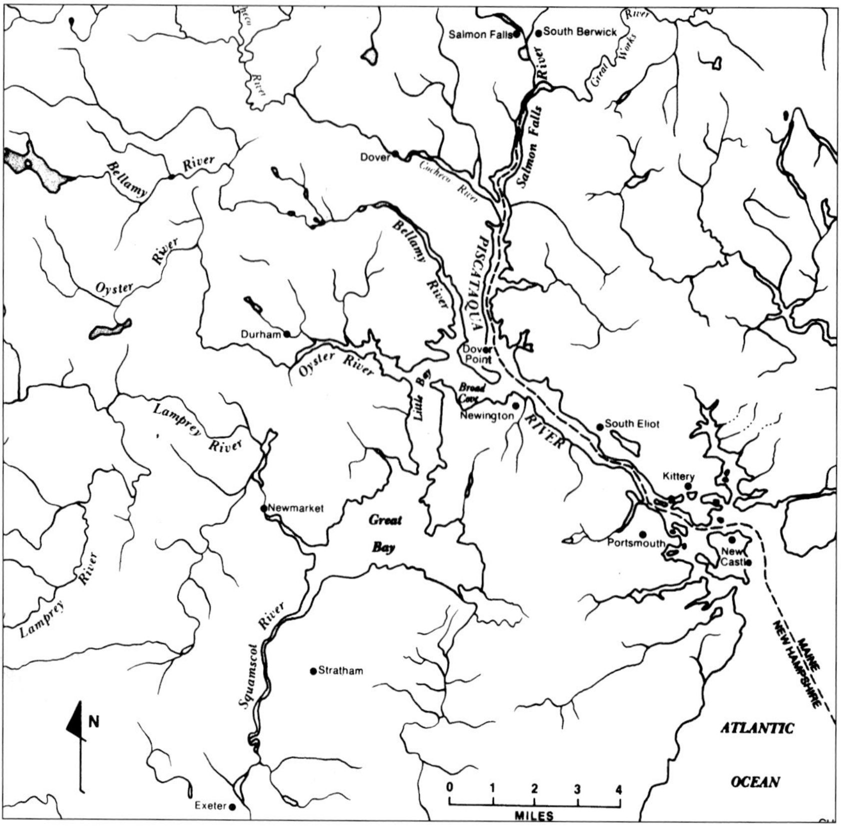

Sketch of Piscataqua River basin (John P. Adams)

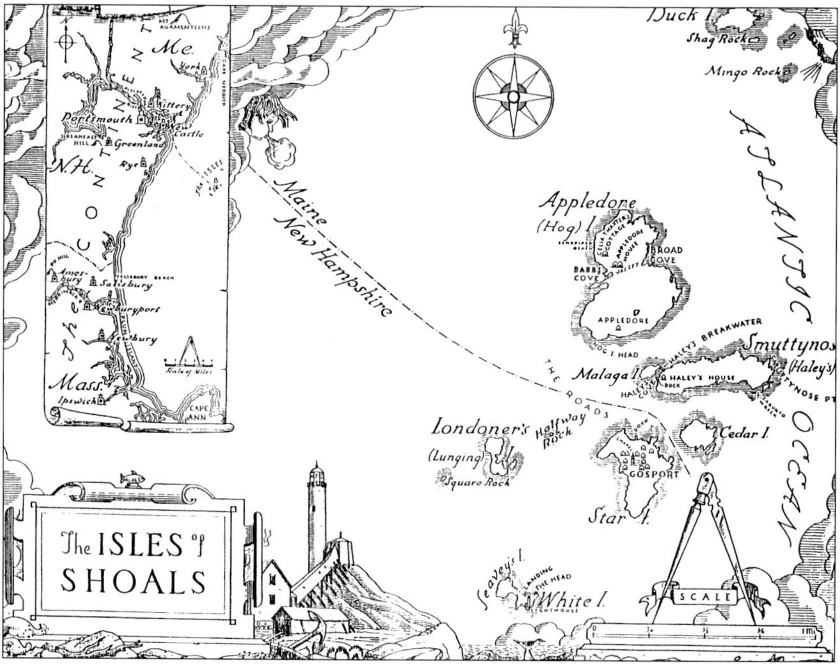

Sketch of Isles of Shoals (Bob Tuttle)

1
LIFE RETURNS

The winds were changing. The sun was reaching higher in the ancient sky and the longer days began to warm the land and its unmarked forests. The birds began their long flight north along the coast, the landscape changing slowly under their flight. The tropic's rich green habitat gave way to thick stands of new temperate spruce, which in turn gave way to shrubs and alder. With each mile north the land became less hospitable to life, less willing to welcome anyone to its barren landscape. Nevertheless, the birds flew on, driven by instincts to nest and fill their craws with food found in abundance along the shore, where the land still refused to bear substance or shelter and the glacier stood tall against the sky.

The birds tore seaweed from rocks along the shore and snatched other materials to build their crude nests in the barren land. Days when strong winds blew from the south the birds soared along a sheer glacial wall which towered thousands of feet over the land. They drifted upwards in effortless spirals to the top. From their vantage point they could see a vast ice field reaching over the northern horizon. To the south lay an inland sea and at its edge stood a cluster of large granite knobs, stripped and polished.

Under the warming sun the ice shield was shrinking after thousands of years expanding across the land. The sea began to rise. As the ocean filled the inland sea, and a new boundary was formed against the land, the cluster of granite knobs became islands. North from these islands the birds could see a rise escaping from under the glacial wall. Still trapped within the ice, it was too soon to tell yet whether it would be a mountain shoulder or one of many granite folds in the landscape. Great rivers erupted from under the ice cap. The exposed land was gouged and cut by the silt-laden water.

At the end of the warm season the shorter hours of daylight and the change of wind brought the birds and their new offspring to wing. They headed south to wait for the land to warm again. In the spring, when they came back, they would find subtle changes. On the rocks where they had made their nests they would see flaky patches of tiny brittle fans that would fall away when pecked. The plant life was returning. The warm winds from the south bore the seeds of lichen. Needing only rain, sun, and the body waste left by birds for their delicate roots to clutch the porous rocks, the lichen thrived. The plant life would die, decay, and provide for a thickening soil with each passing year.

Many generations later the birds could see that the rise of land to the north had escaped from the ice cap. A small mountain rose over 600 feet from the coastal plain.

Flying above its summit the birds could make out, far to the north, the last of the glacier and a new mountain range reaching high above the foothills. To the south were their nesting islands. To the southwest, along the new coast, a large river cut deep into the land. The run-off water from the glacier also flooded the region with many smaller rivers colored turquoise in the sunlight as they carried organic material to the sea. As it settled to the bottom, the material would become suspended in a thick caldron of nutrients by strong currents upwelling across the ragged ocean bottom, thus attracting an endless abundance of marine life.

The rising sea pushed back the river and made its strong current run both north and south on the rise and fall of the tide. It pushed inland, spilling over banks and flooding a low-lying valley to form a swollen bay pressed against the surrounding hills.

Soon the land was no longer barren. A lush blanket of green invaded the land and grew into a tangled maze of life. Forests thrived in the fresh crisp air. The roots of soaring trees filled with nourishment from the soil held firmly against the cycle of storms that moved against the land.

One day, long after the ice cap had left the valley and the forest was well established, a bird landed on a tree limb to look around before committing itself to the ground. A strange scent filled the air. No life in the forest stirred. The bird looked off to the island where its partner pecked twigs into place for their nest. Something was wrong, but nothing it had known before warned it of the danger. It looked again to the island and knew it had to reach its mate. On the first stretch of its wings it heard a rush of wind and felt something slam into its heart. It tried again to unfold its wings. Instead it fell from the tree, fighting to fly until the last of its life had spilled from the wound. Humans had followed life into the river valley. These people called the river the *Pascataway*, "where three rivers make one . . . and pour their waters into the Atlantic Ocean."[1]

The rise in the land seen from the islands became a place for native Americans to look out over the land also. They called the rise "Accominticus". They called themselves Abenakis. In the warm months of the year they came down from the inland forests and lakes to harvest lobster and fish from the sea.

The land of the "*Drowned Valley*",[2] with its thick stands of tall white pine and oak, its abundant wildlife and rivers, created an abundance of food that attracted the humans. Soon these same elements would welcome the fair-skinned men who came from the sea, the men who had outgrown an island kingdom and an old, tired continent. They saw this new land differently from the native Americans. They did not share the native's relationship to the natural world — killing only what they would need for food, cutting down only trees needed for shelter, and trapping only those furs needed for warmth. Europeans saw the land in the light of opportunity. Commerce, enterprise, personal gain, and wealth were the raw fuels driving the engine of European expansion. They came not only with their desires, but, unwittingly, the infections of western civilization. In time disease all but annihilated the coastal nations of the native northeast Americans who soon learned to trade furs with the people who had come from the sea and so killed more game than they would ever need.

Each spring the birds returned to the north country along the coast. With each new season came change and new threats. Old nesting sites left in the fall would be gone by spring. In time the islands off the Piscataway where they had their rookeries would become the Isles of Shoals,[3] islands settled by humans. Yet, even with the presence of people, the birds were compelled by instinct to return to the islands, compensate for change and lay their eggs, listening carefully in the darkness and be forever watchful of new dangers.

2
THE PEOPLE FROM THE SEA

The lands of the northern latitudes from Scandinavia to North America are maritime stepping stones (Iceland, Greenland, Labrador, Newfoundland, and Nova Scotia). Following that route provided the earliest fishermen and explorers with the shortest distance between the two land masses of Europe and the New World.

Vikings sailed from their homeland and settled Iceland about AD 874. Eric the Red moved farther west and established a colony on Greenland's coast about 986. Then fourteen years after that Leif Ericson explored North America. Ericson most likely made contact with native Americans who were descendants of what anthropologists call the Red Paint People. He could have seen them far offshore fishing in their own great boats.[1] Over the next two decades Scandinavians continued to explore westward and supposedly found the northeast coast from Newfoundland to Cape Cod. History is unclear as to the reason why the Vikings failed to survive in America. Recently, archeologists have discovered remains of soft-shell clams, *Mya arenaria*, off northern Europe carbon-dated to the thirteenth century. There is no natural distribution process to explain how the clams got to Europe, giving support to the argument held by many historians that the Vikings had preceded Columbus to North America.

From John Cabot's first exploration of the Canadian Maritimes in 1497 to John Smith's mapping of the New England coast in 1614 many European explorers investigated the land and its countless nooks and crannies, inlets, bays, and rivers. By the time the first settlements were established in the seventeenth century the eastern coast of America had been thoroughly explored by the French, Dutch, Spanish, Portuguese, and English, as well as by the Scandinavians.

Each time they returned home the adventurers told tales of a land rich in natural resources, and of a native population with a social class structure not unlike England's, with its own line of nobility. There were even David Ingram's tales of 1568 in which he claimed he had found "a magic City of Norumbega. The houses had pillars of crystal and silver.

The natives showed him a peck of pearls and rubies six inches long."[2] Norumbega was thought to have been located along the great river flowing through Acadia, New France, known today as the Penobscot River of northern Maine.

Each new generation of European fishermen was drawn farther and farther west in the hope of finding new codfish grounds. They followed the fishing banks that radiated like mantles from the stepping stones. These "banks" led the way to New England. It is suspected that these men were fishing American waters long before European explorers gained fame for their journeys and discoveries.

By 1600 the ambitions of several wealthy English merchants and members of the nobility became more focused. Understanding that America was a promising territory for trade, they designed a simple plan. After trade had been established with native Americans and the land possessed, British settlements would be developed and the land secured for England before France had a chance to do so.

In 1603 a young man from Bristol, England, was given the opportunity to lead an expedition to America. Martin Pring's mission was to explore the northern latitudes of coastal America, map the land and its rivers, and chart the waters while establishing contact with inhabitants in order to trade. The root of the sassafras tree was to be harvested as well; it was thought to have medicinal benefits and would command a high price among apothecaries, thereby paying for much of the expedition.

Pring, only twenty-three years old, held the confidence of Bristol's local merchants, who encouraged the mayor to sponsor the expedition and to hire the young man. Pring was given two ships: the *Speedwell* and the *Discoverer* of fifty and twenty-six tons respectively. Most likely these ships were not more than fifty to seventy feet in length and carried a complement of forty-eight men and cabin boys between them. They had food stores for eight months and articles for sale or trade once they made contact with the native Americans. These articles included brightly colored hats, stockings, thimbles, pins and needles, as well as axes, spades, saws, knives, and hatchets.[3]

The two ships sailed from Kingrode, Bristol, on 20 March 1603. On 7 June Martin Pring wrote that they were close to a "multitude of small islands. . . . [He] was not looking for islands . . . he was looking for safe harbors and rivers that led far inland. . . . He was not looking for a place of immediate settlement, but was making a map which would guide later settlers. Maps came first. He was also looking for Indian camping grounds and a chance to establish the beginnings of trade."[4]

The islands Pring had referred to were most likely the islands of Casco Bay, Maine; later he wrote of exploring four rivers to the south. He started with the Saco, Kennebunk, York, and finished with the "Piscataway," now pronounced Piscataqua, the most promising river, as the others did not reach far enough inland to be of great interest. The Piscataqua had the depth and inland range ideal for trade and development. After a sail of twelve miles upriver in the *Discoverer*, "Captain Pring moored the ship and the entire party went ashore. As far as anyone knows, their feet were the first of any white men's to step on the New England mainland at this point."[5]

A search of the area for sassafras proved hopeless. They were too far north. During the previous year Bartholomew Gosnold had led an expedition to the region and explored lands farther to the south around Cape Cod. There, along the western shorelands of the large bay formed by a cape, both Gosnold and Pring had found enough of the valuable root to fill their ships' storage holds.

Before leaving the Piscataqua Pring drew a detailed chart and noted how thick, endless forests grew from the river's edge and reached far inland, how the deep water ran into a tranquil bay, and how several large islands two leagues off the river's mouth showed signs of use by the native inhabitants. However, no contact was made with them.

The small ships turned south out of the harbor and sailed to the sandy shores of Cape Cod Bay and an inlet Martin referred to as Whitson's Harbor, in honor of the Mayor of Bristol, who had financed the expedition. Though Whitson's Harbor was changed eventually to Plymouth, Pring did live to see Britons settle a colony there.

Through the fair-weather months of July and August Pring and his men went about gathering sassafras root and cedar, clearing land for gardens, and planting a variety of seeds to test the soil. Within a few weeks the wheat, rye, barley, and peas all grew into good crops, though they were planted late in the season. By late July the *Discoverer* was loaded. Pring ordered the crew to set sail for Bristol, and told its captain to inform the mayor that the *Speedwell* would soon follow. In mid-August the remaining men were ready to leave. As Pring weighed anchor the natives, who had caused the men little problem, laid a strip of fire in the

Coat of arms of Sir Ferdinando Gorges (author's private collection)

woods that rimmed the expedition's camp sight. Ola Winslow wrote that this strip possibly was the one which the Pilgrims found bare of great trees seventeen years later.[6]

Martin Pring returned to America on later voyages as navigator and captain. Though no subsequent trip of his would be as historic as the one of 1603, he did prove that future ventures to New England offered prosperity for those who dared to gamble their wealth in New World trade.

Inspired by the successes of explorers such as Gosnold, Weymouth, and Pring, Sir Ferdinando Gorges of Plymouth moved to secure land and establish settlements in northern coastal America. He was a man of means and influence who had dodged his way through political turmoil from loss of wealth and incarceration to full pardon and return to financial well-being. His timing seemed perfect. He was back in power at the right moment in history to see his dreams materialize. On 10 April 1606, James I granted Gorges a charter for the right to

> Establish two separate colonies in Virginia. . . . The "first" colony under the London Company was authorized to settle somewhere in southern Virginia between 34° north latitude, (Cape Fear River near Wilmington, N.C.), and 41° north latitude, (southwest corner of Connecticut).

> The "second" colony, under the Plymouth Company, was authorized to make a settlement in northern Virginia, (later named New England. . .) between 38° north (southern Maryland) and 45° north (southeast corner of Maine).
>
> Thus there was an overlap of three degrees of latitude from 38° to 41° in which either company could make a settlement. However, the charter stipulated that the two settlements must be at least 100 miles apart. The land grants extended along parallels of latitude across the continent to the Pacific Ocean.[7]

The sites for these two settlements were established even before the grants were issued. The London Company located near the thirty-seventh parallel in what became Jamestown. The Plymouth Company was located midway between the forty-third and forty-fourth parallel near a river then known as the Sagadahoc, now the Kennebec. Gorges joined forces with Sir John Popham. Together they worked with the Plymouth Company to settle "northern Virginia."

In August 1606 they sent two ships out to confirm that the site they had chosen was still best suited for them. The most ideal spot would have been farther to the south with its milder climate, but the Plymouth Company had another motive. It had to establish a British stronghold in the heart of Acadia to challenge the French colonies there.

Ferdinando Gorges's ship, the *Richard*, never made landfall at Sagadahoc. The captain, taking a southern route against orders, was captured by Spanish sailors who took his ship to Seville.[8]

Sir John Popham's ship, the *Mary and John*, under the command of Thomas Hanham, left later that year in October. Martin Pring was among the crew and served as master navigator and guide. Their part of the expedition was to provide the *Richard* with support, but they were forced to carry out the mission alone. Despite the loss of the *Richard* they were successful. Their findings at Sagadahoc, now the area near Bath, Maine, were so well received in England, that the Plymouth Company immediately arranged to send a number of people over to establish a plantation.

The London Company was already far ahead of the Plymouth Company in implementing its own plans to establish the Jamestown settlement. In December 1606 a ship had sailed with settlers on behalf of the London Company. Another six months passed before the Plymouth Company's two ships were ready to sail. The *Mary and John* and the *Gift of God* departed Plymouth on 31 May 1607 with one hundred men on board bound for Sagadahoc. Captains Raleigh Gilbert and George

Popham were in command of the ships, with Popham serving as leader of the expedition.

Among the crew on Gilbert's boat, the *Mary and John*, was Skicowaros, a native American, home bound. He had been brought to England along with four others from the western shores of Cape Cod Bay by George Weymouth in 1605. Though they were seized and taken on board Weymouth's ship against their will, the natives had soon realized no harm was to come to them, "after perceiving by usage we intended them no harm, they have never since seemed discontented with us, but very tractable, loving and willing by their best means to satisfy us in anything we demand of them. . ."[9]

Though the native American culture of the time did have a well-defined social order English royalty considered them *salvages* (to use the Old French spelling). The five Abanakis brought to Plymouth, England by Weymouth were: Tahanada, a Sagamore or chief; Amoret, Skicowaros, and Maneddo, all gentlemen in their tribe; and Sassacomoit or Squanto, a servant, who befriended the Pilgrims.[10]

While in England the five men were given David Thomson, a teenage boy of Plymouth, who served as their guide and confidant. Thomson's father had himself been a servant of Gorges for many years. Gorges was particularly fond of the boy, and under his guidance the young man was kept very busy.

When Thomson turned fourteen he began his seven-year apprenticeship in a chosen trade. Apothecary Dr. Richard Vines, the ship's doctor and former crew member on Pring's voyage of 1603, was seeking permanent employment with Sir Ferdinando Gorges. He proposed to take charge of medicines on future trips to northern Virginia, and, after several conversations, the doctor agreed to take the boy on as his new apprentice. Already skilled in reading, writing, and calculating, Thomson would prove to be a valuable associate.

Both Dr. Vines and his apprentice were assigned to the crew billet when the *Mary and John* sailed from Plymouth in 1607. During the long voyage Thomson would learn seamanship from ship's navigator Robert Davies. In return he would serve as interpreter and help where he could in securing friendly relations with any natives they might encounter in America. His earlier friendship with Weymouth's five native Americans soon earned him respect among the crew.

In late July the *Mary and John*'s crew sighted southern Nova Scotia, where the next several days were spent fishing the local waters. While the crew were thus employed, some natives went in their open boats to investigate the men who had come from the sea. It became obvious to the ship's crew that these natives had had previous contact with Frenchmen as they occasionally used French words and phrases. "David and Skicowaros had difficulty communicating with the Nova Scotia Indians. Their language was quite unlike Skicowaros' dialect with which David was familiar. Communication was largely by gestures and signs."[11]

On 4 August the *Mary and John* sailed around Cape Sable, Nova Scotia, and into the Bay of Fundy, then changed course to south by southwest to follow the eastern shore of North America. After a two-day sail they were within sight of mountains and hills familiar to Skicowaros and the island where Weymouth had erected a cross in 1605. He had named the island St. Georges.[12] As they approached the island's cove Captain Gilbert noticed a ship already at anchor there. It turned out to be the *Gift of God*.

With it being early August no time was lost in searching the coast for an ideal site for their settlement. The day after they arrived Captain Gilbert and fourteen men including Skicowaros, Dr. Vines, Thomson, and Davies set out for the mainland making landfall at Pemaquid Point. Skicowaros guided the party into the Pemaquid River, now the Damariscotta, to Tahanada's village. At first they were met with hostility until Tahanada heard Thomson calling out to him. The chief immediately ordered his men to lay down their weapons as he welcomed his friend from England.

Though friendly contact had been made a degree of doubt concerning the explorers' safety remained. Within a few days the entire expedition sailed from St. Georges Island making good a course for the Sagadahoc River.

Navigator Davies made the following notes; they appear as recorded:

> Mundaye beinge the 17th Auguste Capt. Popham in his shallop wth 30 others & Capt. Gilbert in his shipes bott accompaned wth 18 other persons depted early on the morninge from thear ships & sailed up the ryver of Sagadehock for to vew the ryver & allso to see whear they myght fynd the most convenyent place for thear plantation. . . .
>
> Tuesdaye beinge the 18th after our retorn we all went to the shore & thear mad chois of a place for our planation whch ys at the very mouth or entry of the ryver . . . on the west syd. . . .
>
> Thursday beinge the 20th of August all our companyes landed 7 thear began to fortefye. Our presedent Capt. Popham sett the fyrst spytt of ground unto ytt and after hem all the rest followed & and labored hard in the trenches about ytt.[13]

Sketch of seventeenth-century pinnace or shallop, typical of first vessels built by the English in America (author's private collection)

For the next five months the one hundred men who were to stay behind spent their time building a fort. St. Georges Fort was built on land native Americans had called Sabino, "Almost an island of good bigness," at the mouth of the Kennebec River.[14] And "In addition the carpenters framed '. . . a pretty pinnace (small boat) thirty tons, which they called the *Virginia*. . . .' It was the first vessel built by the English in America." [15]

The men first attended to their safety. Preparation against a potential attack from the natives, French, or Spanish took longer than necessary. This would prove a tactical mistake. The already difficult situation facing the leaders was further complicated by their arrival late in the season, which put them four months behind in preparations for winter. To have arrived in April would have been better, giving them time to establish gardens, cut fire wood, and hunt wild game for furs and meat.

In October, with cold weather approaching, the *Mary and John* was ordered back to England under the command of the newly appointed captain, Robert Davies. Dr. Vines and Thomson were among the crew. The *Gift of God* followed on 16 December with a load of masts to be sold to English boatyards. When the ship finally arrived home, the crew

". . . brought back the news to England of the bitter cold in Maine, and that a fire had destroyed much of their provisions . . . [they] also brought back more than half of the discouraged colonists."[16]

In February the forty-five men who had remained at Sagadahoc were faced with yet another serious setback. On the fifth Captain George Popham had died, turning the command of the colony over to 24-year-old Captain Raleigh Gilbert.

With the approach of spring the men had already survived the worst of winter. The *Mary and John* had just recently returned from England, laden with supplies, all of which should have uplifted the settlers' spirits. But it did not. The warming spring could not revive their hopes. To ensure that spirits would indeed remain defeated they were told that Gilbert's brother, Sir John, had died. This required Gilbert to return to England to resolve problems concerning his brother's estate.

With no one left to inspire the men their will to carry on vanished. The settlers all boarded the waiting ship and their own pinnace, the *Virginia*, and left Sagadahoc. Did they realize how close they had come to achieving immortality in New England history? Fort St. Georges continued to provide fishermen a base of operations during spring and fall trips to the Gulf of Maine.

Dr. Vines and David Thomson went on working for Sir Ferdinando Gorges as agents in the affairs of the Plymouth Company in northern Virginia. They returned to America several times in the ensuing years. Thomson matured into a hard-working man. His early experiences in America nurtured a dream—that one day he might develop his own settlement there. Someday he would break the cycle of servitude his family had endured. History remembers him today as New England's original Yankee.

Seven years passed before the English looked again to settle northern Virginia; seven years passed before the dream of living and trading in North America struck a chord in the imagination of Sir Ferdinando Gorges once again. Inspired by Captain John Smith's voyage of 1614 Gorges, along with many others, began again to focus on America.

In 1614 Captain Smith, already famous as a soldier and a leader at the Jamestown settlement, found employment with three wealthy London merchants. They gave him instructions to explore northern Virginia for gold and silver, probably inspired by the lingering hope that David Ingram's tale of Norumbega was true; or maybe their interest in finding gold was just a ploy, " '. . . For our golde, it was rather the Master's

Captain John Smith (*History of New Hampshire*, Stackpole)

device to get a voyage that projected it, then any knowledge he had at all of any such matter.' "[17]

The merchants included in their instructions a more practical assignment for Captain Smith. He was to hunt for whales; but above all else he was to do whatever was necessary to make the voyage pay for itself. As in previous ventures there were always alternative missions, if primary ones failed. They were to explore the land and fill the holds with commodities for English markets.

On 3 March 1614 Smith set sail from London. He made landfall in America in late April at Monhegan Island, an established center of English fishing in the Gulf of Maine.

From his island campsite Smith searched for the purported silver and gold mines to no avail. Neither did he find one clue as to the whereabouts of Norumbega. Further to frustrate the captain, his men and ships had proven poorly equipped for whale hunting.

Two months passed before Smith sent his men codfishing and trapping for mink, martin, beaver, and otter. In the meantime he had become intrigued by the vastness of the coast and the endless inlets and rivers. He decided, " 'Whilest the sailers fished, my selfe with eight or nine others of them might best be spared; range the coast in a small boat, . . .' "[18]

Provisions for the captain and his men were stowed in a small sailing vessel, called a pinnace, which they had built; it was no more than thirty-five feet long and had one or two masts. Instructions were left for the others to continue filling the ship's hold with furs and codfish. In the month Smith and his men were gone the remaining crew dried codfish and stowed 11,000 fur pelts traded from the natives in exchange for inexpensive trinkets. The expedition took Smith from Penobscot Bay to Cape Cod as he surveyed the coastal contours, taking depth soundings along the way, more out of necessity than design:

> I have had six or seven several plots [charts] of those northren parts, so unlike each other, and most so differing from any true proportion, or resemblance of the countrey, as they did mee no more good then so much waste paper. . . I have drawen a Map from Point to Point. . . Ile to Ile,. . . with the Soundings, Sands, Rocks and Land-marks, as I passed close aboord the Shore in a Little Boat.[19]

As he sailed along the coast Smith recognized the broad opening of the Piscataqua River described by Pring. Apparently Captain Smith did not explore the river. It is assumed that if he had, he would have made

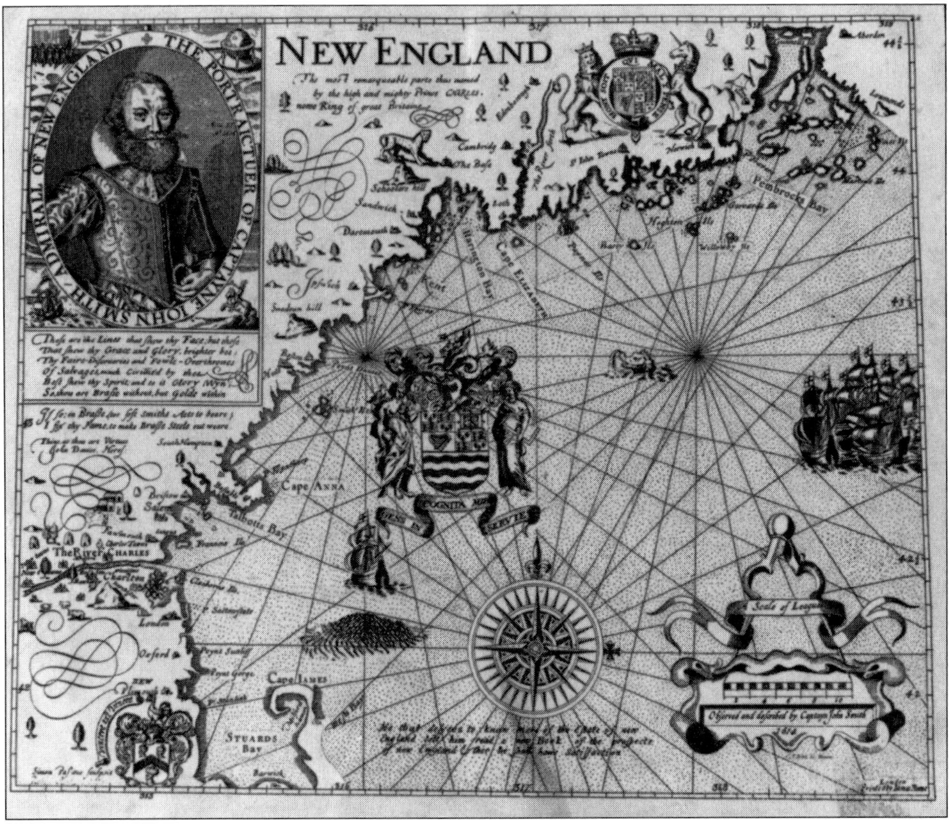

Captain Smith's map of 1614 showing for the first time in history the term "New England" (Star Island Corporation Private Collection)

mention of the exploration in his *Description of New England*, the journal he wrote of this voyage. Smith did, however, take notice of a cluster of rocky islands standing just southeast of the river's mouth. He explored and mapped them, and called them his own, Smyths Isles.

All nine islands and surrounding ledges were accurately depicted on his chart. Smith's detailed journal reveals how impressed he had become with America:

> Smyths Isles are a heape together, none neere them, against Accominiticus. . . . And of all the foure parts of the world that I have yet seene not inhabited, could I have but means to transport a colonie, I would rather live here (New England) than anywhere; and if it did not maintaine it selfe, were wee but once indifferently well fitted, let us starve.[20]

Smith accomplished much during his time in America, aided by the two natives, Tahanada and Squanto, who returned home with him from yet another trip to England. He went on to make several contacts with tribes in the area, "The principall habitation Northward we were at, was Penobscot; Southward along the coast and up the Rivers we found Mecadacut, Segocket, Pemmaquid, Musconcus, Kenebeck, Sagadahock and Aumoughcawgen;"[21] all were located within the land that became known as Maine.

His enthusiasm was contagious. Upon returning to England Smith authored an exotic tale of America that passed among his countrymen and ignited their imaginations which for so long had had so little reason to be aroused. His men brought back tales of unbounded resources of animals, fish, lobster, and timber. Soon, merchants and sailors began planning their own trips to what was now known as New England. When Smith presented his map to Prince Charles, soon to become Charles I, he inquired as to what the broad land mass standing unexplored behind the coast should be called. The prince replied simply: "Call it New England."[22] Upon completion of his journal and map the title of First Admiral of New England was bestowed upon Captain John Smith.

Several years would pass before a group of merchants and lords was able to establish permanent plantations in New England. When the time came to divide the land they gave Smith only his isles off the Piscataqua River. This could be construed as an insult to Smith if one considers his own words on the matter,

> "But not one lot for me", wrote the Captain, "But Smith Isles, which are a many of barren rocks, the most overgrown with such shrubs and sharp whins you can hardly pass them, without either grass or wood, but three or four short shrubby old cedars. . . ."[23]

Despite this obvious affront to his great stature among the people of England, he managed to bring matters to a positive conclusion: the great wealth of New England was to be realized from the sea, and his isles, "were in the heart of 'the strangest fish-pond I ever saw.'"[24]

Captain Smith held the opinion and nurtured his dream that one day he would return to New England and establish his own settlement. Four times his ship set sail from England; four times it was driven back by misfortune. A violent storm, the ship's inadequacies, and pirates robbed him of the opportunity to realize his final goal. He never saw New England again. He did, however, live to see the Pilgrims settle New Plymouth, and to see for one last time Princess Pocahontas, who as a girl of twelve had persuaded her father, Chief Powhatan, to spare Smith's life:

> As a child Pocahontas had sat at the feet of her father's prisoner, Captain John Smith, and had listened to him tell wondrous stories of the fabulous white man's world. After six weeks of captivity, John Smith became the object of an Indian ceremony which was a combination of mock execution and salvation as a token of adoption into Powhatan's tribe. It was Pocahontas, the chief's daughter, who was to act as the intercessor to stop the execution of the doughty captain. Subsequently her father . . . and Captain Smith became friends and sworn blood brothers. To Pocahontas, Captain Smith was like a God.[25]

Pocahontas had traveled to England from Virginia with her husband John Rolfe and her son in 1616. While in London she met once more with the man who had been so dear to her in America. They rekindled their admiration for one another as Princess Pocahontas humbled the commoner Smith by calling him father. She would hear nothing of his protest, declaring that she had always thought he was equal to her own father Powhatan.

After several hours reminiscing on a life they had known so far away in Virginia they said their farewells. By March of the following year the despondent Pocahontas had fallen ill. Little time could be wasted. Pocahontas had to return to her homeland or die from the diseases of England which her frail body could no longer withstand.

Sadly, on the day of her departure her condition worsened. Before the ship's sails were filled with the winds of the English Channel she was near death, "At Gravesend (the mouth of the Thames) she was taken ashore. There Pocahontas died."[26] She died aged twenty-two. Her body remained in the foreign land and was buried at St. George's Church, Gravesend.

John Smith, who died in 1631 at age fifty-four, managed to attain legendary stature within his lifetime. Nevertheless, Smith's accomplishments, from the Middle East to America, were feeble compensation for the loss of his last unfulfilled dream: to return to his beloved New England. His body was laid to rest in St. Sepulchres Church, London. His fellow countrymen, who, with the fullness of love for a man who had dispensed so valiantly England's influence throughout the world, inscribed on his tombstone:

To the living memory of his deceased friend, Capt. John Smith, some time Governor of Virginia and Admiral of New England, who departed this life 21 June, 1631.

Here lies one conquered who has conquered kings,
Subdued large territories, and done things
Which to the world impossible would seem,
But that the truth is held more in esteem. . . .[27]

3
DAVID THOMSON AND HIS DREAM

David Thomson was born in Clerkenwell Parish, a suburb of London, in December 1592, three years before Shakespeare penned *Romeo and Juliet.* His birthplace lay in the shadows of Newgate Prison where debtors and tardy churchgoers were kept. Death by hanging could come to many prisoners due simply to poor reading skills, since without them inmates could not protect themselves against a prejudiced clerk who used false journal entries unjustly to influence a judge or jury. In 1603 Thomson's father, Richard, moved his family to Plymouth where he continued in the service of Sir Ferdinando Gorges, then commander of Plymouth Fort.

In Plymouth Thomson met the shipwrights, sailors, captains, and fisherman who made Plymouth England's busiest seaport. He met old seamen who had sailed with Sir Francis Drake on his world voyage. He met William Hawkins whose son, Sir John Hawkins, built the ships that defeated the Spanish Armada in 1588.

From this seaport sailed not only Drake, but Sir Walter Raleigh, John Hawkins, Cavendish, and the Pilgrims. Yet, Plymouth, with all of its great and famous seamen, was foremost a fisherman's port. Thomson's imagination was sparked by the tales of these men upon their return from months at sea. Earlier, at the beginning of each season, a hundred ships had set sail for the western cod grounds of the North Atlantic. One can imagine Thomson spending hours on the docks watching in fascination as men hustled about readying their ships for a new voyage, and watching out in the harbor the great white sails flap slowly into billowing sheets of canvas, nudging the ships forward. And as the fleet rounded Fisher's Nose, gliding down to the English Channel, one can imagine the young Thomson dreaming of the day when he would join those men and their ships.

In 1616, nine years after his first trip to America, Thomson returned with his friend and mentor Dr. Richard Vines. They were once again in the employment of Sir Ferdinando Gorges, who maintained the power and influence required to convince merchants that an investment in New England settlements would prove not only wise but profitable. He ignored the advice of some who had been to America, who saw it as a waste of money and time, since the horrible winters made the land uninhabitable.

Thomson and Dr. Vines left Plymouth in March aboard the 200-ton ship *Abraham*, rigged for a fishing expedition to Monhegan Island. Their mission, similar to that of Pring's, was to explore the coast for suitable sites near mouths of large rivers; also to establish a winter camp to prove that Englishmen, when properly prepared, could survive winters in northern New England. Once found and surveyed and so noted these sites would serve as potential locations for future settlements.

Once the *Abraham* made landfall at Monhegan Island Thomson, Dr. Vines, and four men set sail for the mainland in a shallop, a small sailing vessel built on the island during an earlier expedition. They went back to Fort St. Georges, where they found a small band of fishermen from Bristol, as well as locating Thomson's friends Tahanada and Skicowaros. After a brief visit, they moved east at the rate of five leagues per day, or fifteen nautical miles, towards the bay Smith had called Pembrock, known today as Penobscot Bay.

They explored this massive recess in the coast and its many islands and inlets. The bay, a deep blue velvet carpet, held the islands against a backdrop of old, round-topped mountains making up the distant horizon. Stands of forests loaded each island with an overburden of timber. Rich green pine, fir, and spruce draped thick canopies above the forest floors. Here and there a shoulder of an island or a point of land escaped from the covering and exposed its white granite skin to the spring sun. Ribbons of granite, skirting the islands in varieties of contours and shadows, kept the soil well above the highest of tides.

Finishing their work in Penobscot Bay the men set a course of S by W. Enroute back to Fort St. Georges they passed several small English fishing vessels just offshore. By then an estimated 200 ships were working the Gulf of Maine cod grounds. Anxious to move on toward the south, they stopped at the fort for only one night.

Thomson and Dr. Vines sailed on through Casco Bay where they found a fine harbor but no sizeable river. They continued south to an area which reminded Vines of his boyhood home, ". . . on the Torridge

River near Bideford in Devonshire."[1] Then on to the mouth of the Piscataqua River, where its currents were so foul that day that they chose not to explore farther. Past the Smith Isles and Cape Ann the men sailed, finding anchorage along the north shore of Massachusetts Bay in a protected harbor that appeared to be among the most ideal so far discovered. Sheltered by a number of barrier islands, the entrance led into a large inner harbor into which two rivers flowed, known today as the Charles River and the Mystic. While there, Thomson explored an island which would one day be his own.

Satisfied with the extent of coastline explored, Thomson considered their first objective completed, but Dr. Vines insisted they circumnavigate the perimeter of Cape Cod. They stopped at Pring's Whitson Bay, which Captain Smith referred to as Plymouth. They sailed around the hook of the cape down the seaward side, stopping before they reached Elizabeth Isle, known today as Cuttyhunk, where Gosnold and Gilbert had found valuable sassafras in 1602. Changing direction, they headed northeast, back along Massachusetts Bay to the Piscataqua River where they spent time making detailed journal entries of the area. This time, taking account of favorable tides, they sailed inland to the bay noted by Pring. They also traded among the now sickly natives for furs, while searching the forest for medicinal plants. By now it was well into August and the men turned their attention to the next phase of their voyage—finding a suitable location for a winter camp.

The men returned to the place that reminded Dr. Vines of his childhood, located just twenty miles northeast of the Piscataqua, which the natives called Sawco. There, behind a long narrow sand barrier, they found an estuary the doctor would name Bideford Pool. The next three months were spent building a shelter with fireplace and enough room for six men to live comfortably throughout the long winter. In the nearby forests they found all the firewood and game they would need. Fresh meat and fish were dried, salted, or smoked and then stored as winter food.

The months passed in relative ease and comfort. The men made every effort to avoid contact with the nearby tribal villages for fear of contracting the disease that was killing their inhabitants. Endless winter hours must have been spent speculating on just how a full-sized plantation might survive and prosper in this hostile land. By the end of February, with the worst of winter behind them, they had accomplished what so many swore could not be done—they had survived a northern New England winter.

Having successfully completed the last of the expedition's goals the six men readied the shallop for the sixty-mile sail back to Monhegan Island and an eventual rendezvous with the returning *Abraham*. The small vessel was filled to the gunwales with the harvest of their year-long trek down the coast. A small delegation of still healthy natives came to bid farewell to the men who had come from the sea. They watched these men sail far offshore until the shallop disappeared beyond where the sea meets the sky.

The campsite was abandoned. Though the men had gone the natives had no room in their hearts to rejoice while the black spirit of death remained.

By May the *Abraham* was ready to sail. On the return voyage Thomson must have been anxious to see his young wife, Amias, and their new baby. For the second time she had given birth, death having stolen their first born shortly after birth. The second baby was to have come last October. If it had survived, it would be nearly a year old when Thomson returned home.

One can imagine Thomson looking up into the rigging, up into the sails far above the deck, then out over the monotonous sea, wishing for more wind, as he nourished within a dream of someday returning to America with his family to set out on a new life.

The crewmen were reunited with their loved ones in Plymouth, June 1617. One can imagine too the cry that must have gone up through the town from the waterfront, "The *Abraham*, she returns!" Thomson learned upon his arrival that their child had survived. Prissilla was a strong and healthy baby.

Thomson soon acquired copies of Captain Smith's Admiralty map and *Description of New England*. He had met Smith in Plymouth when the captain had called on Sir Gorges in August 1614. Thomson found encouragement in Smith's narrative, "here [in New England] every man may be master and own labour and land . . . If he have nothing but his hands he may set up his trade; and by industrie quickly grow rich . . . "[2]

Over the ensuing years fishermen and adventurers continued to set course for New England in late winter and early fall. The fishing grounds from Sagadahoc to Martha's Vineyard became the most productive in northeast America. By 1618, 135,000 lb of fish were being landed annually in New England. With each returning ship there came more reports of unprovoked acts of aggression inflicted on the native Americans, who, as a result, were becoming more militant. This unfortunate development posed a threat to Sir Gorges and his plans. In 1619 he organized another trip to New England, this time led by Captain Thomas Dermer. David Thomson was appointed to the crew billet. The native servant, Squanto, was to return home aboard ship yet another time. Included among his numerous ventures away from his homeland was one episode where the ship on which he sailed fell into pirates' hands.

Gorges instructed Captain Dermer that upon his arrival in New England he should make every attempt to reestablish friendly relations with various Sagamores and their tribes. With Squanto's help the Englishmen pursued peace. Squanto enlisted the wisdom and help of Samoset, the Sagamore from Pemaquid, to facilitate negotiations between the tribes of Massachusetts Bay and the English. Samoset convinced Sagamore Massasoit to trust the English and agree to honor a treaty between the two nations. The treaty was to be short-lived.

Since 1606 Gorges had immersed himself in various plans which would lead one day to his plantation in New England. The available journals on the subject of America, with which he was well versed, all confirmed his beliefs. However, one major obstacle stood in his way. Though empowered by James I in the Virginia Charter to create such settlements, Gorges felt a new entitlement, a new charter was called for, enabling him to delegate grants and authority to plantation leaders.[3] With this power would come the right to control the fishing grounds off New England one hundred miles out to sea to impose taxes. The Jamestown fishermen argued vehemently against such taxes. Their position was that over the years they had earned the right to fish the waters of New England free of restrictions and taxes. The seeds of revolt were sowed.

Fortunately for Thomson his life's ambition was on a similar course to Sir Ferdinando. The town's wealthy merchants no longer considered the idea of investing in America absurd. Listening to his exciting narratives, they finally acknowledged the country's potential.

Thomson's promotion of a permanent settlement in the form of a traders' outpost in New England was based on a sound business proposal. Profits for the merchants could be substantially increased by taking greater advantage of a second fishing season.

For years the fishing fleet would leave Plymouth after the winter gales had passed and arrive off New England at Monhegan Island in time for the spring fish run. Later that spring, with their ships full, they would head for home. Thomson, on his journeys to America, discovered another run of codfish was available in the fall. The run could not be exploited if the fishermen had already left with their ships. He promoted the concept of a year-round fishermen's colony. This would allow the fishermen to stay, without interruption, through the two seasons, while the ship's crew made two round trips a year rather than one. His interests went beyond this initial plantation, to the island he had discovered with Dr. Vines in a protected harbor of Massachusetts Bay. It was there that he would eventually move his family and operate his trading business.

Besides fish the ships could bring back greater quantities of furs and desperately needed American timbers. Thomson concluded that in time this trade route could be expanded to the shores of Europe. The merchants of Plymouth were well aware that when Gorges did receive his new charter Thomson would be among his first grant holders. The aroma of future success and profits filtered up from the "quay" and intoxicated the entire town.

Captain Smith's Isles off the Piscataqua River played a key role in Thomson's plans. Ideally located in deep water and central to where he believed the majority of New England settlements would be established, the islands could offer merchant tallships easy access and anchorage for lightering cargo. The isles, too, were not far from the fishing grounds that were already yielding an unlimited source of 100 lb codfish. Thomson's promotional efforts included persuading fishermen to leave the remote islands of Monhegan and Damariscove and develop a new staging area for their dry-fish processing in the Gulf of Maine at Smith's Isles.

The dry-fish technique was different from that already developed by the Portuguese fishermen off Newfoundland. With unlimited quantities of salt the Portuguese wet stored their fish directly into ships' holds for the relatively short voyage home. Wet storing was not practical for the English. They had salt but not in the quantities needed for this process, and they had farther to travel. By dry storing their catch a greater tonnage of fish could be stowed for a longer period of time with limited threat of spoilage. The dry or dunfish process employed the help of a land-based crew that cut, stripped, and filleted the fish on wooden piers or floats along a protected shore. The most critical part of the whole process was preserving, "The dryness and salubrity of their atmosphere [the Smith Isles] . . . enabled the fishermen to prepare by a process of alternate drying and sweating, without salt, the famous 'dun' or 'dumb' fish, which could not be rivaled elsewhere."[4]

Thick fillets were placed on wooden racks called flakes and dried to a rich mahogany brown, then packed in shipping casks or kegs. The end product was a preserved fillet of fish that still maintained a certain bulk and moistness characteristic of a fresh fillet; thus, "The market price of these fish was three or four times that of the Poor John and Haberdine, made at Newfoundland."[5]

After their fishing seasons were over Thomson's men could return to a trading post he hoped to establish at the mouth of the Piscataqua River, spending the remainder of fall preparing for winter. The more ambitious men could venture inland and harvest timbers and trap wild game for their valuable pelts, while David could maintain friendly contacts with the natives for fur trading.

Throughout the summer of 1620 Thomson and Gorges went about their separate but converging ways, continuing to market New England's future potential. Then, in late August, two ships, not known to the locals, came past Fisher's Neck and approached Plymouth's inner harbor. This chance visit was made by the *Mayflower* and the pinnace *Speedwell.*

The *Speedwell* had been brought into the quay for much needed repairs before sailing the Atlantic to a place in Virginia located near the Hudson River. The Pilgrims on board these vessels had recently gained a charter from the London Company. Numbering over a hundred men, women, and children, the Pilgrims were anxious about leaving England on an unseaworthy ship.

Thomson's biographers, his descendants, have claimed that during this call on the port of Plymouth, Pilgrim leaders led by Miles Standish, William Bradford, William Brewster, and Christopher Jones, the *Mayflower*'s captain, sought information on America from Thomson. If so, he could have offered little information on the area they wished to settle. On his numerous travels to America he had not ventured farther south than Cape Cod. His biographers indicate that Thomson spent his time with the Pilgrims sharing tales of Massachusetts Bay and discussing how the place noted as "New Plimouth" on Smith's Admiralty map, called Accomack by the natives, held the most promise.

Thomson's biographers further imply that the Pilgrims were quite impressed with what they were told, but were faced with the dilemma of being already committed by contract to Virginia. By the end of their interview, questions concerning the land of "New Plimouth" dominated their conversation. Thomson supposedly gave a detailed description to Jones of the best course to take if they chose to land at "New Plimouth". (The captain had been on previous whaling trips to Greenland, but none to the continent.) The following quotation from the biography is a fair representation of how ships in those days might have made a westing voyage from Plymouth. Thomson apparently told them to

> make good a compass course of west-northwest . . . for about 400 leagues. The course would take them along between 51° and 52° (north) latitude. The compass variation will slowly increase from 10° west to 25° or 26° west. When he came to where the variation was 25° west and he was around 52° latitude, he should shift his course a little to port to[wards] compass west. This will move the ship southwesterly more or less parallel to the American coast. The variation may increase to as much as 27° west and then will gradually fall off. Of course, the latitude will also decrease.[6] When the vessel gets to 42° latitude he should shift his [course] to starboard to true west and aim to ride the 42nd parallel right into Cape Cod or Cape James on Smith's map.[7]

Centuries of world travel had produced such navigational instruments as the log line used by mariners to estimate roughly how much east or west distance was being made. Accurate calculations were not possible until the chronometer was invented in the seventeenth century. North and south distances could be established accurately with the astrolabe; a forerunner of the sextant. If, indeed, the Pilgrims had met with Thomson and had had prior knowledge of the area known as "New Plimouth", then it is unlikely that Captain Jones had failed to recognize Cape Cod when it came into sight.

Even without this chance meeting, doubt continues to be raised about the Pilgrims' intended destination. For any seasoned mariner of the day, such as Jones, would have had at his disposal the latitudes of all the major landmarks on the east coast of America and would have had little trouble making close landfall to any desired destination. Captain Jones must have known he was 120 nautical miles too far north. Early histories also surmise that he was more than glad to discharge his difficult passengers at the first bit of land he came upon.

Speculation as to whether Thomson met with the Pilgrims may never be verified, but history does confirm that the *Speedwell* was left behind in

Plymouth, also that all 102 Pilgrims were bound for America aboard the *Mayflower* on 6 September 1620, and that in mid-November they landed not on the Hudson River, but on Cape Cod. Was this by chance or design?

Two months after the departure of the *Mayflower*, the bureaucratic logjam that had thwarted the dreams of Thomson and Gorges finally broke. On 3 November 1620, Sir Gorges received his long sought-after charter. Immediately, he established the Council for New England. The charter gave the council sweeping authority over New England. With its new and far-reaching powers, the council was authorized to issue grants for plantations, townships, and cities, to establish laws, and to regulate commerce and taxes. However, this would all ring hollow if Gorges, who was in London at the time, could not find the means to enforce this new power.

Gorges quickly sent orders to Thomson in Plymouth to commence with plans and outfit yet another expedition bound for New England, this time to construct a base of operations. The new plantation would be located at the Piscataqua River entrance, and centered on Fort Pannaway. Gorges expressed his hope to join the new settlement in 1622, a wish he would never realize.

Gorges's instructions were explicit: the fort was to be built,

> so it would dominate the "two mouths" of the Piscataqua River with long range cannons, thus denying the use of the river to any potential European enemy. The fort also must be able to withstand a land attack. . . .
>
> The site chosen for the fort was on a rise of ground overlooking the mouths of the river.[8]

In December 1620, Thomson and his advance team left Plymouth aboard the fishing vessel *Johnathan*. At Smith's Isles, a few men disembarked to prepare for the new fishing season. The *Johnathan* continued on to the Piscataqua, where Thomson led his men ashore and began staking out his new plantation.

Within hours, natives came from the forest displaying great excitement and agitation over stories they had heard from the Patuxent people concerning the men who had come from the sea in greater numbers than ever before, and how they had made homes for themselves at Accomack. The men and women and their children were not only invading the land, but

> Groups of armed men from this ship [*Mayflower*] would go ashore . . . and tramp among the sand dunes digging into Indian graves, stealing cached Indian seed corn. They desecrated an Indian cemetery and robbed some vacated Indian dwellings. When the white men saw an Indian, they chased him.[9]

Thomson was distressed by the reports. Those settlers, who were neither fishermen, nor woodsmen, nor traders had let it be known from the outset that they possessed more contempt than compassion for their savage brethren.

Thomson divided his time between the burgeoning fishing industry at Smith's Isles, which the fishermen were calling the Isles of Shoals, and erecting the fort as ordered by Gorges. Samuel Maverick described the fort during a visit later in 1623,

> . . . a strong and large house, enclosed with a large and high palizado and mounted gunns, and being stored extraordinarily with shot and ammunition was a terror to the Indians. . . . This house and effort he [Thomson] built on a point of land at the very entrance of Pascataway River.[10]

In 1622 Thomson's men had completed their work on Fort Pannaway. Though no diagrams or descriptions have been found concerning the fort other than Maverick's brief account, Thomson notes the following in support of the fort's existence:

> Listed in the Acts of the Privy Council of New England (at the time the holder of real power in England) 1622–1623, in the Public Record Office, London, is a letter from the Privy Council to Lord Carew, Master of Ordinance, dated 17 February 1622, directing him on behalf of the Council for New England to grant a license to Thomas Weston, merchant of London, to send over to New England in the ship *Charitie*. . . thirty pieces of iron ordinance, namely fifteen demi-culverines (long range guns), weighing 1.5 to 1.8 tons each; ten sakers weighing 1.0 to 1.4 tons each; and five minions, 0.7 to 1.0 tons; totalling over forty tons.[11]

Assured that his men were handling details properly and with the fort completed, Thomson returned to England. There he received his long-awaited reward. The Council of New England issued him a grant for a 6,000 acre Pannaway Plantation on the Piscataqua River entrance. The parcel of land extended from Fox Point on Great Bay, down the Piscataqua and four miles down the coast to the south.

During this last trip to England, Thomson strengthened his financial status by creating partnerships in his venture. In January 1623, with all

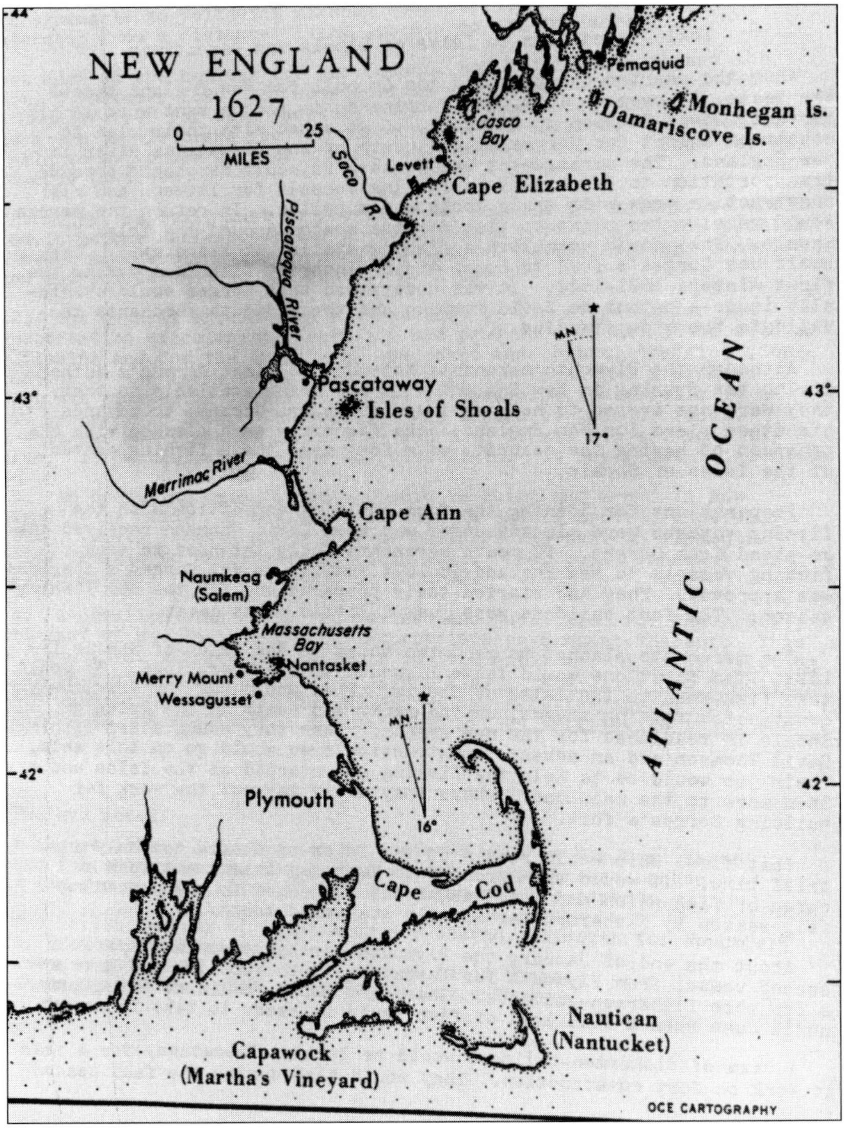

Coastal sketch showing Pannaway related to Massachusetts Bay Area and Plymouth, as well as Monhegan Island (*First Yankee*, Thompson)

details and business activity concluded, Thomson, his wife Amias and their second child, the four-year-old John, sailed from Plymouth on board the *Johnathan* with a contingency of seven men who would help develop the settlement. It is wondered if Prissilla, who was left behind with her grandparents to finish her formal schooling, ever contemplated the possibility that she might never see her family again.

There were many men besides Thomson who had helped Sir Gorges and sought his good favor. Among them were those who aligned themselves with powerful lords. The political chess game of their lives was underway as they pursued their own agendas. Among Gorges's forty council members were Mason and Argall.

In 1613, Sir Samuel Argall had led a force of Englishmen from Jamestown to Acadia and destroyed the French settlements of St. Souveur on Mt. Desert Island, St. Croix and Port Royal, Nova Scotia. These attacks effectively removed the early French threat to English plans for developing New England, thus paving the way for Gorges to gain control of commerce and the taxes he needed to justify project investments. This would effectively end the French threat to New England until the French and Indian War of 1745.

Captain John Mason, in March 1621, had received a patent from the council for land found between Salem and the Merrimac River, Massachusetts. The following year, Mason allied himself even more closely with Gorges as they jointly issued between them a patent for all the land along the New England coast from the Merrimac River to the Sagadahoc River and extending sixty miles inland. This land represented an area stretching from today's Massachusetts/New Hampshire border, to Bath, Maine on the coast, and a line stretching roughly from Nashua, New Hampshire, to Mt. Chocorua, and Bethel, Maine. They called it the Province of Maine.

That grant was split in 1633. The land north and east of the Piscataqua was called Maine, and went to Gorges. (The northern five islands of the Isles of Shoals (this name change, from Smith Isles to Isles of Shoals is dated as early as 1623 by Christopher Levett) were added to Maine in 1635. They are called Appledore, Smuttynose, Malaga, Cedar, and Duck.) Mason received the land from the Merrimac to the Piscataqua. He called it New Hampshire, after his home county of Hampshire, England. (The four southern Shoals Islands were incorporated into New Hampshire in 1635. They are called Star, Lunging, White, and Seavey.)

Reasons given for a territorial split of the isles were twofold: the separation blocked the growing Shoals' populous from uniting their islands into a separate and independent state; second, the division gave the leaders of each territory an opportunity to realize profits through taxes from the burgeoning fish industry there.

Meanwhile, the Pannaway Plantation was attracting more men from England. Edward Hilton had arrived with Thomson in 1621; later he was joined by his brother and family in what is now Dover Point, New Hampshire, in 1623. William Jeffrey was another who sought prosperity in the new land. He became the first person on record to live at the Isles of Shoals in 1628. Today his name marks the fishing grounds lying just twenty miles east of the Isles of Shoals, Jeffreys Ledge, where, as recently as the 1970s, Soviet trawlers would fish under the veil of darkness, vanishing beyond the horizon to international waters during daylight hours.

Thomson had developed a dream for himself, and a vision for the new settlers. A vision that showed how one should live in the land. His actions indicate that he had been troubled over stories of the natives' mistreatment. His vision went beyond the intoxicating moment of self-indulgence to embrace future generations of Americans. The desire to bequeath the children of the new land a life without conflict with the natives seemed to be paramount for him.

Though he was not pleased with the Pilgrims' conduct concerning native American affairs, Thomson did provide Plymouth Colony with assistance while at Pannaway Plantation. On at least one occasion Miles Standish went out in search of desperately needed food and supplies. Bradford's writings make reference to one such trip, indicating that Standish, ". . . must have been at Pannaway about the last of June [1623], as he returned to Plymouth in July laden with provisions he was in quest of, and bringing along in his company our Mr. David Thomson from Pannaway."[12]

In 1623 ships commissioned by the Council of New England which were seen in the Gulf of Maine fishing grounds tried to enforce council policy while gathering taxes. Already the new settlers displayed signs of resistance and independence, as indicated in this passage:

> About the latter end of June came in a ship, with Captain Francis West, who had a commission to be Admiral of New England, to restrain interlopers and such fishing ships as came to fish and trade without a license from the Council of New England, for they were too strong for him, and he found the fishermen to be stubborn fellows.[13]

After the construction of Fort Pannaway, Thomson oversaw the building of homes for the fishermen and their families. Soon this group was joined by men skilled in a variety of trades. Fur trappers, woodsmen, farmers, and sawyers had made the plantation the earliest diversified commercial center of New England. This new interest in the Isles of Shoals rendered Monhegan and Damariscove Islands and their difficult approaches much less desirable. By 1626, Monhegan had been all but abandoned, and the hub of commercial fishing had shifted to the Piscataqua River and the Isles of Shoals.

Amias Thomson undoubtedly wasted little time settling into her new home. Natives indentured to serve the needs of the new plantation came every day to help with her chores. Throughout the long days she crafted a home out of the wilderness. She adjusted to the raw uncivilized life of the Pannaway Plantation and accepted her husband's preoccupation with his work. Amias would have to plan her day's activities independently. Having grown up on the waterfront of Plymouth similarly unassisted, Mrs. Thomson undoubtedly found adapting to this new life exciting. Her father had been a noted woodworker and shipwright, and far too busy to see after his daughter's every need. At a young age, Amias learned to get along by means of her own devices. At Pannaway she continued to do what was needed to make her life in America work.

Thomson designed his plantation around this premise, that once his men had created a workable living area, the region would, on its own merits, attract new and self-sufficient settlers. He seemed to have had no desire to start out with a settlement consisting of naïve people who had little or no knowledge of how to survive, such as was the case at the Plymouth Plantation. Building self-reliance would have taken Thomson too much time.

In early December 1623, Pannaway received unexpected visitors. Sir Ferdinando Gorges's son Robert, the newly appointed governor general of New England, sailed into the Piscataqua with twenty would-be settlers on board. Gorges's plan had been to use the dwellings of a settlement in Massachusetts, but the site apparently did not suit the needs of young Gorges, who was two years younger than Thomson and had been a companion of his in their youth in Plymouth, England.

The well-intentioned governor general had trouble fulfilling any of his responsibilities while in New England. He and Captain West had failed to collect taxes and regulate the fishing industry along with their failure to establish his settlement. Discouraged, he was ready to leave that hostile environment on the next available ship bound for England. Unfortunately, with winter fast approaching, Gorges would have to wait until spring.

Gorges needed shelter for his people. One can imagine the humiliation he endured at having to ask a commoner to take care of his group. Thomson agreed to assist, most likely from a sense of obligation to Gorges's father. However, it seems he placed a few stipulations on the agreement: that he, not Gorges, would be in charge of the group; and, secondly, that Gorges himself must make the public announcement that Thomson would be their leader while at Pannaway.

All survived with relative ease that winter through proper management and rationing of food. With the approach of spring Governor General Gorges fled New England on the earliest fishing vessel to leave Monhegan Island. However, before departing America, Gorges exercised one last right as governor. He ordered the men of Pannaway to build a house for Samuel Maverick, a friend who had accompanied him from England. The house was to be located on the shores of Massachusetts Bay, in an area known today as Boston, and to be armed with guns from the Pannaway fort. Gorges further instructed Thomson to care for those people in his party who chose to stay behind. Crippled by instincts of servitude and humbleness, which likely fueled his desire to be free from such class slavery, Thomson's indebtedness to the governor's father tempered his anger and compelled him to comply with the orders.

During that summer the men from Fort Pannaway followed Thomson to Massachusetts, where they found a spot suitable for Maverick to live. Maverick recorded, in 1660, that in 1625 his house had been located "Two miles sowth from Rumney Marsh on the north side of Mistick River . . . [and] fortified with a pillizado and flankers and gunnes. . . ."[14]

By 1630 Maverick's fortified home was a well-known trading center and social gathering place. Edmund Johnson had arrived in Massachusetts, along with the great Puritan migration, and made this comment:

> [Winnisime was] . . . where Mr. Samuel Maverick then living . . . had built a small fort with the help of one David Thompson [all future generations would use the 'p'], placing four murtherers [cannons] to protect him from the Indians.
>
> . . . neare an island called Thompson's Island lived some few planters more. These persons were the first Planters of those parts having some small trading with the Indians for beaver-skins."[15]

Thomson built a house of his own on the island that stood not far from Maverick's across the harbor, the island he had visited with Dr. Vines many years earlier. During this time he brought Amias and son John to visit their new home. It was July and the season held great promise for the young family. He showed them how the new home and trading post would work, then his son John went out to explore the island with the native servant Wat Tyler.[16]

The Thomson house was located

> on the bank, on the east shore; just south of the center of the island . . . [it was] set by the four points of the compass facing the south. It was probably twenty-five or thirty feet square . . . one story high and built of logs. . . . Inside was a large room, at the back of which stood the broad and deep fireplace four feet across, which served both for cooking and warmth. . . . The cellar walls as well as the chimney were built of large rough field stones, and the cellar floor was laid with bricks ten inches square, which must have come from England by way of Little Harbor [Pannaway Plantation].[17]

Later that season Thomson and his family left the harbor for the sail back around Cape Ann and through Ipswich Bay to Pannaway Plantation. There, he saw that the men were managing well without him, especially since they had recently learned of Parliament's revocation of the fish tax in New England, with its Bill for Free Fishing. The original tax set by the Council of New England had been "5 pounds for every 30 tunns of fish."[18]

A slight but steady flow of new settlers was leaving Plymouth for Pannaway. Unwilling to live under the Pilgrim's strict government, these people were "dissatisfied with the high-handed way the Brownist 'saincts'[sic] were running the colony."[19] Settlers developed homesites from Little Harbor to Great Island and along the southwest shore of the Piscataqua to a place upstream known as "the bank with the wild strawberries." Located two miles from the fort, the steep bank rose thirty feet above the river. From the top of this rise the land fell away in a mantle of rich growth, gently sloping back towards both the downriver and upriver shores. On the upriver side, a natural freshwater spring was discovered in a nook down near the water's edge. The high ground of the bank served as a vantage point from which settlers could detect an approaching enemy. Additional protection came from the river itself, as the tidal flow there was at its worst. The main axis of the powerful current collided with the river bank on the ebb tide, making boat or canoe handling at times of strongest flow extremely dangerous. Today, the Piscataqua is rated among the top ten fastest navigable deep-draft rivers in the world.

After one last winter at the Pannaway Plantation, in 1626 Thomson readied his family for the move to their new home. Little is recorded of Thomson's life once he moved to Massachusetts. What does emerge is evidence that two years later he was dead. His death may be surmised from Bradford's writings where reference is made to an incident in 1628, when one Thomas Morton was forcibly removed from Merry Mount in Massachusetts by New Englanders. It seems that Morton was selling guns and liquor to the natives, and was openly defiant about his dealings. After repeated attempts to reason with him failed, several settlers and the colonists of Pannaway and Plymouth, led by Miles Standish, contributed the money needed to deport Morton back to England via the Isles of Shoals. Amias Thomson's name was among the individual contributors, noting she had given fifteen shillings. No further mention of her husband has been found. Within the year, Amias was remarried to Samuel Maverick. The circumstances surrounding Thomson's death may never be known.

Mrs. Maverick and her new husband lived at Winnisime, and soon established the early social center of Massachusetts. There they entertained Governor Winthrop and the newly arrived Puritan immigrants in 1630. The friendliness between the Mavericks and the Puritans soon weakened; the open display of frivolity at Winnisime did not sit well with frowsty Brownists. In 1651, the Mavericks fled to Saco, Maine, but the Puritans crept slowly out from Boston, and in time all of coastal New England fell under their influence.

Nine years later Maverick sailed to England upon the restoration of the Stuart monarchy. Having exposed the intolerable conditions colonists were subjected to under the Puritan rule, he submitted a list of demands to Charles II, requesting an immediate response. Maverick returned to New England with authority from the king to take what action he deemed necessary to improve the situation. However, even with royal support Maverick could not stem the spread of Puritan control over New England. By the 1670s the Mavericks were living in New York, where Amias died in that decade.

John Thomson followed a life at sea, returning to Massachusetts in the 1640s to take rightful possession of the deed to his father's island, which after much hassle was awarded to him. However, since 1634 the island had been occupied by the settlers of Dorchester for the operation of a school. John was unsuccessful in removing those people. It is assumed that daughter Prissilla lived out her life in England.

In many ways David Thomson was the "original Yankee." A man whose vision fostered a persistent, stubborn, and singular minded people whose descendants today are known for their great uncompromising traits. Those people are the people of New England.

At the age of thirty-six David Thomson was denied the summit of his dream from where he had hoped to look out over his accomplishments. He was denied the years of a man's life when he can reflect with wisdom that is simple and direct. However, Thomson did live to see his dream begin to draw character in the new land. His legacy is obvious. He, as much as any other man of his time, should be considered a leading pioneer in New England history.

4
NEW ENGLAND LOST AND GAINED

The native American looked down from Agamenticus to the broad valley of his forefathers. One day soon he would turn to the interior, to a land not yet settled by the men from the sea. No longer could the native look forward to the freedom of warm months by the shore. Lost were the days of great feasts on the food that had come from the sea. Lost were the rich low plains with their crops of corn and beans and squash for the harvest in the cooling months. Lost were the countless families whose life lines reached back to the days of the great wall of ice and beyond. And most of all were lost the many women of his nation who had carried the stories of their people, stories from when the first of their tribe had opened his eyes upon this land.

A deadly and evil darkness had spread across the land. It flowed through the forest on a thin whisper of air drifting from the dwellings of the people who had come from the sea. The deadly contagion stemmed from the diseases brought to America by the white man, diseases against which the natives had no natural immunity. A whole nation died at the hand of this unseen enemy. The native searched the forest where the spirit of his forefathers once resided with honor in war and peace; he found it gone. He turned to the men who had come from the sea, and they showed a veil of friendship, which soon fell, to expose a people without knowledge of the spirit of the land. They showed little desire to learn of the spirit or care for the traditions of the people who were already at home in the land.

Year after year after year more people came from the sea. Some became friends. Most became enemies. At first they had come only when the land and sea were ripe for harvest in the months of the fairest weather, yet more and more stayed. The native turned from the sea and looked to the forest and to his people. The spirit that had brought them laughter and joy was gone.

Many times the native returned to Agamenticus in search of the spirit, but it never again touched his soul. He looked far off to the great mountains whose peaks lay white beneath the winter's snow, though the valley was green. A pall of sadness descended on his shoulders, a sadness soon to be worn like a black robe by the people of his nation. A robe which in time would be worn as a symbol of resignation, not in resignation to the people who had come from the sea, but as a mark of resignation that the great spirit of the land had left them and was no longer there to give them guidance and protection.

To the Europeans, America was perceived for the most part as land open for the taking, void of domestication (*Vacuum Domicilium*), void of a law to be respected or feared. Put simply, the native American nations did not count. They were seen as subcultured and, at best, as only a brief, inconvenient distraction.

One can only imagine how rich life would be today if the collision of two cultures had rather been a fine blend where the identity of both could easily be discerned.

The destruction of the native American culture and way of life was accomplished not by any great military strategy, in the honor and the glory of battle to which the natives were accustomed, but rather, unwittingly, by the early explorers, who naïvely brought with them a variety of diseases. From first contact with Europeans in the fifteenth century, when the natives of New England numbered an estimated 100,000, to 1620, 80 percent of the native population was lost to European disease.

Demoralized and drained of strength, the coastal natives offered little resistance; such as there was, was easily suppressed by local militia until the upland natives gained support from the French in 1745. They watched the people who had come from the sea erupt from their ships in wave after wave. Between 1630 and 1640, 20,000 Britons came to New England. Starved for freedom they soon involved themselves in a life they had once found distasteful. Their new villages bore reminders of the very English towns and cities they had left. Their laws and regulations became strict and confining. They had missed an opportunity to blend their lives with the spirit of the land and the people who had come there first.

The men cut long narrow wounds in the forests for their carriages and wagons, linking town to town. Other roads were cut into the depths of the woods to harvest timber for homes and ships. Large open tears in the forest canopy began to appear. By the eighteenth century only one quarter of the forests stood in New Hampshire. (Today 87 percent of New Hampshire is forested; it is the second most forested state by percentage in the country.)

The native, for one last time, went to Agamenticus to search the land. From the corner of his eye, he caught the glimpse of a bird rising from the sea. He watched the bird soar above the valley and swoop down along the contours of the forest. The bird, an eagle, spiraled skyward high above until she was lost for a moment in the sun. Then she descended to a tree limb and stared down on the native for the longest time.

With a cry that echoed across the valley below and with a great stretch of her wings, she lifted off with slow, powerful strokes. As the eagle circled above, she let out another cry which sent a sudden chill through the native's soul. He ran to the tree and climbed as high as the limbs would allow and watched the bird fly off towards the great white mountains. Did he sense that the bird was carrying the spirit of the land to a new place far beyond where the sky makes love to the land and the sun hides in the darkness of the night?

The angered spirit lived among the peaks of the White Mountains where it never slept. Its anger turned into raging winds that swept across the summits, tumbling violently, aimlessly through the notches and valleys. These were winds the likes of which the world had never seen before.[1] From time remembered, the natives traveled little in the mountains of the angry winds.

In the absence of the spirit, the land of the coastal plain also became possessed of an anger that filled the hearts of its people.

Sir Ferdinando Gorges's monopoly over New England was severely hindered by the establishment of the Massachusetts Bay Company and Colony in 1629 and the Puritan immigration that began the following year. To counter the growing influence of the Puritans, Gorges and Mason created the Laconia Company. They attempted to control the successful fishing industry at the Isles of Shoals, the fur trading on the rivers, and inland timber cutting. With the blessing of Charles I, they also organized a group of settlers, numbering fifty families, to establish a village on the Piscataqua River. These settlers arrived in 1630 aboard the *Reliance*. The site chosen had been inhabited by earlier traders and proven ideal for a settlement. It was situated on the level ground just down and inland from the high river bank which was covered with vines of wild berries.

Sufficiently impressed with the abundance of these wild berries, the settlers called their new town Strawbery Banke Village. Soon a large fortress-like building known as the Great House was erected a few hundred yards from the embankment, toward the south. It became a general purpose building and provided shelter for the people when they were threatened by natives. These settlers also established, in 1638, an Anglican Church of England to help stem the spread of Puritan influence northward.

Gorges lost his monopoly with the abolition of the Council for New England in 1635, the year his partner John Mason died. The division of the land in the northeast established the territorial boundaries of what eventually became the six states of New England. The Massachusetts Bay Company had gained control and ruled with a strong Puritanical hand.

Trade activity increased with the homeland. Manufactured goods from the homeland were exchanged for fish, fur, and timbers, at first with little actual exchange of money. England resisted monetary exchange for as long as it could for fear that the new colonists would be able to finance an army and navy and trade their products elsewhere. When the colony became more self-sufficient, thus lessening its dependency on English merchandise, a step towards commercial autonomy was made. The exchange of money for goods sold was inevitable.

Each day brought new confidence that gains were being made in dealing with adversities and in controlling the land. Dams to operate saw mills were built far inland along the deepwater estuaries of what became the Berwicks and Dover. Farmers made wooden casks in the winter to hold fish bound for Europe. Fishermen built shallops. Lands were cleared for farms. By the mid-eighteenth century, agriculture, the raising of livestock and vegetables, would contribute £73,000 per year to the economy of New England through exports alone, while the fish industry generated £152,000.

Soon claims and counter-claims on the land were filed by feuding colonists. New grants were issued on top of old ones. Puritans came north and forced upon the settlers an agenda for strict living. "Thomas Warnerton, of Strawbery Bank, said: 'They are all rogues and naves at the Bay, and I hope to see all their throats cut.' "[2] Indeed, the Puritans managed to make life very difficult for everyone living within their sphere of influence.

Many settlers chose at this time to remove themselves from these conflicts and to live in more remote places such as the Isles of Shoals, where they hoped to be free from direct Puritan rule. However, in 1641, when New Hampshire finally fell to the Puritan Bay Company, the people of the Shoals "openly revolted against the Puritan roundheads, and declared their independence."[3] Their Church of England minister, Reverend Gibson, enthusiastically supported them, a direct act of defiance against the authority of Oliver Cromwell. But, in 1652, when Maine was drawn into the Puritan Bay Company, the Isles of Shoals people were unable to continue their revolt. A Harvard-educated Puritan minister was sent to them, named John Brock.

The year Brock arrived at the Shoals a petition to allow women to live on the Isles of Shoals submitted to the Massachusetts General Court proved successful, "It was ordered, upon the petition of William Wormwood, that as the fishermen of the Isles of Shoals WILL entertaine womanhood, they have liberty to sit down there, provided they shall not sell neither wine, beare, nor liquor."[4]

Women, until this court action, had been forbidden to live at the Shoals. Yet, in 1647, John Reynolds defied the courts and the wishes of the other island men and brought his wife to Hog Island, known today as Appledore. It seems, however, that the islanders had an even greater concern about Mr. Reynolds's other interests:

> It is by mutual consent of this Court ordered, that Mr. Renolds shall, within twenty days, remove his swine and goats that he hath at Hog Island from thence. . . . And as for the removal of his wife, it is thought fit, if no further complant come against her, she may as yet enjoy the company of her husband.
>
> Dated the 20th day of October, 1647.[5]

Apparently, the women whom the fishermen chose for wives were generally thought to be on the outer reaches of proper social behavior. They were

> like fishwives the world over, the mistresses of shrewd and biting tongues. . . .
>
> For instance, at the court held in Saco, in 1665, Joane Forde, wife of Stephen Forde, of the Isles of Shoals, was presented and convicted for "calling the constable Hornheaded rogue and Cowhead rogue." "Joane Forde," continues the record, "was punished for this offence by nine stripes given her at the post, at a Court holden in York, Decem. 2, 1665."[6]

The Isles of Shoals population soon increased with the repeal of the ban on women. By the end of the 1650s, the several hundred inhabitants petitioned the court in Boston for township status. In 1661, on the third petitionary attempt, their wish was granted and their town was named Appledore after the town of the same name found in North Devonshire, England, a small fishing village on Barnstaple Bay. This fledgling town was furnished with courthouse and fort, minister and church, meeting house and livestock, gardens and a thriving fishing industry, along with an already established academy on Appledore for boys of the best families of the new colonies.[7]

To the islands came such noted families as Cutts, Pepperrells, Wormwoods, Seeleys, and such men as Reverend Richard Mathers, Reverend Joseph Hull, and the notorious Philip Babb, among many others.[8] The fishermen among the Shoalers, in time, gained a knowledge of the island waters that bordered on the subliminal. From the mere sound of surf breaking on one cliff or nook or cove, a man could tell what particular landfall he was near, even while sailing in the thickest of fog.

Over seventy small cottages, each measuring approximately fifteen by thirty feet, soon dotted the islands. They were constructed with wood acquired from the sawmills inland near the great bay, or even torn from boats that had been discarded or wrecked. These homes were erected on mortared stone foundations and built like ships, tight and sound. A number of the homes were located along the rim of the islands, perilously close to the water's edge. Most, however, managed to withstand the elements, except for one.

In the summer of 1635 a powerful storm hit the coast—some historians believe it to have been a hurricane. On or about 14 August, at the height of the storm, the home of the Tucker family, situated on the eastern point of Smuttynose, was swept out to sea. Several weeks later that house washed on to Cape Cod, eighty miles to the south, "where it was hauled ashore and identified by a box of linens and papers. The Tuckers had fled uninjured as their house was wrenched from its foundation."[9]

During these early years of development, the Shoals became the contact point between Britain and the rest of New England. For captains and their navigators, the isles were easy to find, their surrounding waters providing deep anchorage and good holding ground for several ships at one time. By creating the Shoals as a hub of commerce, valuable time was saved transporting goods back to England. These same ships would return months later carrying letters and news for the people of New England. From the Isles, the colonists learned that the Puritan rebels beheaded King Charles I on 30 January 1649.[10]

While these new Americans were enjoying virtually unbridled expansion, the coastal native Americans mounted only feeble attempts to resist the taking of their land. Among the most notable attack by natives was that on the settlers of the western frontier, in an area known as the plains. In June 1696, natives came by canoe from York to a location just south of the Piscataqua River entrance. From there they moved overland to the plains where they slaughtered fourteen people and took four hostages. A village militia went after the natives and caught them early the next morning while they ate. Captain Shackford and his men routed the natives and freed the captives at what is called today Breakfast Hill, south of Portsmouth.

An attack at the Isles of Shoals occurred during Lovewell's War in 1724:

> the savages made up a flotilla of fifty canoes and cruised the mainland coast to the terror of all settlements. They captured twenty-two vessels, several of good size, one armed with swivel-guns, and made a foray on the Isles of Shoals, where they cut out two shallops but committed no other depredations.
>
> The old fort on Star was manned by Shoalers, and the whole village must have assembled there, except for Betty Moody who hid with her small children in a tiny cave at the opposite side of the island (eastern end). The long-accepted tradition is that once in the cave the smallest child would not stop crying, and the distraught mother, in attempting to stifle its cries, she stifled its life.[11]

New settlers to the Piscataqua River basin and the Isles of Shoals generated international commerce, to Spain, Portugal, and the Caribbean Islands. This region became the center of commercial activity in young New England. And so fears of vulnerability soon became everyone's concern. In 1632 a new fort was established on Great Island on the Piscataqua River, one of an eventual nine forts built over the years on the river basin, five of which remain today. Though crude in design the fort would serve to protect upriver settlements at the first sharp bend in the river, where it narrows and heads inland. This location served as a better vantage point for protection than the one chosen by David Thomson in 1621.

In 1653 local residents were still expressing concern for their safety and petitioned the general court at Boston for help,

> for want of some necessarie meanes to withstand any forraine forces & being not unsensible of the considerable trade both of fish and timbers exportable amongst us,. . . and also humblie to make request that yee would be pleased so to consider of our desires as that wee may truly be well fortified against any forraine assaults.[12]

As a result, a new fort was erected on the western rise of Star Island, Isles of Shoals. A rebuilding of that fort in 1692 measured fifty square feet when it was fully equipped with nine four-pounder cannons to complement the two existing guns and the forty-man garrison.

Strength and security came with the increase in settlers. Strength and security came with the building of villages and forts. Strength and security came, in time, as the people shed the very image of being settlers. Soon a new generation would be set upon the land, a generation retaining only faint images of how life in New England had been for their forefathers. A foothold on the land had been gained and won. They had become, themselves, native Americans.

5
STABILITY AND SELF-RELIANCE

While the New England colonies were prospering, in the 1640s England was reeling from civil war. The struggle between Parliament and Crown peaked with the overthrow of Charles I and his public beheading in 1649, effectively ending the power of the throne over Parliament. The sum total of these events for New England was that, with minor exceptions, the homeland left the colonies alone for vast periods of time.

One cannot discount the influence the religious conflicts in Europe had on the burgeoning colonies. From the moment that Martin Luther nailed his theses to the church door in 1517 there was no turning back the rising tide of Protestant sects and schisms. For each religious group struggling in Europe, whether Catholic or Protestant, a similar group could be found (but a few years later) in America, where often they continued to fight the religious wars. Puritans readily passed laws openly hostile to the Church of England and other religious sects. Thus Roger Williams was forced to flee Massachusetts in 1635 because of his radical ideas. Yet, by and large, the colonists of New Hampshire were more concerned with survival and profits than religion.

The Bank of Amsterdam and the Bank of London, both founded in the seventeenth century, initiated the breakup of the banking monopolies of private families. During this period the mercantile system gained complete control over Europe. Indeed, it was this system of high tariffs and domestic monopolies that would eventually fuel the American Revolution.

Meanwhile in Portsmouth and the islands off its coast the issues were far more simple. Would the crops come in on time? Who would help the widows of fishermen lost at sea get through the long winter? Their's was a struggle for more gains than losses, more strength to endure than weakness. They needed then more than ever a sharp focus on the tasks at hand and far fewer distractions.

By 1653 the villagers of old Strawbery Banke felt a need for change. A failure properly to honor the man who had made their new life in

The Jackson House located on Christian Shores, Portsmouth's northend, is the oldest house in New Hampshire, 1664 (still standing today) (NHHS #387)

America possible, John Mason, inspired them to adopt a new name. On 28 May 1653, by petition to the general court in Boston, their town name became Portsmouth in honor of their late founder, who had been governor of Portsmouth in the county of Hampshire, England.

Though life in Portsmouth was becoming more civilized the frontier still clung to the outskirts of town. Dangerous wild game continued to menace the local folk. In 1662 a bounty of £5 was ordered to be paid for any wolf shot within town limits.

Struggles over the issue of autonomy continued to strain relations between Portsmouth and Boston. Yet, despite the tension, the wealthy and educated of Portsmouth managed to persuade other local inhabitants to allocate £60 in 1669 for a new building at Harvard College, established in 1638.

Not unconnected with their agitation for autonomy was their most unpuritan regard for alcohol. The New Hampshire settlers' thirst for dark imported rums from the Caribbean Islands became legendary. They were not to be denied their grog no matter how strong the protest from

Boston might be. In March 1669 a tavern license was issued to Henry Sherburne and his wife. Their establishment became known throughout the area for its abundant rum supply. Other taverns were better equipped for ale drinkers.[1]

On 18 September 1679 New Hampshire became an independent royal province freeing them from the forty-year rule of Massachusetts. Maine would not be as lucky, remaining under Massachusetts rule until 1820. John Cutt became New Hampshire's first governor and Portsmouth its first capital.

This newly found independence reverberated throughout the region, and was directly responsible for a major change in life at the Isles of Shoals. Within three years of the severance from Massachusetts no fewer than forty families left the town of Appledore, Maine, province of Massachusetts to live on Star Island, province of New Hampshire. Little did Ferdinando Gorges and John Mason realize in 1635, when they had established the territorial boundary through the middle of the isles, that they would eventually provide the Maine Shoalers an alternative to life under the repressive rule of Massachusetts. The exodus left so few people on Appledore Island that the town was dissolved in 1682. By 1688 the island was all but deserted. In just twenty years it had lost virtually all of its estimated 600 residents.

With most of the Shoalers living on Star Island, it became necessary to petition for a new township, which was granted in 1715. The New Hampshire General Assembly designated Star Island as the site for the town of Gosport, the name of a small town near Portsmouth, England.

These young coastal villages were coming of age. By 1700 Portsmouth alone had a post office, hospital, prison, and headmaster, though its first public school was not built until 1708. By 1761 America's first regularly scheduled stagecoach run was in operation between Boston and Portsmouth, "Fare, 13sh. 6p. Capacity, three passengers."[2] In the 1690s a new trade was introduced, shipbuilding, which would dominate the Piscataqua tidal basin and its people well into the twentieth century.

Ever since the first fishermen came to the Gulf of Maine, the building of small pinnaces or shallops had become a daily necessity. Once settlers were established on a permanent basis, woodsmen expanded the search for New England white pine, which towered 200 feet over the forest floor, for export to England. These men were hired to cut the finest trees for the English shipyards' masts. Penalties were levied on those who cut

A view of Gosport village, Star Island, looking from Smuttynose Island. Though the photo was taken in mid-1800s, it likely shows the village as it would have appeared in much earlier times (NHHS #4030)

trees marked with the broad arrow. The king's surveyors reserved all trees they found with a base width greater than twenty-four inches. Only certain timber could be cut for home building, fencing, or burning as firewood. Whether driving through Wolfeboro, New Hampshire, past Kingswood High School, or hiking along the Mast Trail in the mountains of Wonalancit, New Hampshire, reminders of these first forest cuttings still remain.

The deepwater river system served well the shipmasters who came for the trees. On flood tides captains sailed their vessels far inland towards the headwaters of the estuaries where the timbers lay on the embankments. Their vessels were especially designed with openings in the hull at either end making below-deck stowage possible.

The natural lie of the land, with the forests crowded against the river's edge, eventually attracted boatbuilders from England. They established their first shipyards on islands near the river's mouth. Then, in time, literally dozens of yards of all sizes and capabilities could be found far inland where the Piscataqua splinters into a number of smaller rivers. White pine, white oak, hackmatack, and cedar grew near the rivers, which made the collection of materials an easier chore. In 1690 artisans from England came to the Piscataqua to construct the British warships *Falkland* and *Bedford Galley*.[3] These ships were the first of their kind built in America to fly the Royal Navy ensign. This marked the birth of naval shipbuilding in North America.

The frigate *Falkland* built along the Piscataqua River in 1690. This ship was the first naval warship built in America by the British (Portsmouth Naval Shipyard Museum)

For what seem purely political reasons no new contracts for shipbuilding in the area were issued until the 1740s. There was a certain fear among some Britons in power that if major ship construction took place the colonies could then develop their own navy or merchant fleet and so threaten England's monopoly over the colonies' economy. Nonetheless, in 1745 William Pepperrell, Jr., who had led 1,000 New England soldiers to defeat the French army at Louisburg, was rewarded with a contract to build the 60-gun frigate *America*, later renamed the *Boston*. The ship was launched from a yard in Portsmouth's North Mill Pond in 1749. Pepperrell went on to become the first native born American to be knighted by the Crown of England. He also headed a successful merchant shipping concern. In years to come the family business interests diversified into manufacturing bedroom linen. Today the Pepperrell name can still be found in the mills of Biddeford, Maine, and on fine bathroom towels.

The control of New Hampshire's politics during the colonial period was in the hands of one family, the Wentworths. John Wentworth became lieutenant governor in 1717. He was followed by his brother Benning, who in turn became royal governor in 1741. Benning held his position for twenty-five years, until he was eased out of office, and his nephew John became governor in 1766.

John harbored many lofty dreams for the future of his province, but youthful naïvety and public revolt denied him the opportunity to prove himself. Governor "Johnny" Wentworth gained the dubious distinction of becoming New Hampshire's last royal governor, the one who lost his province to street mobs in 1775.

Many wealthy merchants prospered during this time. As Portsmouth continued to dominate commerce in the northeast, merchants consolidated their trade interests with the West Indies and the colonies to the south. A variety of wood products and fish were exchanged for rum, molasses, sugar, and slaves. Merchant tallships became more frequent on the river. The prosperity brought a wonderful display of opulence to the streets of Portsmouth. The most obvious exhibition of wealth was reflected in the magnificent mansions built during the period just prior to the Revolution. Many of these colonial homes remain today and make the area one of the finest for viewing colonial period mansions in America.

Prosperity was not confined to the Piscataqua River basin. Spanish merchant ships were a familiar sight at the Isles of Shoals, swinging gently on their anchors as they were filled with dry fish and products from the mainland. Evidence of Spanish influence at the Shoals remains today in the name of Malaga Island, loosely shackled to Smuttynose by the 1820 Haley breakwater. Island town meetings dealt with such issues as what fines should be levied on those who left fish heads to rot above the tide line. Actual fines were instituted in 1755. Meantime they had more important matters to attend to—finding ways to avoid sending delegates to the general assembly on the mainland, along with their overdue taxes.

For a brief time prior to the Revolution, colonial New England enjoyed relative peace and tranquility, except for the grumbling concerning taxes. Had the Parliament of England been more responsive to the signs of unrest and had it dealt with the rise of resentment against its tax policy, a tax war might have been avoided, or at least postponed.

Governor Benning Wentworth (author's private collection)

Warner House stands on the corner of Daniel and Bow Streets (NHHS #A78)

Nowhere in New England was the resentment of taxes felt more keenly than in the Portsmouth area. From the fight to repeal the fish tax to the fight for eventual independence, the people of New Hampshire were determined to control their own destiny.

Self-reliance and self-determination grew in the men of the Isles of Shoals from their will to survive and to be free. By 1650 the isles were settled by a determined but unruly people. Reverend John Brock, a shining light in the repressive Puritan era, came to the Shoals that year to bring the fear of God and a lifestyle of temperance to the 600 Shoalers, who maintained the largest settlement in the eastern provinces at the time. During his twelve-year tenure Reverend Brock molded the islanders into one of the most self-sufficient communities in New England:

> Many substantial and well-furnished houses had been built. . . . Herds of cattle and flocks of sheep abounded. Some of the richest men . . . lived there, and left large estates valued at from two hundred to seven hundred pounds. It was an important center of trade, and had its large distribution warehouses.[4]

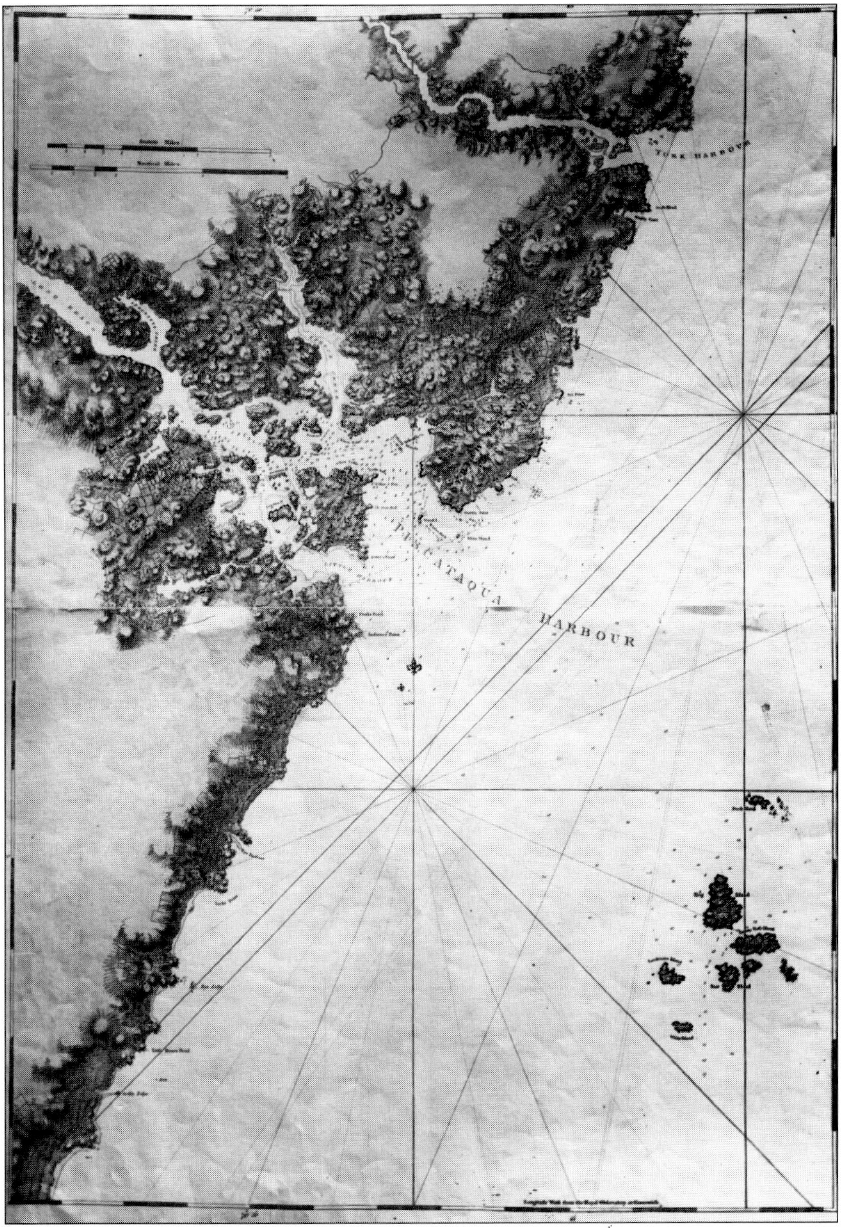

Joseph F.W. Des Barres' map of Portsmouth and Piscataqua harbor, with Isles of Shoals, 1779 (NHHS #1720)

Cargoes of all description were measured in hogsheads or quintals, several hundred of which were distributed to market from these warehouses during the height of the islands' commercial activity.

The demands and rigors of their daily work routine forged the fishermen into a new breed. From the beginning of time people of a lesser spirit have avoided putting to sea altogether. Even today few people can say that they understand fishermen or comprehend how they can live on the sea as they do, faced with daily perils as common as potholes during spring thaw. From the early morning hours to well past sundown they labored at setting and hauling back their gear. They stripped and stowed fish all day long as their boat pitched and rolled unpredictably. This was a life of extremes and hard work which afforded no time for show of emotions, for debate, for conflict from within. It was a life they grew to accept, stoically. And when one was lost at sea—or worse yet, when a whole crew was lost—the community placed their grief in balance with their acceptance that this was part of a life that had to be, with little time to spend grieving their loss.

Brock was the consummate man of God laid at the feet of "heathens." In time, his persistence won the Shoalers' faith and following, but not without some help from above. Any two parsons would have felt their task had been accomplished in the eyes of God when Reverend John convinced his flock to set aside the Lord's Day for worship. Not Brock. He pushed the issue, requesting one extra day every month in the "worship of our Lord Jesus Christ." The fishermen went to Brock and protested that they would defy his wish and go fishing on the day of his "extra worship." They claimed too many days had already been lost due to "the foulness of the weather." Though Brock must have sensed their wish for his blessing, he knew they would leave with or without it. He replied:

> "If you will go away, I say unto you 'catch fish if you can'! But as for you that will tarry and worship the Lord Jesus Christ this day, I will pray unto Him for you that you may take fish till you are weary." Thirty men went away from the meeting and five tarried. The thirty who went away from the meeting, with all their skills, could catch but four fishes. The five which tarried went forth afterwards, and took five hundred. After this, the fishermen readily attended whatever meetings Mr. Brock appointed them.[5]

Brock quickly ascended to a position of universal respect among the Shoalers.

It was among the best of times the Isles of Shoals would ever see as a village center:

> with all the reckless and improvident habits of the sailors and fishermen, and with all their hardihood, courage, and spirit of adventure . . . their "fearful trade" taught them such life-long lessons of self-reliance as almost to obliterate from their minds the very sense of divine protection and aid.[6]

After Brock's departure in 1662, for the next seventy years, life on the Isles of Shoals became a series of peaks and valleys under the guidance of a whole host of ministers, until 1732. That year Reverend John Tucke was ordained, on 26 July. By 1732 the Shoalers "were noted for their indifference to the law, their insubordination, their hostility to taxation, and their habits of gross intemperance."[7]

Born in the town of Hampton, New Hampshire, on 23 August 1702, Tucke was a fourth-generation New Englander. His family was well enough off to send him to Harvard College, where he graduated in the class of 1723 ranked seventeenth out of forty-three students. Until 1770 all Harvard graduates were ranked, not by scholastic achievement, but in the order of their social position. Reverend Tucke's family enjoyed a modest ranking.

Nine years after his graduation Tucke found his calling in life. Upon hearing that a position had become available in the town of Gosport, Isles of Shoals, Tucke applied and was given the post. Initially, it had to have been the lure of the liberal compensation that drew him to this remote outpost, where life was as base as anywhere he could find in all New England.

The islanders agreed to pay him £110 per year, plus £50 towards the construction of a home on a lot of his own choosing where he and his wife could live.[8] Within a few years, with his work at the Shoals fully appreciated, his salary was increased to include one quintal of fish from each man per year. They also took the time from their daily chores to make sure the reverend and his family were never in want of fuel for their stove or fireplace. His became one of the best compensated ministries in all the New England colonies.

Tucke became the only minister in Isles of Shoals history to spend his entire ministry in the service of its people. He shepherded the islanders with constant care far beyond the confines of his church duties, as he also attended to their medical needs, brought them together in regular town meetings, and kept, for the first time, records of such gatherings. He also ran the general store. In 1734 he won a vote from the Shoalers to open a school for their children, of which Tucke would be its first tutor. Such a selfless and dedicated man had little trouble winning his people's respect.

Tucke could easily have found a position of status and comfort on the mainland. He chose instead to go to sea, to live his life where the surf wraps a perpetual fence along island shores. A fence without form, better than any built on land, willingly kept the shepherd and his flock in place. Late in August 1773 sometime after conducting baptisms for two children, Reverend Tucke passed away. His death marked the end of the golden era of the Isles of Shoals fishing villages and a lifestyle the islanders would never see again.

In 1800 Tucke's grave was discovered and properly entombed in a raised crypt covered with a stone tablet inscribed with words of praise. Led by Edward Tucke in 1914 descendants acquired from the Piscataqua Savings Bank of Portsmouth, then owner of Star Island, the rights to a sixty-by-sixty foot plot of land with the grave in its center. After Tucke's remains were relocated on more level ground, workers erected a granite obelisk above the grave.

Crypt placed over Reverend John Tucke's grave in 1800. Note sparse vegetation not yet recovered from days of greatest population of Star Island during the fishing era (NHHS #4028)

Tucke monument under construction in 1914 (NHHS #2911)

The base of the monument encircled the vault and original redstone cover, but at no point did it bear weight upon the crypt. Each block of granite was locked into place on top of one another by "gun metal dowels" two and a half inches thick by six inches long, all secured with Portland cement and molten lead. Granite for the project came from the Pigeon Hill Granite Company of Rockport, Massachusetts. The blocks were brought from the flooded quarry by barge, with draft horses and buckboard wagons to haul them to the construction site. Once completed, the monument measured ten feet square at the base, rising forty-six feet six inches above the ground, and followed a design "after the Egyptian dimensions established as a standard thousands of years ago."[9] It is today the tallest tombstone in New Hampshire.

The impressive monument seems much taller than its forty-six feet, as it rises nearly a hundred feet above the immediate shore line. Inscribed on the monument's polished east face in half-inch deep letters are the words transcribed from the original vault lid of 1800:

Underneath
are the Remains of the
REV. JOHN TUCKE, A.M.
He graduated at Harvard
College A. D. 1723, was ordained
here July 26, 1732,
and died late in August, 1773,
Aet. 71.
He was affable and polite in his
Manner, amiable in his disposition,
of great Piety and integrity,
given to hospitality,
Diligent and faithful in his
pastoral office, well learned
in History and Geography as
well as general Science, and a
careful Physician both to the
Bodies and the Souls
of his People.

Erected 1800 in the memory of the Just.

Living at the Shoals during the time of Reverend Tucke was another man who helped guide the Shoalers' spirit and commerce. Samuel Haley and his family lived on the Maine side, on Smuttynose Island. He represented the essence of a "Shoaler," embodying what was eventually to become the essence of the American Yankee. Referred to as the "King of the Islands," Haley came to the Shoals in about 1750 and bought Smuttynose Island. Captain Haley's ambition was simple: to help the islanders gain self-reliance and independence from mainland merchants. He soon gained recognition for his entrepreneurial qualities; he was the man to see for nearly all the supplies anyone would need, from rope to liquor.

When Haley arrived at his island he constructed a home, which still stands today and has been dated to at least 1750. Over the years Haley developed, "a grist mill, lined out a ropewalk 270 feet long (for manufacturing fisherman's line), a windmill, salt-works, bakery, brewery, distillery, blacksmith's shop, and cooper's shop, and planted a cherry orchard."[10]

Captain Haley married and had two sons, one of whom, Samuel, Jr., carried on many of his father's businesses after the elder Haley's death in

Captain Sam Haley's house, *c.* 1750, is located on Smuttynose Island (photo by Rob Karosis)

1811 at the age of eighty-four. Haley was laid to rest in the family plot on Smuttynose and the inscription on his gravestone reads:

In memory of Mr. Samuel Haley
Who died in the year 1811
Aged 84
He was a man of great Ingenuity
Industry, Honor and Honesty, true to his
Country & A man who did A great
Publik good in Building A
Dock & Receiving into his
Enclosure many a poor
Distressed Seaman & Fisherman
In distress of Weather.

The "Publik good" referred in part to a longstanding tradition established by Haley. Throughout the years, when storms blew wild across the Shoals and horrible seas churned up the ocean, the isles became an oasis, a God's Port for mariners "caught out" in the storm. In the days before a lighthouse was erected on White Island, Captain Haley would rest a lantern on the upstairs windowsill that faced east towards the vast ocean. This guiding beacon became known as a symbol of hope for distressed sailors, who were guided by its warm glow to the island where they would find shelter and care.

6
PIRATES AND GHOSTS

When the subject is pirates little can be done to separate fact from fiction. Pirate legends have drifted down on the whim of history's gentle breath.

The high seas during this period of expanding world commerce were void of a common or enforceable code of law. The number of English merchant ships sailing the trade routes to India, China, and the Americas could not keep pace with the competition. The English fell behind the Dutch, French, Spanish, and Portuguese in securing a niche for themselves in maritime trade. The Crown was virtually bankrupt and unable to fund a merchant fleet or a navy. Internal problems and civil unrest crippled England's maritime interests, forcing a turn to wealthy lords and merchants with incentives such as Letters of Marque. These letters or commissions allowed privately owned ships (privateers) to sail under full authority of the Crown with the right to seize any ship flying the flag of an unfriendly nation. The captured cargo and vessel were taken to England where the privateers received handsome rewards. This joint venture brought great wealth to the Crown's Treasury and made development of a formidable Royal Navy possible. By 1696, "There were 234 ships with a total complement of 45,906 men and officers."[1] When its navy was well enough established England repealed the Letters of Marque.

Life on a pirate ship was not always filled with the swashbuckling, romantic, mutinous rogues and deeds of novels and movies. For many, the raids on world shipping were just part of doing business. The captain's job was simple: produce, or step aside. Granted, some captains had to be slain, but many were simply voted out of their position when another pirate who had gained the confidence of the crew took over.

Depending on rank and tenure, sailors were given a predetermined percentage or share of profits when the goods were sold. American colonial traders felt no particular sense of loyalty to any one country. Pirates sold their booty to them with few questions asked. New York harbor became a haven for the sale of such goods, and a place where pirates found retirement with the help of the local magistrates.

Once a pirate had acquired enough wealth, he had the option to leave his shipmates; he was not necessarily doomed to a life of endless piracy. With the money a new identity could be bought from corrupt magistrates. Within weeks of "retirement" the one-time pirate might reappear in society to walk freely and without fear among the village streets in the best English attire.

The Isles of Shoals, due to their remote location, also proved a favorite refuge for pirates. Throughout the colonies it became general knowledge that Shoalers were an independent lot with little regard for mainland life or authority. Pirates bartered with island traders for food, supplies, water, and spirits, usually without fear that one of them might sail away to alert the militia. Nonetheless some islanders were tempted by bounties which were paid for information concerning the whereabouts of pirates:

> In response one Robert Saunders in 1724, brought intelligence of a (pirate) ship haunting these waters. The general court allowed him forty shillings "To be paid by the Constable of Gosport, as he is behind in the payment of his Province rates for the year 1723." No more intelligence of this nature was advanced by Shoalers![2]

This time spent among the isles offered a moment of rest for the marauding corsairs from their endless voyaging.

Among New England's most notable pirates were Quelch, Hawkins, Bellamy, Bonnet, Avery, Dixie Bull, Bradish, Scot and of course, William Kidd, and Edward Teach known to history as Blackbeard. The earliest recorded pirate conflict in the area occurred in the 1630s when Dixie Bull terrorized America's new settlements. A band of local militia from the Piscataqua River successfully defended themselves and chased the pirates down the coast of Maine.

New England raised its own breed of pirate such as Low from Boston. During a raid on the Shoals he took three fishermen hostage and threatened them with death if they refused to curse three times the hated Reverend Cotton Mather. "Mather was detested by all pirates because he was so fond of preaching long funeral sermons to condemned pirates as they were about to be hanged."[3]

Stories of pirates cannot be told without conjuring up images of men with pierced ears and bandanas swarming over a remote isle to bury their treasure, and swear, on pain of death, never to reveal its whereabouts. In reality, treasures were often "stashed" out of necessity when conflict was unavoidable, since the pirates had no desire to be caught with the stolen goods or cash on board. The normal routine called for the booty to be sold for preferred monetary payment as soon as possible, with shares distributed in short order to maintain harmony among the crew. Nevertheless, tales of buried treasure persist to this day, and make the Isles of Shoals modern-day "Treasure Islands."

According to legend, Captain Quelch buried $275,000 at the Shoals in 1702. As a privateer out of Boston aboard the brig *Charles*, Quelch's captain, Plowman by name, was in possession of a commission which called for the seizure and destruction of any pirate ships he came upon. Quelch, being first mate, took command of the vessel when Plowman died. For reasons that seem obvious, Quelch and his men lowered the privateer flag, abandoned the commission and hoisted the skull and cross bones.

Two years after his visit to the Shoals in 1702 Quelch and all twenty of his men were captured, tried, and convicted of piracy. On 30 June 1704, along with six crewmen, Captain Quelch was hanged in Boston. Little of his treasure has been found.

Blackbeard, who died from twenty-five wounds inflicted by colonists in 1718, had also sailed the Gulf of Maine. In the early 1700s during a voyage through New England, Blackbeard sailed to the Isles of Shoals where he reportedly stashed several bars of silver. Though he spent the majority of his days along the east coast, records show that Blackbeard sailed to Scotland where the following tale evolved into one of the great lores of the Isles of Shoals and one which may provide a link with those bars of silver:

> On one of his cruises, while lying off the Scottish coast waiting for a rich trader, he was boarded by a stranger, who came off in a small boat from the shore. The newcomer demanded to be led before the pirate chief, in whose cabin he remained some time shut up. At length [Blackbeard] appeared on deck with the stranger, whom he introduced to the crew as comrade. The vessel they were expecting soon came in sight, and after a bloody conflict became the prize of Blackbeard. It was determined by the corsair to man and arm the captured vessel. The unknown had fought with undaunted bravery and address during the battle. He was given the command of the prize.
>
> The stranger Scot was not long in gaining the bad eminence of being as good a pirate as his renowned commander. His crew thought him invincible, and followed where he led. At last, after his appetite for wealth had been satisfied by the rich booty of the southern seas, he arrived on the coast of his native land. His boat was manned and landed him on the beach near a humble dwelling whence he soon returned, bearing in his arms the (near dead) form of a woman.

Captain Teach, better known as Blackbeard the Pirate (author's private collection)

> The pirate ship immediately set sail for America, and in due time dropped her anchor in the road of the Isles of Shoals. Here the crew passed their time in secreting their riches and in carousal. The commander's portion buried on an island apart from the rest [possibly White Island]. He roamed over the Isles with his beautiful companion, forgetful, it would seem, of his fearful trade, until one morning a sail was seen standing in for the islands. All was now activity on board the pirate; but before getting under way the outlaw carried the maiden to the island where he had buried his treasure, and made her take a fearful oath to guard the spot from mortals until his return, were it not 'til doomsday. He then put to sea.
>
> The strange sail proved to be a warlike vessel in search of the freebooter. A long and desperate battle ensued, in which the cruiser at last silenced her adversary's guns. The vessels were grappled for a last struggle, when a terrific explosion strewed the sea with the fragments of both. Stung to madness by defeat, knowing that if taken alive the gibbet awaited him, the rover [Scot] had fired the magazine, involving friend and foe in a common fate.
>
> A few mangled wretches succeeded in reaching the islands, only to perish miserably, one by one, from cold and hunger. The pirate's mistress remained true to her oath to the last, or until she also succumbed to want and exposure.[4]

The most infamous English privateer to hold a letter of marque was Captain William Kidd, feared by foreign merchants from Madagascar to the West Indies. When the commissions were revoked, Kidd, forced by a mutinous crew, continued to seize foreign ships. Considered a rebel by England, Kidd was pursued from the Indian Ocean, across the Atlantic to the West Indies where he stashed much of his wealth. He would argue his case without the incriminating evidence on board.

As Kidd sailed off the coast of southern New England, faced with certain capture, he was quickly running out of room to hide. He knew he would not escape. Through the Earl of Bellomont, then acting governor of New York, a meeting was arranged between Kidd and the Council of Massachusetts located in Boston. Kidd was confident that, if he were allowed the opportunity to present his case, he could reason his way back into the Crown's good graces. Just days before the meeting was to be held Kidd gave several thousand pieces of eight and valuable merchandise worth over 10,000 pounds to loyal friends and to his wife Sarah, who lived in New York at the time.

One story in the legend of Captain Kidd persists to this day. While he sailed off New England Kidd took one last bag of coins, weighing 40 lb, and hid it. Speculation as to where the treasure may be has persisted in local histories from New York to Nova Scotia. So grew the legend of Kidd's treasure being stashed among the rocks of the Isles of Shoals. The legend today goes as far as to identify a probable location: on the eastern shore of Star Island far below the high cliffs where a trap-dike forms in the tide zone in an area known today as the marine gardens. It is here, below the monument to Captain John Smith, that legend places Captain Kidd's treasure.

Kidd went to his meeting in Boston on the strength of Bellomont's assurance, " 'I make no manner of doubt but to obtaine the King's pardon for you. . . . I assure you on my word and honour I will perform nicely what I have now promised tho this I declare before hand that whatever treasure or goods you bring hither I will not meddle with. . . .' "[5]

Bellomont went back on his word. Potential rewards for the capture of Kidd lured him into a conspiracy against the pirate. His moral fiber dissolved, Bellomont sprung the trap, "with Kidd's cries ringing in his ears, Bellomont could start to count his profits."[6]

Kidd was sent back to a country unsympathetic to his plight. In London his once influential position had vanished. Old friends who had helped when he was a privateer failed to come to his defense. They regarded Kidd as one who no longer served their needs. Captain Kidd pleaded his case: it had been his mutinous crew who had forced him to commit acts of piracy. If he failed to persuade them, the alternative was death. His cry fell on deaf ears. England wanted a message sent to all pirates of the high seas. A trial, whose outcome was already assured, commenced. The verdict: guilty of piracy.

On 23 May 1701 Captain William Kidd, along with three other convicted pirates, was taken from Newgate Prison to Wapping on the Thames. Along the route the public crowded the street for a sight of the famous pirate, and to offer him a last bit of spirits. By the end of his journey he was pretty near drunk. He remained his unrepentant and defiant to the end, though it took two attempts to kill him. The first time the rope broke.

A common practice of the day was to throw the pirate's body over the bank at Wapping to drift out to sea, but this would not do for Kidd. In death his body served those who had prosecuted him as a warning to all his kind. England now had a new policy for dealing with pirates: relentless pursuit, capture, a merciless trial, and humiliation after death. Kidd's body was stood upright in a wire cage and hung from a tree at Tilbury Point, by the entrance to the Thames, a grim symbol marking the beginning of the end of the classic age of piracy.[7]

Stories of ghosts tag along at the heels of pirate tales like so many lost puppies. Through the ages, Isles of Shoals legend has provided us with one tale where the spirit of Scot's mistress haunted the Isles:

> [Her ghost] has been seen more than once on White Island—a tall, shapely figure, wrapped in a long sea-cloak, her head and neck uncovered, except by a profusion of golden hair. Her face is described as exquisitely round, but pale and still as marble. She takes her stand on the verge of a low, projecting point, gazing fixedly out upon the ocean in an attitude of intense expectation. A former race of fishermen avouched that her ghost was doomed to haunt those rocks until the last trump shall sound, and that the ancient graves to be found on the islands were tenanted by Blackbeard's men.[8]

Celia Thaxter, nineteenth-century poet laureate of the Isles of Shoals, perpetuated this romantic tale in her account:

> I have before me a weird, romantic legend of these islands, in a time-stained, battered newspaper of forty years ago. I regret that it is too long to be given entire, for the unknown writer tells his story well. He came to the Shoals for the benefit of his failing health, and remained there late into the autumn of 1826, "in the family of worthy fishermen." He dilates upon the pleasure he found in the loneliness of the place, "the vast solitude of the sea; no one who has not known it can imbibe the faintest idea of it." "From the hour I learned the truth," he says, "that all which lives must die, the thought of dissolution has haunted me;—the falling of a leaf, a gray hair, or a faded cheek, has power to chill me. But here in the recesses of these eternal rocks, with only a cloudless sky above and an ocean before me, for the first time in my life have I shaken off the fear of death and believed myself immortal."
>
> He tells his strange story in this way: "It was one of those awfully still mornings which cloud-gazers will remember as characterizing the autumn months. There was not a single vapor-wreath to dim the intense blue of the sky, or a breath to ruffle the almost motionless repose of the great deep; even the sunlight fell seemingly with a stiller brightness on the surface of it." He stood on a low, long point fronting the east, with the cliffs behind him, gazing out upon the calm, when suddenly he became aware of a figure standing near him. It was a woman wrapped closely in a dark sea-cloak, with a profusion of light hair flowing loosely over her shoulders. Fair as a lily and as still, she stood with her eyes fixed on the far distance, without a motion, without a sound. "Thinking her one of the inhabitants of a neighboring island who was watching for the return of a fishing-boat, or perhaps a lover, I did not immediately address her; but seeing no appearance of any vessel, at length accosted her with, 'Well, my pretty maiden, do you see any-thing of him?' She turned instantly, fixing on me the largest and most melancholy blue eyes I ever beheld, said quietly, 'He will come again.'" She disappeared around a jutting rock and left him marvelling, and though he had come to the island,. . . for a forenoon's stroll, he was desirous to get back again to Star and his own quarters after this interruption. . . . Finding nothing—no woman on the island resembling the one he had met—and "hearing of no circumstance which might corroborate the

unaccountable impression," he resolved to go again to the same spot. This time it blew half a gale; the fishermen in vain endeavored to dissuade him. He was so intensely anxious to be assured of the truth or fiction of the impression of the day before, that he could not refrain, and launched his boat, which sprang strongly upon the whitened water, and, unfurling his one sail, he rounded a point and was soon safely sheltered in a small cove on the leeward side of the island. . . .

Then he leaped the chasms and made his way to the scene of his bewilderment. The sea was rolling over the low point; the spot where he had stood the day before, "was a chaos of tumult yet even then I could have sworn that I heard with the same deep distinctness, the quiet words of the maiden, 'He WILL come again,' and then a low, remotely-ringing laughter." He went on to return day after day until he recorded his last visit. "The last time I stood with her was just at the evening of a tranquil day. It was a lovely sunset. A few gold-edged clouds crowded the hills of the distant continent. . . . The ocean lay blushing beneath the blushes of the sky, and even the ancient rocks seemed smiling in the glance of the departing sky. Peace, deep peace was the pervading power. The waters, lapsing among the caverns, spoke of it, and it was visible in the silent motion of the small boats, which, loosening their white sails in the cove of Star Island, passed slowly out, one by one, to the night-fishing." in the glow of the sunset he fancied the ghost grew rosy and human, in the mellow light her cold eyes seemed to soften. But he became suddenly so overpowered with terror that "kneeling in shuddering fearfulness," he swore never more to look upon that spot, and never did again.

Going back to Star he met his old fisherman, who without noticing his agitation, told him quietly that he knew where he had been and what he had seen; that he himself had seen her.[9]

It had been the "old fisherman" who handed down from early times the tale of how the pirate's maiden had come to be on the Isles of Shoals.

Other ghost stories tell of how a man out with a party of friends exploring Duck Island saw, peering through a window of an old abandoned fisherman's shanty, the face of a beautiful woman. Upon further investigation, he found no such person when he entered the shack.

Perhaps the most famous ghost of the Isles of Shoals was that of Philip Babb. He came to the Isles in 1652, appointed by the magistrate of Boston to the post of constable. In his lifetime he managed a tavern, a trading post, and served as butcher. It seems possible that he held little regard for the Puritan authority. Being highly motivated by the potential profits to be realized at the Shoals, it is speculated that Babb conducted business not only with legitimate business people but also pirates. There is no evidence to bear out the rumor that he actually sailed with them.

In his book *Ninety Years at the Isles of Shoals*, Oscar Laighton, son of Thomas Laighton, who founded the hotel era at the Isles of Shoals in 1848, goes on to tell his own account of Philip Babb's ghost:

> Appledore House stood in the valley between the north and south hills of the island. The valley terminates on the east in Broad cove, on the west in Babb's Cove . . . Babb's house was on the south hillside near the cove. When we first came to Appledore (1839–40) there was a large excavation at the head of the cove, where Babb had dug for treasure. There has always been a story that Captain Kidd buried money over these islands, as Sam Haley's find of silver on Smuttynose would seem to prove.[10] Babb made a big effort to dig up something. The pit he made was thirty feet across and ten feet deep, as I remember it. The place was filled up level in the great storm of 1851. Father told Judge Whittle that Babb at last discovered a big iron chest at the bottom of the pit, and, with his friend Ambrose Gibbons tried to lift it out, but it was too heavy, and with a hammer and cold chisel they finally started the cover a little, when smoke, like burning sulfur, came from under the lid; that when at last they burst it open, red hot horseshoes flew out. Babb and his friend escaped, but the chest is still there. Just at dusk on pleasant evenings we would see Babb's ghost standing at the head of his cove near the pit he dug. It was very real and no islander would venture near after nightfall. Babb's ghost persisted until the Coast Guard built their boathouse over his treasure (1908), when it [the ghost] disappeared.[11]

The following descriptions detail the image of Babb's ghost:

> The face of the spectre is pale, and very dreadfull to behold; and its neck, it is averred, shows the livid mark of the hangman's noose. It answers to the name of "Old Bab [*sic*] ."[12]

> [One] could see the face and recognize the butcher's frock and the belt of Babb. . . . The white stripes in the frock gleamed like phosphorescent light, so did the awful eyes . . . the shape grew indistinct, first thick and cloudy, then thin, dissolving quite away. . . .[13]

During his lifetime, Babb became a very successful business man. Upon his death, in early 1671, his estate was worth £320 6s. 8d. Philip and his wife had five children, all boys. Today, well over 150 families throughout the country have traced their roots back to Philip Babb and his sons.

Stranger tales than even those of pirates and ghost were being told along the waterfront well into the nineteenth century. Tales that were far more common and believable in the days before enlightenment. The 9 June 1827 *Portsmouth Journal* reported,

> An account of a terrible Sea Serpent seen by the crew of an Irish ship, the *Quebec-Trader*, Captain Cleary . . . a boat's crew was sent from Q.T. to board a wreck; the man first on deck was seized and devoured immediately by a monster; the rest pulled for the ship. The wreck drifted near the ship, and enabled those on board to discern the serpent distinctly. He was coiled up on deck—they fired at him, and he went overboard. They supposed him to be 60 feet long, and 9 feet in girth.

7
SEEDS OF REVOLT

For a century and a half Britain continued to use the colonies as an all-purpose dumping ground. From various religious groups whose presence in England was a bother to the Crown or Parliament came much of the population of New England by 1760. That history is written by the victors would seem to be borne out by the perceptions of the American revolutionaries handed down through time. They were firmly convinced that the colonists' loyalties were evenly split between the Crown and the separatist movement, when actually the overall sentiment among the American intelligentsia was support for the king and opposition to the revolutionaries.

It is also important to understand that the hallowed political cry, "Taxation without representation," did not stand alone as the prime mover of revolt. By 1760 England had invested over £20 million in the American colonies. It also had become increasingly dependent over the years on American raw materials such as tobacco, fish, food, and other staples. Britain could ill afford to lose its monopoly over those resources and would use the hugh debt to supress cries for autonomy.

Nevertheless, for much of the time between 1640 and the 1760s the British Parliament had virtually ignored the signs of growing independence and coming of age burgeoning in the American colonies. However, when William and Mary came to power in 1689 they quickly moved to accommodate many of the colonists' complaints, for due to their financial burdens caused by the wars with France, they were faced with no other choice—they had to turn to the wealthy Americans for funds. Parliament, with the blessing of the Crown, began over the following years to pass a number of tax laws directed against their colonies. The taxes provoked such anger that the most radical colonial leaders were able to play upon it and begin a series of agitations aimed at severing ties with England, activities which began to escalate in the 1760s.

There was no one better to serve as prime agitator than Sam Adams, who was a "nagging malcontent that you want to poke in the nose and yet the kind of fellow you want on your side in an eye gouging fight. . . . He was the seven-year-itch. He was a burr under the saddle. . . . Such men breed revolutions. . . . Adams . . . kept things in a hassle. . . . This is the man who, as much as any other, nudged and nagged us into revolt.[1]

In Portsmouth nothing since the great earthquake of November 1755 shook the town so completely as the Stamp Act. By September 1765 effigies of the local stampmaster, an employee of the Crown, were hung in Market Square, paraded around town by an angry mob, and later burned.

In October the *New Hampshire Gazette* editors orchestrated a mock "two days of mourning" over the Goddess of Liberty's death. The Liberty Pole, erected near the bridge by Puddle Dock, where the Strawbery Banke Museum is today, flew the first revolutionary flag, on which was emblazoned a snake and the phrase "Don't Tread on Me". The next year protests escalated with mobs rampaging through the streets of Portsmouth. On 9 January 1766 they converged on the doorstep of George Meserve and compelled him to surrender his commission as stampmaster. Their persistence finally drew results. In May 1766 Portsmouth and the colonies celebrated the repeal of the Stamp Act .

This repeal, a brilliant political retreat by the English Parliament, was soon followed by an act which fell off the chart of common sense. With the passage of the Townsend Acts—known in the colonies as the Intolerable Acts—by Parliament in 1767 the protest began anew. The American colonies were now subject to an import tax on tea, which inspired the Boston Tea Party of 1773. In Portsmouth, locals seized the cargo of the brig *Revolution* from the tax collector who had taken possession of it when local merchants failed to pay the appropriate duty. In fact, on 15 December, the day before the Tea Party, the people of Portsmouth voted against the tea tax.[2] When the British navy blockaded Boston harbor following the Tea Party the people of Portsmouth responded quickly with aid. On 10 October 1774, the town voted publicly to send the people of Boston and Charlestown relief of £200.

By the end of 1774 when the British placed a restriction on gunpowder imports, the Boston revolutionaries turned to their comrades in New Hampshire once again. On 13 December 1774 Paul Revere was given instructions to deliver a letter to Captain Samuel Cutts, of the New Hampshire Militia, who was then living on Market Street in Portsmouth. Revere, a silversmith from Boston, had spent much of the past year avoiding the British regulars while transporting communication between the Boston revolutionaries and the Continental Congress meeting in Philadelphia.

That very evening, upon receiving his orders, Revere set out on the sixty-mile ride through the back roads to avoid contact with British regulars. That ride provided the Americans with a critical turning-point in what was quickly becoming a full-fledged revolution.

The letter Revere delivered contained information that a British warship would soon be dispatched from Boston to Portsmouth harbor. Troops on board were either to remove all 100 gunpowder kegs, 50 muskets and 16 small cannons from the site of the 1635 fort, then known as Fort William and Mary in New Castle, or to occupy and defend the fort. In either case, immediate action had to be taken since only a light detachment of five soldiers under the command of John Cochran stood guard at the fort. In light of the embargo against gunpowder imports, confiscation of the munitions was imperative.

Within twenty-four hours, on 14 December, 400 men calling themselves the Sons of Liberty sailed down the Piscataqua River in shallops and gundalows, led by John Sullivan and John Langdon. Once the men made landfall at New Castle at mid-afternoon they were deployed on all sides of the fortress. Cochran yelled to the mob to disperse or face the anger of his cannons. The cry to advance went out and in turn was answered by errant bursts of fire from just three four-pounders and one badly aimed round from the defenders' muskets. Before the British could reload, the colonists seized the fort. For the first time a British flag was lowered by American colonists.

By dusk the men made their way back into the headwaters of the Piscataqua River basin, vanishing into Exeter and Durham. The powder was stored beneath the pulpit of the meeting house in Durham until needed by the patriots of Boston. That night, as they reviewed the day's events, it came to their attention that they had failed to secure the muskets and small cannons for one reason or another. The men returned the next night and again met with little opposition. These acts of treason directed against a fort flying the British flag were among the first recorded overt military actions taken by colonists against England.

It is reasonable to suppose that the stolen armaments and powder were transported to Massachusetts to become part of the stores hidden at Lexington and Concord by the rebel colonists.

The New Hampshire Militia rallied to support the rebel cause almost immediately after the skirmishes at Lexington and Concord. It was well represented in Boston at the Battle of Bunker Hill. They numbered over 2,000 strong and were led by General John Stark, who stands with two other men credited with the most famous battle cry in American history. After the patriots had exhausted their ammunition, Stark directed his men to cover the retreat behind a fence. He stood before them and, not wanting to waste the last of their shot, cried out, "Wait till you see the whites of their eyes! Pick out the officers. Aim low. Fire at the crossing of the belts."[3]

Despite the victory of the colonists at Lexington and Concord and the subsequent siege of Boston, time and extraordinary discipline were needed to fashion the colonial mobs into a disciplined army which could meet the challenges of war against British regulars. Luckily, the British delayed their military response, giving the weaker and less organized rebels the desperately needed time to gain strength and training.

Among the mistakes made by the British was a failure to give Portsmouth proper status as a potential battle front, though the small seaport was on the outer fringes of the conflict.

In August 1775 at a session of the General Court of New Hampshire in Exeter, Colonel John Fenton of Plymouth displayed contempt toward the rebels and was quickly expelled from the chamber. He fled to Portsmouth, where an angry and drunken mob found him sheltered in Governor Wentworth's home on Pleasant Street. The mob demanded Fenton's surrender, or the governor's home would be torched. Fenton courageously gave himself up to spare the governor and his family inevitable harm.

Wentworth knew that Fenton's surrender would quiet the mob for only a short while. He quickly gathered a few valued belongings and family and fled to Fort William and Mary, which was still in the possession of loyalists. A messenger rowed out into the harbor to the anchored British frigate *Scarborough* and told its captain of the trouble. Interrupting his duties of blockading the port of Portsmouth against any vessel bringing supplies and food to the insurgents, Captain Barclay took the governor and his family on board for safe keeping. Wentworth and his family were eventually taken to Boston, then under British control.

The youthful governor refused to believe he had lost his colony to what was no more than a handful of irrational rebels. When he had become the newly appointed governor in 1767 Wentworth had been filled with a sense of righteous ambition and naïvety. He expected his subjects to share in his dream, that one day his province would become the gemstone of the colonies.

Grossly overextending his expense allowance and neglecting his subjects, Wentworth, who had attended Harvard with John Adams, ordered the cutting of new roads from Portsmouth to the lakes region, where he had his men build a mansion near what is now Wolfeboro. His vision for the future of the colony focused on the heartland, where wild game and forests were still to be found in abundance. His plans were one day to move the seat of government there, bringing with him a good deal of the population. He reasoned, wrongly, that his pride and enthusiasm and general sense of fair play toward his people would override the rebels' defiant behavior.

Wentworth simply failed to understand the colonists' basic needs and frustrations. He was offering a dream when all they wanted was food and free trade. Confident that he could restore reason to the general court and regain order in "his Province," on 21 September 1775 Wentworth sailed from Boston aboard the *Scarborough* to Gosport harbor, Isles of Shoals, which were not yet showing a preference for either Crown or colonies. Undoubtedly the islanders were more concerned with day-to-day existence than with the issues of revolt.

By means of messengers Wentworth sent communiqués to the general court in the form of proclamations calling for the legislature to come to its senses and denounce the revolt. This futile gesture became the last act of a royal governor in the province of New Hampshire. The colonial rule of 150 years came to an end in an ugly, disorganized manner.

Governor Wentworth was a man of concessions who ultimately fell victim to the overwhelming movement of revolt. Discouraged, Wentworth left the Shoals and New Hampshire never to return again. Soon he would send his family to England and later, when all hope was lost, he too would leave America. After the war, England gave him the governorship of Nova Scotia, where many of the colonial loyalists had fled during the conflict.

It was common knowledge throughout Portsmouth that the independent Shoalers were still trading with the British, even though on 11 March 1775 the British flag had been lowered there for the last time. Rebel leaders expressed concern that if the islanders were left alone, the

Interior photograph of sitting room of York Harbor Inn, York harbor, Maine. This section came from the Isles of Shoals during the Revolutionary War (York Harbor Inn, photo by D. Armsden)

British navy would use their harbor and islands, posing a direct threat to Portsmouth's safety. On 5 January 1776, the order came from the New Hampshire assembly to evacuate the Shoals. The evacuation began eleven days later.[4]

The exodus was slow, but complete enough to warrant the removal of the ministry to York, Maine. During this period many island homes were actually removed intact by barge, or dismantled and reassembled along the coastal region. Counted in those buildings that still stand today are the Star Island parsonage, located on the shore road from Kittery to York, and the center structure of what is today a fine food and lodging establishment in York Harbor, Maine, The York Harbor Inn and Restaurant.

Some historians are quick to blame the Revolution for the downfall of the Isles of Shoals' fishing and trading industry. It is true that it serves well as a benchmark for the decline, but it is evident that even before John Tucke's death in 1773 the Isles' influence as a major commercial center was fading. From 1767 to 1775 Gosport's population fell from 284 to only 44. Islanders had realized that nearby ports were becoming the new centers for fish trading, and that the Isles were slowly being passed over by merchants in much the same way that Monhegan Island had been abandoned for the Shoals in 1628.

While this struggle for national freedom consumed the colonies, a small tremor rattled the distracted village of Portsmouth. It rose from the murk of the river in thick fog, creeping over damp cobbled streets where cautious men stopped in pools of light shed from corner lamps, looking back over their shoulders into the black night before moving on.

On 12 November 1779 at the height of the American Revolution a petition was sent to the New Hampshire legislature by twenty slaves, held in Portsmouth, requesting the mens' freedom. "This was not accomplished."[5]

Portsmouth's own signatory to the Declaration of Independence, William Whipple, was a trader in slaves. He moved slaves through a secret tunnel which passed under Market Street between his home, the Moffat-Ladd House, and the waterfront docks on Ceres Street. However, Whipple was not without compassion. When facing Burgoyne's army at the Battle of Bennington, Whipple's slave, Prince, cried, "Master, you are going to fight for your liberty, but I have none to fight for." "Behave like a man and do your duty," said General Whipple, "and from this hour you shall be free."[6]

8
JOHN PAUL JONES COMES TO PORTSMOUTH

With war against England imminent a local militia was soon established under the leadership of William Whipple and John Sullivan. Teams of men were assigned to watch the harbor entrance for British cargo ships and intercept them if possible. What confiscated material was not needed would be sent on to Boston and other contact points within the colonies. Many items were taken directly to General Washington, who called on New Hampshire for men, clothing, blankets, and general supplies throughout the entire war.

Once Governor Wentworth had been overthrown, fear of reprisal forced many Portsmouth residents to flee inland. Leaders of the revolt moved the seat of their new government for the same reason. They chose Exeter, a small town ten miles inland on the Squamscot River, still accessible to Portsmouth by small shoal draft boats, but not by a British man-of-war. In 1805 the permanent capital was located in Concord.

Among the immediate tasks of the Continental Congress was establishing a naval fleet. With New Hampshire forests free from English control, woodsmen had unlimited access to the timbers required for ship construction, and Portsmouth had the shipwrights.

On 13 November 1775 the situation deteriorated drastically. The General Court of Massachusetts, still loyal to the Crown, began issuing letters of marque to any privateer willing to help rid coastal America of ships attempting to deliver aid to the revolutionaries. The Continental Congress countered with their own measure on 13 December calling for the construction and outfitting for war of thirteen ships, "five to be of thirty-two guns, five of twenty-eight, and three of twenty-four."[1] Construction time was to take no more than three months, a seemingly impossible demand.

To help finance the project Congress relied heavily on funds and support from colonial patriots. On 21 March 1776, construction began on the 32-gun frigate *Raleigh* at Ringe's Wharf, North Mill Pond in

Portsmouth. The vessel measured 131 feet and became the first Continental Navy man-of-war built on the Piscataqua. Senior builder William Hackett and construction supervisor Captain Thompson, inspired by the call to nationalism, launched the *Raleigh* just two months after her keel was laid!

If Congress had had to rely solely on itself to fund its navy, without private contributions, the final chapter of the war with England might have had a very different ending. Among the wealthy revolutionaries of Portsmouth was John Langdon, a businessman, statesman, and financier of privateers.

However, wealthy individuals such as Langdon were not driven by the thirst for freedom alone. They saw the war as an opportunity to help and profit. Congress, unable to afford a full-scale navy, was forced to enlist its own fleet of privateers, whose owners would share in profits from captured enemy ships.

It is interesting to note that though the United States has not openly taken part in privateering since the war of 1812, there has never been a law passed by Congress disallowing its use. Not even an international treaty, the Declaration of Paris, signed in 1856, could pressure the United States into officially outlawing privateers.

John Langdon soon offered the services of his Kittery island shipyard located across from Portsmouth, where shipwright Hackett was ready to take on any new assignments. The next of which would be to build the 18-gun sloop, *Ranger*,[2] the namesake of Roger's Rangers, who distinguished themselves during the French and Indian War.[3]

On 10 May 1777 the *Ranger* slipped from her ways to become the first United States congressional warship to have raised aloft the Stars and Stripes of America. Several local women had busied themselves in a great rush to have the flag completed before the *Ranger* sailed from Portsmouth. They managed to piece together the ensign with remnants taken from their own garments.

Awaiting the launching of the *Ranger* was its captain, John Paul Jones. A Scotsman by birth, Jones held a natural antipathy for the English, those who were mishandling his beloved homeland. He was born John Paul on 6 July 1747 in Kirkcudbright. He added the Jones years later while visiting his brother William, then an American by adoption living in Fredricksburg, Virginia. The possibility exists that John Paul had assumed the name to disguise his true identity if captured. Already a wanted man

Bust of John Paul Jones (U.S. Navy)

The Bell Tavern and boarding house where John Paul Jones stayed while in Portsmouth. Today it is called the John Paul Jones House (NHHS #N651)

before the Revolution, Jones was known among the British naval forces as an ex-slave trader, merchantman, fugitive, and the "terror of the seas, the hero of a hundred fearful legends, and subject of . . . jealousy in the most brilliant courts. . . ."[4]

The service record Jones presented to the Continental Congress contained a glowing report on "his extraordinary intelligence and aptitude for acquiring knowledge in naval matters."[5] While promoting his superior knowledge of navigation, he declared to the revolutionaries that he was ready to serve for the greatest cause of all, "Freedom—the cause of human nature."[6]

> "When I entered into the service, I was not actuated by motives of self-interest. I stepped forth as a free citizen of the world, in defence of the violated rights of mankind, and not in search of riches, whereof, I thank God, I inherit a sufficiency. . . ."[7]

In December 1775, at the age of twenty-eight, John Paul Jones received his appointment from Congress as first lieutenant. Though the official date of the Act of Congress issuing appointments of rank was 22 December, actual commissions had been issued on 7 December. Jones received both his officer's papers and orders to report to Commander-in-Chief Hopkins aboard the *Alfred*, after which he was appointed captain of the *Providence*.

Jones quickly proved himself an able leader and seaman, scoring one victory after another along the coast. He was ordered to Portsmouth in 1777 to supervise the completion and assume command of the new sloop of war *Ranger*. He had with him, when he arrived, orders from the Secret Committee of Congress to sail for France to deliver an important message intended to help the American delegation in Paris convince Louis XVI to finance the Revolution. As added incentive for Jones the secret committee instructed him to take command of a new ship under construction in Holland after completing his mission.

Frustration became commonplace throughout Jones's service to America. He had assumed before arriving in Portsmouth that the *Ranger* would be ready for commissioning. Not only was the ship not ready, the non-navy shipfitters were up in arms over their back pay. Captain Jones, realizing the urgency of his new assignment, assured the men that he would see to their pay, from his own funds if needed.

An English biographer wrote,

> It is singular that during the first years of the American Navy, with the exception of Paul Jones, no man of any talent is to be found directing its operations. Had it not been for the exertions of this individual, who was unsupported by fortune or connections, it is very probable that the American naval power would have gradually disappeared.[8]

During his visits to Portsmouth in 1777 and again in 1781, at which time he supervised construction of the 74-gun ship of the line *America*, Jones boarded at the Bell Tavern, known today as the John Paul Jones House. After a good day's work, a little freshening up, and a good meal at the tavern, he would find among the town's fair ladies one with whom to stroll the city streets.

By the end of October 1777 the *Ranger* and her hand-picked crew (among them two free blacks) were ready for sea, along with a shipful of supplies, armaments, and spars too large, making her "cranky."[9] At the ebb tide on 1 November Captain Jones called for his men to cast off all lines. The *Ranger* moved out into the falling tide, on past Fort Point, out through the broad harbor opening, then out beyond the Isles of Shoals. Once cleared of land, she made good a course for France where the Revolution's destiny lay.

The urgency of Jones's mission became more evident as the war with Britain escalated. The Continental Congress and the independently wealthy leaders in its ranks were desperately low on funds. Without sufficient aid the revolt would die. In 1776 Washington and his army had been driven from New York City. Only a lightening raid on Trenton at Christmas gave the revolutionaries hope. However, in late 1777 the rebel cause was given a military victory of immense proportions.

On 16 August 1777 an advance column of British army regulars, under the command of General John Burgoyne, driving south toward the Hudson River Valley was intercepted by American forces. The New Hampshire Brigade, under command of John Stark, confronted a Burgoyne advance column west of Bennington, Vermont.

In the ensuing battle, the British were turned back by an American force that was inspired to arms by Stark's cry, "There, my boys, are your enemies, the Redcoats and the Tories; you must beat them or Molly Stark sleeps a widow tonight!" followed by, "Live free or die!" Facing the combined forces of Stark, Gates and Whipple, also from New Hampshire, Burgoyne's troops were decisively beaten. Today Molly Stark is commemorated by a mountain named in her honor near Lincoln, Vermont. Burgoyne, despite his defeat at Bennington, continued his sweep south until October 1777 when the Americans defeated him at Saratoga, New York. Burgoyne surrendered 5,000 men.

On 2 December 1777 the *Ranger* sailed into the port of Nantes, just one month after leaving Portsmouth. Jones busied himself with overseeing repairs and restocking his ship, waiting for word as to when he might take command of the ship *Indian*, under construction in Amsterdam.

Soon after the *Ranger* arrived in France, Jones sent Jonathan Loring of New Hampshire to Paris with the secret committee's letter for Dr. Franklin's delegation. The message contained news of Burgoyne's defeats at Bennington and Saratoga. Louis XVI was urged to grasp this opportunity to repay Britian for its capture of Canada twenty years before. The Americans urged him to come to their aid immediately with currency, troops, ships, food, and general war supplies.

The French king promised the American delegation full support. He guaranteed that they would receive everything needed to assure victory. France's entire resources were at their disposal. Louis XVI's investment in the American Revolution totalled $240,000,000.[10]

After two months of waiting for his new ship, Jones learned that he was not to be the *Indian*'s next commander. Her constructors had decided to keep her. All was not lost, however. Jones had recognized that it would be futile to build a navy designed solely to combat Britain's men-of-war. He urged the American delegation in Paris to recommend that Congress authorize the construction of smaller, more maneuverable and faster ships. He also stressed the importance of implementing orders for American ships to strike where the Britons were most vulnerable—at home in their own ports as defenses there were light. This would serve to distract the British command from its blockade of American ports. In effect, Jones was suggesting maritime guerrilla warfare. When the strategy was adopted, Jones received his orders to conclude his work on the *Ranger* and get on with the plan expeditiously.

The *Ranger* sailed from her berth in Nantes on 13 February 1778. Jones set her course for Quiberon Bay, where a French squadron was waiting to escort a convoy of American vessels into the English Channel. Realizing that he was to receive a salute of four gun volleys fewer than the thirteen he would be giving French commander Picquet, Captain Jones ordered his men to "Drop anchor!", while he engaged the French Admiralty in a debate as to whether or not he would receive "shot for shot" as was appropriate for an admiral, citing the fact that as he was indeed the "senior American officer (regardless of rank) at present in Europe, it is my duty to claim an equal return of respect to the flag of the United States. . . ."[11] However, his eloquent and haughty protest failed to win him the proper salute.

Nevertheless, on 14 February 1778, Jones maneuvered the *Ranger* into Quiberon Bay flying the Stars and Stripes of America. As his crew fired a salute of thirteen guns, Picquet's salute of nine guns became the first such recognition received by a vessel commissioned by the United States Navy from a sovereign nation.

Captain Jones sailed the *Ranger* with great dignity past the French fleet into the English Channel, where he attacked enemy ships whenever possible. He moved freely up and down the English coast, striking at will, including staging a land assault on Whitehaven, a town in which he had once lived. All of England was startled by Jones's bravado. He had brought the war home to them.

Several weeks after a treaty of alliance was signed between France and the United States on 6 February 1778, Jones received under his command the French ship *Duc de Duras*, renaming her *Bonhomme Richard* out of respect for Benjamin Franklin and his writings in *Poor Richard*.

In late September of 1779 Captain Jones and his men were sailing for The Texel in the Netherlands when, "on the 21st we saw and chased two sail off Flamborough Head. . . ."[12] This chase led to the greatest sea battle of the Revolution, between the British *Serapis* and the *Bonhomme Richard*. The *Serapis* was in every respect the superior ship, but Jones countered this advantage with a series of brilliant maneuvers. Even as his ship settled lower in the water from irreparable damage, he managed to lock the two vessels together and rally the spirit of his crew, crying out defiantly, in response to British Captain Pearson's order to surrender, " I have not yet begun to fight!" This set the stage for an unprecedented American victory in full view of thousands of Britons standing on shore under a full harvest moon. On 25 September as the *Bonhomme Richard* slipped beneath the sea Captain Jones took command of the *Serapis* and sailed her on to The Texel.

George III and his Parliament made a gross tactical error when they failed to place Sir George Rodney as commander-in-chief of the navy early in the war. Rodney was the only British admiral capable of matching strategies with the likes of Jones. During this time of national peril a man of Rodney's stature should have been recognized for his obvious talents and placed where most needed instead of spending the majority of the war in a debtor's prison. By the time Rodney was given the opportunity to deploy his talents, the war was lost.

Jones and his previous ship the *Ranger* returned to Portsmouth before the end of the war. The sloop of war escorted the captured British sloop *Chance* and a brigantine into the Piscataqua River on 22 April 1779.

Early in 1781 Jones returned to oversee construction of the 74-gun ship of the line *America*, and remained with the vessel after commissioning to serve as commander. When he arrived, he soon realized that the new ship, like the *Ranger* before her, was far from completed. Its outfitting was in desperate need of supervision.

Throughout the next sixteen months rumors persisted concerning an impending sabotage attempt on the *America*. Jones recruited a number of the boatbuilders to watch over the craft at night, paying them with his own funds. A whaleboat loaded with British regulars did row with muffled oars up the Piscataqua, passing astern of the *America* several times as she stood on the ways, but that was as close as they ever came to inflicting harm.

In September of 1782, as the *America* was nearing completion and Jones was preparing for the difficult launching, the captain received distracting news. He would be giving the ship to the French upon its completion, as reparation for the man-of-war *Magnifique*, lost in Boston harbor earlier that summer. This was the tenth time the Congressional Maritime Committee had promised Jones a ship and then reneged. His spirits undoubtedly were uplifted during this time by the visit of the Marquis de Lafayette, a longstanding friend and compatriot.

Jones set aside his personal problems and focused on the difficult launching of the *America*. The far bank of the river on the Portsmouth side was a sheer rock cliff, directly behind and down river, only 600 feet from the railway on Langdon's Island. If not careful, the men in charge of the launch would cause the *America*'s momentum to carry the ship on to the far shore, or, if miscalculations were made determining the strength of the flood tide, the ship would be lost on a submerged ledge just upriver from the launch site. An eyewitness account of the launching explained:

> It was necessary to launch exactly at high water. . . . It was impossible to fix stockades in the river on account of the current and the rocks. This defect could only be supplied by anchors and cables. A large anchor was fixed in the ground under the bow, from which depended cables of a proper length and ranged in a manner so as to be drawn gently after the ship, so as to diminish her velocity by degrees.
>
> When everything was prepared, Captain Jones stood on the highest part of the brow, or gangway, that ascended from the ground to the bow of the ship. From that position he could perfectly see the motion of the ship; and determine by a signal the instant when it was proper to let go one or both of the anchors that were hung at the bows, and slip the end of the cable that depended on the anchor, fixed in the ground on the island. The operation succeeded perfectly to his wish, and to the admiration of a large assembly of spectators.[13]

Jones left Portsmouth after the *America*'s launching ceremony with orders to serve on a French ship of another name.

John Paul Jones never attained a higher U.S. naval commission than captain. Individually, the members of the Continental Congress praised the defiant Jones, but as a body they failed properly to recognize, honor, or reward the man who had said,

> "When the American banner was first displayed, I drew my sword in support of the violated dignity and rights of human nature; and both honor and duty prompt me to steadfastly continue the righteous pursuit and to sacrifice to it not only my private enjoyments but even life, if necessary."[14]

They did, however, manage, after much debate, to award him a citation and gold medal in 1787.

No matter where Jones traveled after the war, whether in America, France, or Russia, where he served as rear admiral in Catherine the Great's navy, controversy and intrigue were his constant companions.

In time, Jones's life lapsed into one of melancholy, lacking direction or purpose, or the urge to join a new cause for humanity. Passion for life which once burned with rare intensity became barely a warm ember in his soul. He was consumed by his own unquenchable thirst for life. His spirit and fight were gone. Jones had become a true citizen of the world, disdaining the art of provincial politics, living without homeland or nation.

John Paul Jones retired to Paris where jaundice and dropsy caused his death on 18 July 1792 at the age of forty-five. Buried in Paris, his body was laid into a brine of pickle juice and sealed in three coffins where, in 1905, his remains were discovered and identified. The French, who had made Jones a chevalier, agreed to allow his remains to be exhumed and returned to America. Jones did receive fitting posthumous recognition from the United States when his body was brought to America by eleven naval warships sent by President Theodore Roosevelt. The vessels included the Portsmouth-built USS *Kearsarge*. Captain Jones's body is today enshrined in a magnificent crypt within the chapel of the United States Naval Academy in Annapolis, Maryland.

In July 1992 the State of New Hampshire and the City of Portsmouth, in recognition of the 200th anniversary of Jones's death, proclaimed, from the grounds of the boarding house which bears his name, that John Paul Jones was the adopted son of the state and city. His soul finally found a resting place in the bosom of the nation he so loved and served.

9
A New Nation

From the mainland, just down from the mouth of the Piscataqua River, the Isles of Shoals appeared on the horizon as they had for many years. Round granite knobs with toupees of shrubs were blemished by small stick homes. Mostly abandoned during the revolutionary war, these few houses stood in need of care as the fishermen and their families gradually returned. Bare poles of fishing smacks swaying to a gentle meter began filling Gosport harbor once again.

From the Shoals, looking out from a high cliff, the mainland also looked as it had for many years. But there, in the shadow of Agamenticus, villages throbbed with new life. World trade ships once again called on the port of Portsmouth. New vessels built along the river basin drifted down on the ebb tide past land's end to join the merchant world. Life quickly returned to a normal routine. However, from time to time important events and individuals would again excite the populous.

Tobias Lear of Portsmouth had during the Revolution become George Washington's personal secretary and confidant throughout the presidency and in his private life. He was among those at the president's bedside when Washington died on 14 December 1799.

Lear was instrumental in organizing George Washington's visit to Portsmouth late in 1789. At the time no greater respect could have been given a small humble town than to have the president spend a few days among its people. Washington had chosen New Hampshire for his first official presidential visit to any state as an expression of his gratitude to its inhabitants for helping to make victory possible. In turn the town bestowed on the president their appreciation for his leadership. With people constantly fussing over him, praises came thicker than flies at haying time. Even so, the president managed to find some private moments away from the crowds. He went fishing. In his own laconic style, the president described the event:

> "Having lines, we proceeded to the fishing banks a little without the Harbor, and Fishing for Cod; but it not being a proper time of tide, we only caught two, with w'ch, about 1 o'clock, we returned to town."[1]

A number of public assemblies were held in the president's honor, including a grand dinner organized by the state's dignitaries to associate themselves more intimately with Washington. The evening was filled with accolades and toasts, twelve in all, including,

> '1st, The President of the United States; '2d, Louis the 16th the defender of freedom; '3d, The Fourth of July, 1776.
> '4th, Our friends and allies throughout the world; '5th, The Vice-President of the United States; '6th, May the illustrious author of our liberties long remain th[e]ir protector; . . . '12th, After the first toast the President arose and very politely gave [a toast to], The State of New-Hampshire.[2]

The evening of "joy and good humor"[3] ended for the president at nine o'clock. The celebration, however, went on for many days following his visit, which ended on 4 November 1789, with his departure to Exeter. A genuine pride beamed in the faces of the town, and glowed for weeks to follow.

It is doubtful that the people of the Isles of Shoals were eager to join in Portsmouth's celebration as their lives were filled with rebuilding the island community. By 1790 life and trade snapped along on the cool sea breeze, with a population approaching 100 inhabitants, an average count that would carry through the 1840s. In the 9 September 1843 *Portsmouth Journal* a correspondent reported that "The population (at the Shoals) is less than *one* hundred. There are among the population men of good information, and business habits. . . . The inhabitants are well and decently clothed, and the children . . . have the advantage too of regular schooling."

During post-revolutionary times Gosport village atmosphere had become void of the strong spiritual guidance experienced during the ministries of Brock and Tucke. Many Shoalers displayed disdain toward that former lifestyle by carrying on like depraved heathens. In the winter of 1790 a band of unenlightened Shoalers destroyed their once sanctified meetinghouse-chapel that had stood since 1720 on Star Island's highest ground. Whether they were motivated by hatred of the self-righteous men who had routed them from their homes during the war, or were simply in need of fire wood, we may never know. In 1800 the new chapel was erected on the same site as the previous one, and would serve well as a guiding beacon, with oil lanterns hanging in the windows for fishermen returning after dark. They built the chapel from stone, removing threats of ill-directed temptations from man and the elements.

Gosport village chapel on Star Island as it appeared during the last half of 1800 (NHHS #A59)

In the 1800s the Shoalers emerged as barely more than anachronisms, novelties of a bygone era. They managed to regain a respectable share of the local fishing industry. Month in, month out, they worked their trade through the years. Ships from foreign ports still called on Gosport harbor though with less frequency; most slipped quietly by to anchor elsewhere. Even so, the Shoalers were able to maintain a respectable level of fishing activity through the 1840s. The 21 September 1849 *Portsmouth Journal* reported that,

> The business of Gosport is almost wholly fishing in boats, consuming 3,000 hhds. [hogheads] salt, worth $900. The annual product is about 2,000 quintals dried fish . . . 1,000 bbls. mackerel . . . 100 bbls. oil . . . With this produce of the ocean, and such as the islands afford, the inhabitants (102) are enabled to live comfortably.

Also, the Isles' foremost entrepreneur of the eighteenth century had passed away on 7 February 1811. Samuel Haley died at age eighty-four. His death marked the end of an era. Only remnants of the life he represented were carried forward. For the most part the spontaneous style by which he had lived would become less distinct in the years following his death.

Some traditions remained, such as his window lantern on stormy nights. His son carried on with the routine there on Smuttynose where the lamp continued to serve as a beacon of hope to mariners in distress. It survived as much for the memory of Sam Haley as for the sailors who fought against the odds on the North Atlantic. Each stormy night, when the wind whistled through cracks in the walls and a banked fire warmed the family inside, the lantern glowed.

The 14th of January was such a night. A severe winter gale swept over the islands. The surf's distempered roar filled the darkness as Captain Haley lit his lamp. Outside, snow ripped flat across the island on a cold wind and danced in the window's glow.

Deep within the storm, somewhere east of Smuttynose, Spanish sailors aboard their ship the *Concepciòn* braced themselves against the wild, confused seas. One can imagine off-duty crewmen struggling with their fears at each gust of wind and violent lurch, and the captain and his watchmen being blinded by the darkness drawn around their ship, a darkness choking and smothering their sense of course and position as the *Concepciòn* drew dangerously close to leeward shores. Helpless against the storm, they were doomed if their ship was not somehow turned back against the wind to safety in the open sea. It was a race against time. If they could last out the night before their ship closed with the land, if they could keep sailing through the darkness until daybreak, they would have a chance to survive.

Hours heaped upon hours as the captain fought to keep his ship before the seas. At times he must have turned an ear away from the wind and sworn that he had heard the crash of surf on an ugly shore. The ship kept on lifting and lurching, riding down the jumbled sea. Dark ocean mounts, gnarled with whitecaps, slid by his ship just off the quarters. In those very moments a chill must have cut deep into the captain's soul when the sounds of surf broke his confidence.

The sound came alive as the ship rode up a wave far bigger and steeper than any other encountered that night. A warning cry to stand off must have frozen in the man on bow watch. The ship kept rising. Did the captain turn to see in the first mate's face what he denied in his own? The wave his ship road was clearly lifting on shoal water heading to crash and vanish in a sea of broken surf. The ship fell from the crest through a seemingly endless moment, a moment in which the captain could have cleared his mind of fear and accepted the fate of his ship and crew, until the *Concepciòn* broke its back upon the eastern rocks of Smuttynose. The sailors' cries, the noise of wood breaking up, and of sails whip-cracking in the gale were lost in the storm.

In a sailor's life on the sea, death becomes his mistress, his constant companion. When luck and fate have run their course, sailor and mistress soon wed.

All hope was not lost for the survivors. They struggled against the frigid storm, as they made their way across ice-gilded rocks toward the house and the promise of shelter. Exhausted, they felt a warm sensation sapping their will to survive. One by one they fell back to rest among the rocks. Their mistress had won, and together they would live on in the winds, forever.

Haley woke the next morning to a bright sun rising. He could hear the still angry sea breaking on his island, and, through a window, he could see the smooth swells lift in the shallows to form thin knife edges, before strong west winds peeled each back into plumes. As he stepped from the back door he looked down and saw a man's form tucked in a thin blanket of snow, looking so peaceful, belying the moments of horror before his death. In time fourteen bodies were found by Haley. Their identity remained the storm's secret. Haley gave each man a proper burial on his island, marking the graves with plain, unetched stones still visible today.

The old Haley homestead also remains on Smuttynose Island, and as one passes to the eastside the little upstairs window can be seen.

In the early decades of the nineteenth century the returning vitality of the Isles of Shoals' fishing industry was much like a match flame when it flares bright shortly before dying, as the local price of fish was still being quoted from the Shoals into the 1820s. The major fish trade throughout the region would eventually be absorbed by Gloucester. The isles' 200-year tradition as a fishing center was drawing to a close.

On 29 September 1839 Thomas Laighton came to the Isles of Shoals intending to fan life back into the embers of the dying industry, to make the Shoals once again an economic hub. However, frustrated by his inability to attract enough merchants and fishermen to his newly purchased islands, Laighton put that dream on the mantle and settled into the job that had brought him and his family to the Shoals in the first place, taking care of White Island Lighthouse, built in 1820.

In March Laighton had purchased Smuttynose (in earlier times also called Smyrna), Hog Island (Appledore), and Malaga with partner Joseph Cheever. In 1828 Samuel Haley Jr. had sold his islands to Benjamin Haley for $200. Today, it is suspected by family members that either

Benjamin or a later relative had lost Smuttynose and Malaga in a poker game before Laighton had bought them.

Between lighthouse duties, serving in the New Hampshire senate, and taking care of his family, Laighton managed to renovate his newly purchased Mid-Ocean House of Entertainment on Smuttynose Island and begin offering overnight lodging for guests from the mainland.

As life on the Isles of Shoals was beginning a new direction, so, too, was life along the Piscataqua River. Impressed with the constructors and the ships they had built during the Revolution, the federal government in 1800 called on Portsmouth to play a major role in its naval strategy. The decision to establish a naval construction yard in the river on Fernald's Island, named after its early landowner in the 1600s, would change the texture of life throughout the region for generations to come.

10
PUBLIC AND PRIVATE SHIPYARDS

Portsmouth harbor had an advantage over most in the northeast. It had deepwater navigation reaching miles inland, placing the vast and unlimited forests within easy access to ship construction yards. Extensive surveys of the forests confirmed that enough good timber could be harvested for construction of a seemingly endless number of ships, even though one large vessel required the cutting of literally hundreds of trees. Admiral Nelson's flagship, HMS *Victory*, now berthed in Portsmouth, England, serves as an example of the demands one ship placed on any given forest:

> "of the line" referred to the largest class of warships, of 64 guns or more . . . the largest ships of the line, mounting 100 guns (measured by the weight of their cannonball shot, ships of the line averaged 12 to 42 pound cannonballs) in three tiers, were 200 feet long, built of oak at a cost of L100,000. The largest, Nelson's HMS *Victory* built in 1776–77, was crewed by 875 men . . . *Victory*, at 220 feet, required for construction 2,500 major trees, equal to sixty acres of forest. It carried a mainmast of fir standing 205 feet above waterline and three feet thick at its base. (Her masts were cut from New Hampshire forests.) Constructed in three sections, the three mainmasts of a ship of the line could suspend 36 sails, amounting to four acres of fabric, and making a speed of ten knots. When masts were bent by a strong wind, the strain on the floorboards caused the leaks that required constant pumping.[1]

After the Revolution four U.S. naval ships, two frigates, a sloop, and a schooner, carrying between fourteen and thirty-eight guns, were constructed on Langdon's Island, today known as Badger's. The last of these to be built was the *Congress*, in 1799, which eventually was given to Algiers. The site of construction on Badger's Island is one of the first unofficial naval yards in the United States.

In 1798 the newly formed Department of the Navy decided to have its own navy yards, the notion being that by owning yards the government could better control costs and quality, thus providing private shipyards competition when bids for government contracts were solicited.

Under-Secretary of the Navy Joshua Humphries, in charge of naval construction and the country's first government naval architect, was ordered to find a suitable site for a yard in New England. John Langdon was anxious to sell his island and considered the probable purchase an appropriate gesture of gratitude from the government he helped create. His modest asking price was $25,000 for the twenty-acre island. Humphries was not satisfied with the price and began looking elsewhere. After some study, he concluded that Fernald's Island on the Piscataqua would be more suitable. The fifty-eight acre island just downriver from Langdon's was one of nearly twenty islands that clogged the broad harbor entrance. The deep and swift tidewaters surrounding the island would serve as a natural moat against possible enemy attack.

Humphries negotiated with a Mr. Dennett who, having already speculated that the navy would be looking for an island, had bought Fernald's for a mere $1,700. Dennett sold it to the government for $5,500. The sale became official on 12 June 1800. Subsequently this became the country's oldest continuously operated government navy yard and the only yard still possessing its old nineteenth-century village, including the house where Admiral Farragut died. Over

Early 1800s view overlooking Portsmouth Naval Shipyard with Portsmouth in the background (NHHS #697)

twenty of these buildings are today on the National Registry of Historic Sites.

At the close of the war of 1812, during the British blockade of the east coast, construction of the yard's first ship commenced. The keel-laying of the 74-gun USS *Washington* came in 1814. It was launched just one year later. Weather delays in construction were eliminated when an enormous house was built over the launching ways. In 1817 the *Alabama* was built in the shed and remained "under construction" for forty-seven years, while Congress trickled money down to the yard designated for the ship's completion. Eventually she was commissioned the *New Hampshire* in 1863, later renamed the *Granite State*, and served the navy until 1922. Her ship's bell was retired to the shipyard's mall.

Piracy emerged once again in the nineteenth century to pose a serious threat to United States merchant ships sailing the West Indies. In the fall of 1820 Congress authorized a series of small vessels of "light-draft and heavy armament" to be built at the yard "for the purpose of exterminating the outlaws."[2] The first effort was the 178-ton schooner *Porpoise*, launched in November, carrying eleven guns, to include ten six-pounders and one long eighteen-pounder.

By August of 1821 pirates began roving north along the coast. A local ship's log entry read, "Yard men at the Isles of Shoals in pursuit of pirates."[3] Protection for yard workers was provided by the Marines who were assigned to Portsmouth in 1813. They built their own barracks in 1827 and served until 1987, when the marine unit was retired from active duty at the yard.

The navy yard would grow from a workforce of fifty in the early 1800s to 20,466 in 1943. A graph of shipbuilding activity at the yard would reveal the periods of heaviest construction: the war of 1812, the Civil War, the Spanish American War, World Wars I and II, and the Cold War.[4] During typical peacetime eras government cutbacks were predictable and created a negative effect on the local economy.

The first talks of shutdown came early in the yard's history, starting after the war of 1812, then again after the Civil War. Yard management and concerned citizens lobbied long hours against government plans for closure, convincing Congress of the yard's worth to national defense.

One influential citizen who came to the yard's rescue after the Civil War was Frank Jones, a simple farmer's boy who had made a fortune brewing beer and building hotels. In 1876 Jones's intensive lobbying in

Washington DC won a reprieve for the yard. However, this should not have been necessary considering that Congress had shown commitment to Portsmouth when, ten years earlier, it had authorized the navy to purchase Seavey's Island, separated from Fernald's on the downriver side by Jenkin's Gut. The 105 acres on Seavey's cost the government $1,000 each, and was paid directly to the twenty-eight separate landowners.

Portsmouth Naval Shipyard workers from the earliest days distinguished themselves by providing high-quality production and development of innovative approaches to shipbuilding. From the 1840s through the Civil War, vessels known as sloops of line were constructed, measuring from 140 to 200 feet long and carrying three masts.

Among these ships was the *Saratoga*, commissioned in 1842. She would help secure trade routes with Japan, along with patrolling the Atlantic against slave smugglers; the USS *Portsmouth* at 1,000 tons, and in her own way a beautiful vessel, set a new sailing record from Norfolk, Virginia, to the Sandwich Islands.

In 1846, while under the command of Commodore John B. Montgomery, during the Mexican War, the *Portsmouth* stood watch in the Bay of San Francisco over Yerba Buena, a small village that stood beneath Telegraph Hill. Today Yerba Buena has become San Francisco. Decades later California tried to have the *Portsmouth* restored after retirement in 1915, but lack of funds and her advanced decay left her as a derelict in Boston where she was burned that same year.

Another celebrated sloop of Portsmouth yard was the USS *Kearsarge*. Built in 1861 she engaged the Confederate raider *Alabama* on 21 June 1864 near the coast of France under the command of Admiral Farragut, who, later that year at the Battle of Mobile Bay, cried the immortal rally to arms, "Dam the torpedoes—full speed ahead!" (The torpedoes he referred to were actually Confederate mines anchored in the bay.) The defeat of the *Alabama* ended for all practical purposes the Confederate navy's fighting effectiveness.

While the Portsmouth shipyard cultivated a reputation for delivering quality warships on time and within budget, it also gained contracts to overhaul or repair ships already in service. A floating dry dock was constructed in 1852 on Pierce Island, across the river from the navy yard. This facility allowed yard employees to work on the hulls below waterline for painting or repairs. A survey team recommended the mobile facility be built rather than going through the time and expense of blasting out a fixed dry dock from the river's hard bedrock.

The new unit was mammoth, measuring 350 feet long and 105 feet wide, with lifting capacity rated at 5,000 tons. The navy eventually replaced it with not one but three permanent dry docks. Also, in 1852, the USS *Franklin* came to the yard for repairs. A 2,000-ton, 74-gun sailing sloop of war, she left fifteen years later, seventy feet longer, doubled in tonnage and equipped with steam power to assist her sails. After all those years with the *Franklin* in building number five, yard management found it appropriate to rename the shed *Franklin*. It was later destroyed by a spectacular fire in 1936.

Another vessel to utilize the new floating dry dock came to Portsmouth harbor on 7 June 1855. The USS *Constitution*, America's oldest commissioned warship, sailed into port for a major overhaul. *Old Ironsides*, being recently retired from active naval duty, was scheduled for conversion to a training ship for navy cadets. This was the first of three visits she would make to Portsmouth harbor before being retired permanently to Boston harbor. In 1882 she returned for decommissioning as an active sailing ship. The *Constitution*'s crew secured her alongside the stone quay below what is now the former submarine assembly shed. A full-size house was soon built to enclose her uppermost deck, with the masts remaining stepped. There, she would serve time as a receiving ship for new recruits and dignitaries during special events.

Faced with a relic no longer serving any practical use, the Department of the Navy drew up plans to have her scrapped in the 1920s. National pride, inspired by the pennies of the children of America, came to *Constitution*'s rescue, seeing her as a monument to the country's naval heritage.

The USS *Constitution*'s last visit to the Portsmouth yard came in the late 1920s, when full restoration work was performed. Archival reference material is still located at the Portsmouth shipyard to assist preservationists with her upkeep. Timbers cut long ago were submerged in navy yard reservoirs to maintain moisture. They were never used and are still sitting on the bottom of those ponds, once used to supply fresh water to yard steam engines.

By the late 1890s it became evident to navy yard engineers that the 1852 wooden dry dock had outlived its usefulness. The idea of fixed dry docks was soon promoted to assist in future repairs and overhauls. This quickly became a priority item in the yard's expansion plans. Before the end of the century, dry dock number one was built on Fernald's Island facing upriver. This was soon followed by plans for the world's largest fixed dry dock.

> The channel between the two islands [Dennetts and Seaveys], formerly known as "Jenkins Gut," proved to have a solid rock bed. A total of 166,000 cubic yards of rock were blasted away using steam drills and dynamite. After the site was excavated, some 18,000 cubic yards of Portland cement were poured as a base for the granite. The floor and walls of the basin were composed of 20,500 cubic yards of granite supplied from quarries on Cape Ann, Massachusetts, and at Mount Desert Island, Fox Island, Sprucehead, Biddeford, and Frankfort, Maine. About half of the granite was brought to Portsmouth in a rough state and cut to final shape by New England workmen employed on the job. Late in 1903, after most of the stone had been laid, a cofferdam broke and the inrush of waters threw down the derricks, engines, and boilers. The equipment was quickly restored to order and the 750-foot dock was completed as one of the worlds largest and finest.[5]

Shipbuilding in the late eighteenth and early nineteenth centuries was not limited solely to naval construction. Private yards prospered during this time due to the new and expanded international trade industry and those Portsmouth merchants who had become involved in privateering.

From the beginning, small utility boats were being produced to transport large quantities of goods along the inland rivers, where only shallow draft boats could pass. One particular boat design was the gundalow, a flat-bottomed barge that first appeared in 1658, designed with a broad beam, two feet of draft and a length of thirty-five to seventy feet. The gundalow was propelled through the river basin on the tidal currents, while, in the narrow parts, the crew would pole it along as needed, assisted occasionally by teams of cattle from the river banks. The vessel's primary cargos were marsh hay and bricks from the two dozen brickyards located along the river basin. The high quality clay found in the area made the best bricks anywhere along the coast. By 1900 upwards of 20,000 bricks were manufactured per year and shipped throughout the east coast. Eventually the clay source was exhausted and the industry disappeared.

Until fitted with leeboards to serve as a keel, along with oversized rudders for steering, the gundalow could not venture beyond the harbor. Powered by a lateen sail, much like the dhows of the Nile, the barges eventually were seen up and down the coast, so laden that they had little or no free board. Gundalows were used extensively as late as the 1920s, until bridges, trains, and trucks better met the needs of a modern world.

With the end of the Revolution Portsmouth's merchants sought expanded trade. Loaded ships carrying cargos of northeastern products would sail south to such destinations as Charleston and New Orleans. From these ports cotton was taken to Le Havre, France, or later to Liverpool, England, and sold to textile mills. A return voyage would bring European shipments of spice and fabric to the States. Bound from Liverpool, ships were often filled with hogsheads of salt from Cheshire. Salt remains today among New England's most enduring import commodities.

Trade imports expanded in Portsmouth to include coal from England, and sugar, coffee, molasses, and cocoa from the West Indies and South America. A dark thick rum from Barbados, medicine to "kill the Devil," also became a frequent import item. From the Far East came the finest teas and spices in the world. These merchants would reach far beyond the safe and familiar routes to trade eventually with all of Europe and indeed the world—part of the reason why Britain declared war on the United States in 1812. Indeed, so imperative was the need for profit that during the war with Britain northern New England merchants secretly refurbished supplies and staples of the Royal Navy blockade ships. Even when merchants were eventually free to trade as they chose, captains were in constant fear of marauders from various nations. Expatriated pirates continued to hit defenseless merchant ships as well.[6]

The golden era of trade occurred between 1783 and 1829, a period of history unequalled in numbers of ships calling on the port, or in the variety of products imported or exported.[7] It began with Eliphalet Ladd.

Captain and part-owner of his own ship at the age of twenty-three, Ladd became a leading merchant and shipbuilder. He was heavily involved in English trade during the first years of the republic. At the time of his death in 1806 he had become one of the wealthiest men in New England. Ladd and his wife raised ten children, many of whom carried on their father's business successfully until heavy commercial activity began to wane on the Portsmouth waterfront in the 1830s.[8]

The Ladds were followed by many successful merchants, among them Jacob Sheafe, who was

> A heavy dealer in molasses, rum and sugar from the West Indies and South America; and salt, coral and various merchandise from England and other European countries. Some of his large cargoes were 25,500 gallons of rum in 1806; 26,500 pounds of coffee in 1798; 23,500 pounds of sugar in 1790 and 12,000 gallons of brandy in 1804. He was active between 1790 and 1827.[9]

Of the five warehouses Sheafe owned in Portsmouth, only number three still stands on the Piscataqua River in Prescott Park and is used today as a museum. Among the merchants who prospered were Amazeen, Chauncey, Chase, Cutts, Dennett, Hussey, Odiorne, Parsons,

Sketch of Sheafe Warehouse once located at the entrance to "Puddle Dock", southend of Portsmouth. Note Franklin building in background, on navy yard (NHHS #386)

Rollins, and Tobey, to name only a few.[10] The merchant trade went into decline quickly. By 1829 annual exports were down to $10,740 from a high in 1822 of $199,699, compared with $446,419 in imports in 1829.

One leg of the cotton trade triangle suffered a lethal blow when New England textile mills were constructed. For a short period merchant vessels simply routed from the south back to New England with cotton for the local mills, such as the Cocheco Manufacturing Co. of Dover, and the Portsmouth Manufacturing Co. of South Berwick, Maine, until train transportation brought even this trade to a halt.

Few local merchants actively pursued the lucrative whaling industry with their ships, as did their counterparts in New Bedford and Nantucket. They did, however, deal in whale commodities. A 9 June 1827 *Portsmouth Journal* advertisement read:

SPERMACETI
OIL
J. G. Clasby,
Church Hill, Bow St. (Portsmouth)

Has received per sloops *Factor* and *Edna*,
direct from Nantucket, 108 casks Summer strained
SPERMACETI OIL;. . . 100 boxes
Spermaceti candles;
Which are offered for sale at unusually low prices.

Even with the unfavorable downturn in various markets, the Piscataqua River basin in the 1800s continued to thrive through private shipbuilding. The merchant-sponsored industry expanded to ships capable of sailing the world trade routes. At their height the Piscataqua River shipyards produced 10 percent of all merchant ships built in North America.

Before 1830 over half the ships constructed were built upriver. However, by 1838 all major shipbuilding had moved to Portsmouth, Eliot, and Kittery.[11] At the Salmon Falls River in South Berwick, Maine, between 1783 and 1829, eighteen full-rigged three-masted ships were constructed, totaling over 5,000 tons. They all measured under 120 feet in length and were capable of deepwater sailing. Builders constructed twenty-eight vessels in Dover, New Hampshire, totaling over 7,000 tons. Among the most active yards at the time was Stephen Tobey's. Its last three-master, the 97-foot *Lydia*, was sold in Salem, Massachusetts, and would go on to sail the world in the Indian Ocean whaling trade.

Throughout the 1800s Dover continued as a major port, remarkable considering that ships' pilots had better than ten miles of tricky inland waters to navigate. Vessels 150 feet long and drafting up to twelve feet were seen tied along the Dover waterfront as late as the 1890s. For seventy years the government had allocated money to keep the very narrow and naturally shallow Cocheco River and port dredged for deepwater ship access. However, in 1896 during a paralyzing winter storm, a flash flood tore through the Cocheco waterfront properties. What had taken the Army Corps of Engineers seventy years to dredge out, took mother nature a matter of hours to fill back in. The port of Dover never recovered from this natural disaster. The government could not justify the expense needed to rebuild a channel already fading from commercial use due to competitive overland carriers.

Other towns along the tributaries had a respectable share of shipbuilders. Durham constructed 46 square riggers, 17 brigs, 11 schooners, 1 barkentine, and 1 sloop. The caulking hammer fell silent for the most part in 1829. Oyster River shipyards have produced just three commercial sailing vessels since then.

Exeter enjoys one of the oldest histories in American small boatbuilding, dating to at least 1651. Later, constructors would launch from the banks of the Squamscot River twenty-three full-rigged ships for a total of 6,378 tons. All were built within a twenty-year span, concluding in 1807. While work on smaller vessels continued throughout this period, among the last upriver towns involved in major shipbuilding was Newmarket on the Lamprey River. The yards here produced twenty-eight full-riggers. If one considers all construction during this period, the Newmarket yards stayed competitive by producing over 10,000 vessel tonnage.[12]

The world shipping industry simply outgrew these upriver yards. However, downriver there were virtually no limitations. With no bridges to contend with, and access to materials made easier when brought in by ship, the lower end of the Piscataqua River continued to flourish.

Shipwright William Badger served his apprenticeship under William and James Hackett on Langdon's Island during the Revolution. After the war, Langdon's failure to sell the island to the government provided William Badger with an opportunity to purchase it himself. From 1800 to 1829 Badger built fifty-three vessels, twenty-four of which were full-riggers. He claimed to have built overall ninety-nine vessels in his lifetime and died while constructing his 100th. The island today bears his name, as he still stands watch over the river from his grave on its upriver end. It is said that from his deathbed in 1829, Badger assured his grieving loved ones that he would indeed return to build a hundred more ships.

Across the river was Portsmouth, the largest town on the tidal basin, producing just 14 ships; 21 brigs, and 24 schooners between the years 1783 and 1829.[13] Many of the Portsmouth workforce had found employment in other yards on the river. Portsmouth's role would prove to serve best as a support for the inland yards. After launching, the unfinished ships were towed downriver to the Portsmouth waterfront where masts were stepped and rigging outfitted before departing for sea.

During this time of shipbuilding prosperity, the Portsmouth Naval Shipyard continued to maintain a leadership position of its own in the eyes of the government. The yard's own naval architects went on to play a major part in the future development of submersible craft technology in the early 1900s. The submarine became the new focus of the yard. Its engineers, following instincts and disciplines long-ingrained, would forge a new era of excellence.

Meanwhile, as life along the river prospered for some and faltered for most, a new era was dawning at the all but forgotten Isles of Shoals. An era was approaching that would overtake the northeast and spark the rise of the Victorian summer resort era of New England, and create America's first artists' colony.

11
THOMAS LAIGHTON AND THE GRAND RESORT ERA

In general the main stream of life had virtually passed by the Isles of Shoals during the 1830s and 1840s. However, the arrival of Thomas Laighton and his family in 1839 would signal a new era and rescue the Shoals from the brink of obscurity. Laighton purchased the three islands of Malaga, Smuttynose, and Hog. He would later change the name of Hog to Appledore out of respect for the township of 1661.

For Thomas this was the fulfillment of a longstanding dream dating to 1831, when, at an auction in Kittery Point, his bid for the islands had fallen short. He was an astute politician and a fine public speaker. While conducting businesses such as shipping and whaling with his brother Mark, he also won a seat as state senator, was appointed assistant postmaster, and served in the customs house; but in 1839 he lost a bid for selectman in Portsmouth. After his defeat he decided to move his family to the Isles of Shoals and take on the lighthouse keeper's duties on White Island. In September Laighton made the move with family and cow.

Laighton's lighthouse post was meant only as a temporary two-year duty while he waited for the then Portsmouth postmaster, Abner Greenleaf, to retire. Being the dreamer and visionary that he was, Laighton had failed to anticipate the degree of controversy that moving his young wife and two infant children to the Isles of Shoals would cause in Portsmouth and throughout the state. Political slandering of Laighton helped to deny him the position. He refused to return to the mainland for the next two years, which allowed time for his bruised pride to heal. Upon his return, Laighton quickly regained favor among the populous, winning a senate seat. During his years in Concord, he had moved his family to the Mid-Ocean House on Smuttynose Island where they would be safer and more comfortable. An employee, Ben Whaling, managed the lighthouse duties while he was away.

Yet as he sat in Concord no doubt Laighton's thoughts were far away standing on his island feeling the wind and hearing the surf, dreaming of a day when once again great ships would call on Gosport harbor.

After two terms in the state senate and a term as selectman of Portsmouth he put his political career behind him. Legend says he never stepped foot on the mainland after the mid-1840s, spending the last twenty years of his life on the Isles of Shoals.

Seldom in the biographical notes on Laighton was an unkind word ever written or suggested; there were mainly warm, loving words of admiration for this romantic dreamer, who passed these traits on to his daughter Celia and son Oscar. He was simply described as a lover of canaries. By all accounts all that he did was neat and tidy, and it was said of him that he would not hesitate to work at even the lowliest tasks.[1]

By the mid-1840s, with his focus firmly directed on the growing potential of his inn on Smuttynose, Laighton began developing plans for a resort on Appledore, an idea which received encouraging words from his Mid-Ocean House guests.

For the Laighton children, the time spent on White Island was a true adventure of grand proportions, their home made warm and cozy by the loving care of their mother, Eliza. Celia was four and Oscar only three months old that first time on White Island. Brother Cedric was born at the Shoals the next year. Eliza's son, Oscar, would later write,

> Many people have said, "You must have been very lonely at the light." They did not know that where our mother dwelt there was happiness also. I am sure no family was ever more united and contented than the Laightons on White Island.[2] . . . I wish I could convey to you how beautiful our mother was . . . she was very fair . . . her great charm was in her interest in and instant sympathy with all to whom she talked . . . father and mother's love and respect for each other would be a supreme lesson for some families of today.[3]

Many years later, Celia wrote her own impressions of the first day at White Island:

> It was at sunset in autumn that we were set ashore on that loneliest, lovely rock, where the lighthouse looked down on us like some tall, black-capped giant, and filled me with awe and wonder. At its base a few goats were grouped on the rocks, standing out dark against the red sky. . . . The stars were beginning to twinkle; the wind blew cold, charged with the sea's sweetness; the sound of many waters, half bewildered me. Some one began to light the lamps in the tower. Rich red and golden, they swung round in mid-air; everything was strange and fascinating and new.
>
> We entered the quaint little stone cottage that was for six years our home. How curious it seemed, with its low, whitewashed ceiling and deep window seats, showing the great thickness of the walls made to withstand the breakers, with

> whose force we soon grew acquainted! A blissful home the little house became to the children who entered it that quiet evening and slept for the first time lulled by the murmur of the encircling sea.[4]

A violent storm descended on the Isles of Shoals during the family's first winter at White Island, destroying everything on the six-acre island except the lighthouse and its cottage. Laighton lost all of his poultry while he was saving the family cow by taking it into Eliza's kitchen. At the height of the storm Celia and her father heard the booming of a ship's guns.

In 1838, Laighton's brother Mark had sailed from Portsmouth as captain on their family's whaling ship the *Pocahontas*, bound for Europe on a trade journey. That was the last the family had ever heard from him. Celia would write many years later,

> we were startled by the heavy booming of guns through the roar of the tempest—a sound that drew nearer and nearer, till at last, through a sudden break in the mist and spray, we saw the heavily rolling hull of a large vessel driving by, to her sure destruction, toward the coast. It was as if the wind had torn the vapor apart on purpose to show us the piteous sight; and I well remember the hand [of my father]on my shoulder which held me firmly, shuddering child that I was, and forced me to look in spite of myself. What a day of pain it was! How dreadful the sound of those signal-guns, and how much more dreadful the certainty when they ceased, that all was over! We learned afterward that it was the brig *Pocahontas*, homeward bound from Spain, and that the vessel and all her crew were lost.[5]

Though there were other vessels carrying that ship's name, a nagging thought prevails, was this the same ship captained by Mark Laighton on a return trip to America? Twenty years later Celia wrote a memorable poem that dealt with this painful experience, "The Wreck of the Pocahontas." The last stanza reads,

> Sighing I climbed the lighthouse stair,
> half forgetting my grief and pain;
> and while the day died, sweet and fair,
> I lit the lamps again.

Unwittingly, Richard Henry Dana, author of *Two Years Before the Mast*, might have jinxed Captain Laighton when he wrote, "No danger on the ship with Mark Laighton at the wheel."[6]

White Island Light Station under seige during a March 1984 storm, typical of great storms of all the ages. Three men were stationed here during the time this picture was shot from Star Island; much the same duties were carried out by these men as were by Thomas Laighton and his family. A 3-ton rock was washed through the cottage door and exited under the kitchen sink. Note: what looks like ice or snow on roof is sea water cascading off cottage (photograph by Dave Pierson, with wife Edith, who are the only year round residents on the Isles of Shoals today)

White Island during a normally calm day (photo by Geo. A. Sylvester)

In the spring of 1847 Laighton moved to Appledore to begin construction on his new resort. Lumber was shipped from Bangor, Maine. By September he had brought the entire family over to join him. They worked alongside carpenters from Portsmouth as he rushed to complete the hotel for its inaugural opening the following June.

Laighton's financial partner in the venture was Levi Thaxter, a Harvard-educated Boston socialite. Thaxter had first come to the Shoals in 1846 and was a guest at the Laighton's inn on Smuttynose. He would eventually be employed as the tutor for the children, during which time a love had grown in Thaxter for Laighton's young daughter, whose natural gift for understanding the movement of poetry and prose was beginning to emerge. The first marriage request to Laighton from Thaxter came when she was but thirteen years old and he was twenty-four, raising such a fury that Thaxter was asked to leave the island.

Nevertheless, by the next year Laighton and Thaxter had formed a partnership so that Laighton could complete construction of his resort on Appledore. Thaxter had financial sources which were unavailable to Laighton. Moreover, Thaxter's influence with Cambridge friends could produce a source of visitors from the first families of New England and the emerging American intelligentsia: James Russell Lowell, Edward Everett Hale, the Saltonstalls and Tuckermans, Sam Longfellow, Henry

Wardsworth's brother, Henry David Thoreau, and Nathaniel Hawthorne.

Thaxter persevered in his desire to marry Celia. He asked once again for her hand in marriage. On 13 September 1851 Thaxter married Celia. She was sixteen, he was twenty-seven. The wedding was performed in the hotel's south parlor with a small group of friends and family as witnesses.

The Appledore House was a success from the first day it opened on 15 June 1848, when, at "about ten o'clock we saw the *Springbird* coming, all sails set and colors flying. She was a handsome sight, running before the fresh southwest breeze. With a . . . big bone [bow wave] in her mouth."[7] The *Springbird* was the first ferryboat in what has since become a long line of vessels providing service to the Isles of Shoals.[8] In the first year, Newburyport was used by the ferry service.

Word quickly spread to all of New England about a wonderful new resort bound by the sea from all points of the compass, which offered elegant service, tasty food, an atmosphere possessing medicinal qualities and, above all else, a warm, friendly family to take care of their every need.

As insistent as Laighton might have been in assuring that his guests were provided with the most courteous service possible, he was still a man who treated everyone with dignity, unless one happened to push the limit of fair play, then he would nevertheless eagerly match the ugliest of tempers. One day while he was registering a couple who had just arrived on the ferry, a man came storming up to the front desk and without apology interrupted Laighton and his guests:

> " 'My name is Whittle, Judge Whittle of Manchester. Get a move on and give me a room, or I will go over to the other island.' And he banged his hat down on the counter. Father turned slowly around, and said: 'you can go to h___ if you like.' "

The "other island" was Star where in 1856 the Atlantic House had been built.

Laighton then returned to his guests and calmly finished assigning their room, while the judge stormed out onto the piazza. Later, Oscar ran out to see if Judge Whittle had indeed gone to the other island:

> "I found him in a rocking chair." The boy at first thought he was laughing but then noticed tears running down his face. Oscar begged him not to feel bad and tried to comfort him. After some time had passed the Judge said: 'Are you Mr.

Right: Atlantic House built in 1856 on Star Island. Left: Gosport and Caswell Houses (Portsmouth Public Library, Isles of Shoals Collection)

> Laighton's boy?,' 'Yes, I said.,' 'Do you love your father?,' 'You bet I do; he is the best man in the world.,' 'You are right, my boy. Try to grow up like your good father, and fear not.'[9]

The second season of operation brought a few changes. Laighton had found property in Portsmouth and moved the *Springbird*. This proved a wise and profitable move. With the distance shortened to less than half that of the run from Newburyport, and the sail from Portsmouth a reach rather than a beat to windward, the *Springbird* prospered. The rewards of the move were immediately felt, with increases in overnight guests and the opening to Laighton of a whole new market—the "daytripper." Eliza recruited women and children living on the other islands to help serve the additional guests. At the height of the hotel operation, several years later, 500 guests could be accommodated in both the hotel and dining room, as the great Irish immigration to America provided a primary source of labor.

The numerous amenities made a vacation at Appledore unique: clean, fresh therapeutic sea air, first-class accommodations, abundance of fish, ghosts, sailing, exploring, swimming, hobnobbing with great literary and artistic celebrities and, above all else, Eliza's wonderful cooking. Visitors left the island resort raving about Mrs. Laighton's chowders and the magnificent way she prepared her fish dinners. Fish and lobsters were still found in great quantities near island shores. Menhaden, mackerel, and herring broke the water's surface in giant schools clear to the horizon. Codfish still tipped the scales at over 40 lb. Oscar declared, "Lobsters were so plentiful that we could see them crawling about near the shore. We thought it was great if we got six cents for a three pound lobster."[10]

Levi Thaxter pranced about the island resort in those early years with his dreams floating among the clouds, eager to show off the island to Boston friends and a number of classmates from Harvard. He, it seems, never exerted himself to become a man of accomplishment outside.

> His abilities were above average, but his nature was restless. He felt his responsibilities but could not face them, which led to morbid introspection. He derived little or no income from his own skill or abilities until late in life.[11]

However, Thaxter had brought to the island, before his marriage, Henry David Thoreau and Thoreau's Bowdoin classmate Franklin Pierce, who would become president in 1853.

In the spring of 1853 Celia Thaxter convinced her husband to take the temporary position of preacher for Gosport village on Star Island, where five years earlier the school teacher, Miss Nancy J. Underhill of Chester, New Hampshire, had lost her life when she was swept by waves from a cliff on the southend of the island. The cliff, which forms a natural step, is known as Miss Underhill's Chair to this day.

They moved there with their infant child, Karl, and lived in the parsonage east of the chapel. Levi began his ministerial chores, while finding time to teach the handful of island children. Many years later Celia confessed to her brother Oscar that those few short months were "the happiest days of her married life."[12]

A major turning point in Celia's life came two years later in 1855. One morning, Oscar, now sixteen, and Levi had sailed to Portsmouth for supplies. Sailing back to the Shoals, about half way, the two men were being closely watched by a host of anxious family members and friends on Appledore. They were praying for the men to hurry along before the tumbling green-black clouds racing down on them from behind caught them. The dark squall line rolled out from the coast; Celia ran to the highest point of the hotel, to the tower where her father had already gone with his spy glass. He was yelling to the men: "Down with your sail!"[13]

At that very moment the squall hit the tiny skiff. The wind blew up violently; the men were lost from sight as the rain and waves engulfed them. The squall whirled out over the island, snapping shingles, making shrubs and tall grass and boats dance violently. Then, "as suddenly as it began, the storm cleared, and the setting sun shone out."[14] One wave rose above the rest during the height of the storm to snatch the men from certain death, lifting them to a high rocky shoulder where no other wave could reach. This experience so frightened Thaxter, "that his one idea was to leave Appledore Island and never return."[15]

Thaxter sold his honeymoon cottage to his father-in-law for $600 in 1858. He refused to visit the island again until the summer of 1879, when "Levi overcame his reluctance and returned to the Shoals primarily because of the presence of his life-long friend, the artist William Morris Hunt, who was ill in mind and body."[16] Later that season Hunt fell into an island pond and drowned. Some believe he committed suicide, but Celia maintained that it was a tragic accident.

Celia reluctantly left all that was dear to her back at Appledore. Their move to the mainland opened a painful rift between Levi and his wife which could never be mended. Instead, Celia found comfort in writing poetry that was often sent on to her family. In the winter of 1860, she was surprised by her husband. Levi showed one of Celia's peoms to his friend James Russell Lowell, *Atlantic Monthly*'s first editor. The poem was published unedited.

Land-Locked

Black lie the hills; swiftly doth daylight flee;
And, catching gleams of sunset's dying smile,
Through the dusk land for many a changing mile
The river runneth softly to the sea.

O happy river, could I follow thee!
O yearning heart, that never can be still!
O wistful eyes, that watch the steadfast hill,
Longing for level line of solemn sea!

Have patience; here are flowers and song birds,
  Beauty and fragrance, wealth of sound and sight
  All summer's glory thine from morn till night,
And life too full of joy for uttered words.

Neither am I ungrateful; but I dream
  Deliciously how twilight falls tonight
  Over the glimmering water, how the light
Dies blissfully away, until I seem

To feel the wind, sea-scenting on my cheek,
  To catch the sound of dusky, flapping sail
  And dip the oars, and voices on the gale
Afar off, calling low – my name they speak!

O Earth; thy summer song of joy may soar
  Ringing to heaven in triumph I but crave
  The sad, caressing murmur of the wave
That breaks in tender music on the shore.

From her first poem Celia's literary career rose to a prominence among Boston poets seldom enjoyed by women of the day. As her poetry gained respect and stature, Celia spent her summers at Appledore, entertaining friends such as Harriet Beecher Stowe, Lowell, Ralph Waldo Emerson, Oliver Wendall Holmes, John Greenleaf Whittier, and artist Childe Hassam. Edgar Allen Poe's name is said to have appeared in the hotel register.

Among the happier moments of Celia's life was her meeting with Charles Dickens on 6 April 1867, when she and her husband had dinner at the home of James T. Fields, who had succeeded Lowell as *Atlantic Monthly*'s editor. Unfortunately, no detailed diary of that evening's conversation has been found. Several years after the dinner, Dickens did have an opportunity, however, to read Celia's new book of prose, *Among the Isles of Shoals*. The following critique was taken from a letter written by Dickens to James T. Fields:

> "I think Mrs. Thaxter's prose is very admirable, but I don't believe it! No, I do not. My conviction is that those Islanders get frightfully bored by their islands, and wish they had never set eyes on them." On reading this, Whittier wrote to Celia, "I wish he could have seen them [the Isles of Shoals] as I have."[17]

Life continued at the island resort, one successful season after another. As the elder Laighton grew old and infirm, his sons, Oscar and Cedric, took over the hotel operations. They built a retirement cottage for their parents, overlooking Babb's Cove, with a view of the distant mainland. Public demands were pressuring the boys for more capacity. They were compelled by their own success to expand the resort until it dwarfed the island's entire northend. The front piazza was extended to over 500 feet long, with grass tennis courts in the front yard just back from the tidal swimming pool, where guests had separate bath houses for men and women. Roadways were marked throughout the island and more guest cottages built. Behind the hotel toward the northeast were all of the service buildings: boiler room, stables, carriage house, etc.

During the resort's period of greatest popularity, when its capacity was reached nightly, scheduled coastal steamers called at the island from Boston, a three-and-a-half-hour trip. For the not so venturous, train schedules were available at distant Philadelphia, New York and Boston, specifically timed to arrive in Portsmouth minutes before the next ferry left for Appledore Island.

The Appledore House resort pioneered the concept of vacation time among Americans. Its success bred more success. Imitators complimented the Laightons by duplicating their formula all over northern New England. By the 1870s many new grand-styled resorts began to appear,

Early view of Appledore House. Center section under cupola was the original building opened in 1848. Wings and buildings to left were added on later due to popular demand (University of New Hampshire Media Service)

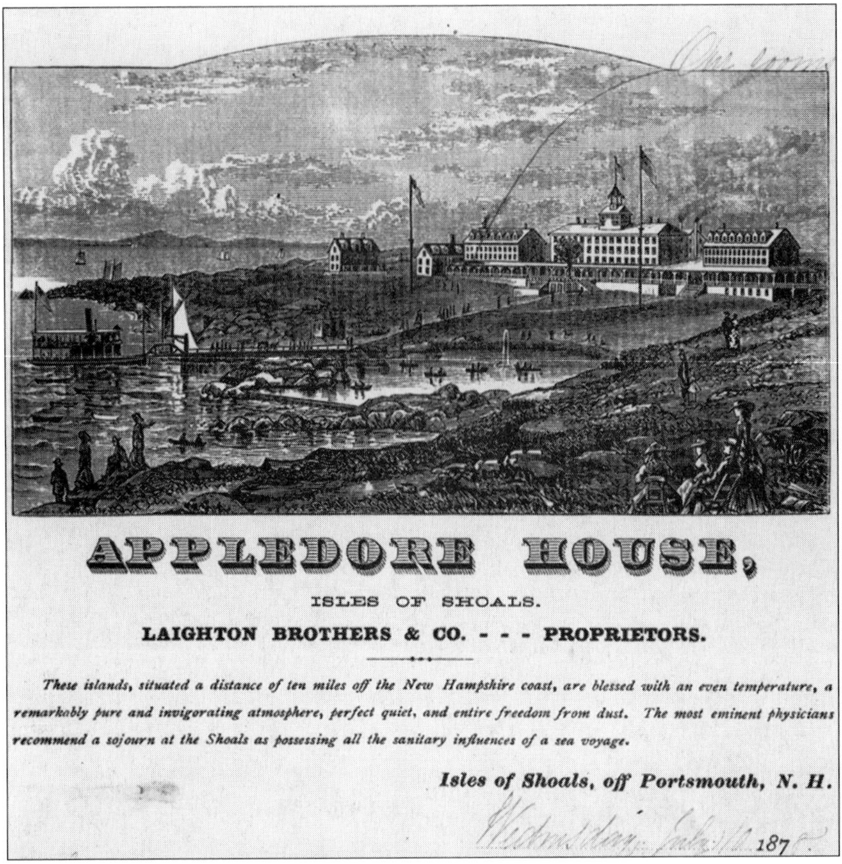
APPLEDORE HOUSE,

ISLES OF SHOALS.

LAIGHTON BROTHERS & CO. - - - PROPRIETORS.

These islands, situated a distance of ten miles off the New Hampshire coast, are blessed with an even temperature, a remarkably pure and invigorating atmosphere, perfect quiet, and entire freedom from dust. The most eminent physicians recommend a sojourn at the Shoals as possessing all the sanitary influences of a sea voyage.

Isles of Shoals, off Portsmouth, N. H.

187

Appledore House 1878. Note continued expansion by Laighton Brothers (University of New Hampshire Media Service)

not only along the coast but inland in mountain valleys and peaks and along lake shores, each providing a new and refreshing twist to attract guests, who in time were ready for a change from the relative limits of an Isles of Shoals vacation.

E.M. Statler came to discover the Laighton secret for himself, which lay in the hands of Eliza and her fabulous cooking. Her popular recipes were featured in the hard-bound *Appledore Cook Book* published in 1878, the year following her death. This visit by Statler established the framework for the Statler-Hilton Hotel Empire. Today most of these hotels are but a memory, gone as the result of fire and decay from a modern world that no longer required the standards of old. However, the

Eliza Rymes Laighton (University of New Hampshire Media Service)

Wentworth-by-the-Sea in New Castle, the Colony in Kennebunkport, the Balsams and the Brenton Woods in northern New Hampshire, and Castle-in-the-Clouds above Lake Winnipesaukee still stand as monuments to this grandeur.

"On December twenty-eight (1865), Cedric wrote: 'Father has paralysis: or something of the kind.' "[18] Their sons had managed to finish the retirement cottage for Thomas and Eliza in the final years of his life. Oscar said, "Father was taken in his chair and mother in a wheelbarrow" to their new home. Eliza had allowed her weight to balloon to a point where she was perfectly round from head to foot.[19]

Thomas Bell Laighton passed away in 1866, "Celia came down at once, and the family was together on May sixteenth as Thomas subsided into dreamless sleep."[20] He was sixty-two years old.

A family plot was prepared on raised ground near the back side of the hotel, where family and friends laid him to rest. From that time on, Eliza had moments of revived zest for life, but each gain was followed by deeper setbacks, which robbed her of strength and the will to live.

Eliza passed away on 14 November 1877. Her daughter wrote, "Dearest Annie [Fields], this morning, at half past seven, the sweetest mother in the world went, God alone knows where, away from us!"[21] Dear Eliza took her place beside Thomas on Appledore. Together, in peace, they waited for their children.

12
THE AGE OF ELEGANCE

People from every corner of the country developed an unquenchable thirst for the resort on Appledore Island. In 1866, the year their father died, the boys decided that traditional sailing vessels, though proven reliable over the years, were not keeping up with demands. That year, they introduced the first steam-powered vessel, the *Pioneer*.[1] The ten-mile trip from Portsmouth to the Isles of Shoals often took the *Springbird* all day if conditions were not favorable. The new steamer, on the other hand, could make the trip consistently in just one hour, guaranteeing a regular schedule to Appledore. With more daily trips available to the Laightons, they could now accommodate far more guests.

In 1869 the SS *Appledore* went into service. On busy summer days, while still several miles from his island dock, the captain of the *Appledore* would sound the steam whistle one time for every ten passengers on board. This alerted the hotel staff as to the number of guests they should prepare for, as telegraph communications had not yet been established between the island and mainland. However, a few years earlier in 1866 islanders stirred with excitement when a large ship sailed by the Isles of Shoals to an anchorage just off Rye Beach. The ship, *Great Eastern*, was laying the first transatlantic telegraph cable to America from England.

The brothers were caught up in the whirlwind of their success. With hotel expansion came an indebtedness to local banks which rose to over $70,000, a primary cause for their financial collapse in the twentieth century. There were other contributing factors. The resort was facing more and more competition. What had been for years a virtual lock on the market, now became apportioned among the dozens of new vacation spots. The supply of new hotel rooms throughout New England grew much quicker than the market demand could absorb. In the summer of 1872, on one overbooked night, the brothers offered Oscar's room to John Poor's wife and children, while John slept in the parlor on a sofa. Other guests had already taken the pool table. The next morning, as people checked out, a room was secured for Poor and his family. Not just any room, but the finest one in the entire hotel! While Oscar and Cedric were innocently flowering the Poors with genuine hospitality, John Poor was secretly buying property on Star Island from the last remaining residents of Gosport village.[2]

Poor's intentions soon became known to the Laightons. He was going to build a 250-capacity resort on Star Island. On the surface, Cedric and Oscar welcomed the new place, declaring that there was plenty of business for everyone, but privately they were very concerned that their comfortable monopoly would be seriously threatened.

On the morning of 6 March 1873 workers on Poor's resort and other islanders woke to the horrible news that bloody murders had been committed during the night on Smuttynose Island. The victims were Norwegian women, Karen and Anethe Christensen. Maren Hontvet, Karen's sister, miraculously escaped the ax-wielding murderer that night. She alone gave the gruesome details of the incident, informing the authorities that the killer was the Prussian immigrant, Louis Wagner, a man who had lived with the family on Smuttynose the year before. He had helped John Hontvet and Ivan Christensen aboard their fishing boat the *Clara Bella*. They surmised that Wagner, knowing the men were baiting trawls in Portsmouth overnight, had gone to the island with the intent to rob his friends. Apparently the family dog Ringe barked and spoiled Wagner's plans, forcing him to kill the women.

Wagner was caught in Boston, returned to Alfred, Maine, and stood trial for murder within three months of the crime.The case presented against him was based on circumstantial and contradictory evidence. After one short week the trial ended on 18 June 1873 with a guilty verdict and a death sentence. Though the prosecution's case was weak by modern standards, the defense could not come up with evidence to corroborate Wagner's story that he had spent the entire night in Portsmouth.

Celia Thaxter, who had just arrived at Appledore the day before the murders with her oldest son Karl, published a fictionalized account of the murders in the May 1873 issue of *Atlantic Monthly*, one month before Wagner's scheduled execution on 25 June. Her motives are unknown. Did she fear that the rising sympathy for Wagner among the citizens of Maine might cause the governor to commute the sentence, or worse yet, reopen the case? Was she trying to protect someone? Why was she compelled to go to such extremes to make sure Wagner would not live? Could she not have waited, allowing justice to run its due course? Or,

Original Oceanic Hotel on Star Island shortly after completion (University of New Hampshire Media Service)

was she simply exercising her literary license to seize an opportune story about which to write? One hundred and twenty years later these questions still linger.[3]

In one year, John Poor managed to build not only the Oceanic Hotel resort, but also a 200-foot stone pier for the steam ferry, and a sandy swimming area in a sheltered cove next to the pier. The sand had been taken from a deep crevasse on the southwest side of Star, which in itself was too narrow and exposed for swimming.

As for a grand opening celebration in 1873, no detail was left undone. Poor sent notices to all yacht clubs and yacht owners throughout New England inviting their members to participate in a sailing regatta at the Isles of Shoals, featuring a race from the Shoals to Boon Island and back. More than fifty magnificent yachts sailed to the islands for the race and festivities. The winner was the *America*, the most famous racing yacht in the world and namesake of today's America's Cup race.[4]

Poor was very successful in the short time he owned the resort. There is no evidence that relations between the Laightons and the Poors were anything but friendly. Oscar already had a small steamship, the *Pinafore*, and a longstanding shuttle service between Appledore and Star Island's Atlantic House, built in 1856 by Lemuel Caswell. He was eager to keep his vessel on line to Star, while still providing freight runs to Portsmouth.

Two years later the Oceanic Hotel was destroyed by fire. Poor quickly rebuilt a replacement over the winter by adding on to the Atlantic

Gosport harbor during the "Grand Opening Regatta" for Oceanic Hotel, 1873 (NHHS #4029)

House, spared from the fire, between the Gosport and Caswell wings. Apparently the fire took the spirit of competition from John Poor. Soon he was negotiating a sales agreement for that next year. The new owners were his "friendly" competitors, the Laighton brothers, who purchased all of Poor's interests on Star Island for $100,000. Only $35,000 had been invested to build the original hotel.

Cedric hesitated at first. The brothers' indebtedness was already great enough. Yet, everyone, including Cedric's banker, encouraged the purchase, assuring him that the future looked bright for both resorts. They insisted that he secure Star Island against future adversaries. With this purchase the brothers assured their eventual demise. Though managing to stay ahead of their creditors for several more years, they would never enjoy financial stability again.

As Celia assisted where she could with the hotel operation, she managed to raise her three sons, Karl, John, who was born in 1854, and Roland, born in 1858. Karl was the only one born on Appledore, in the North Cottage, and was "said to be the first child born on Appledore in more than a century."[5] The others, John and Roland, were born in Massachusetts. All survived into the twentieth century, with Roland passing away in 1932, at age seventy-four.

First *Oceanic* approaching Star Island pier, around 1883. Oscar Laighton's *Pinafore* is seen heading for Appledore (University of New Hampshire Media Service)

New Oceanic Hotel annex added to Atlantic House after fire destroyed the first Star Island hotel two years after it opened (NHHS #A58)

Karl suffered from "congenital lameness and retarded mentality."[6] He was subject to violent outbursts and Celia removed him from school at age seventeen and continued to mother and protect him until her death. John and Roland went on to lead successful lives away from the island, with Roland becoming a doctor and professor at Harvard, and John a farmer.

After her father's death, Celia kept in touch with island life through frequent letters received from her brother Cedric over the winter. On occasions, one can imagine her looking up from the letters out over the landscape, seeing in the distance an imaginary wave breaking on familiar rocks among her islands. Celia finally saw the fulfillment of her dreams to be near her beloved islands when Levi agreed to sell their home and move to Kittery Point. This move was helped along by the death of their longstanding friend William Hunt in September of 1879. After the funeral, "with sadness of heart the Thaxter family returned . . . directly to the home on California Street [Newtonville] . . . perhaps the old joys would return to the fireside where Hunt had read his 'talks.' The ceiling was still black with the smoke which Hunt humorously said had pickled so many pleasant evenings."[7]

Time passed painfully slow that winter in the Thaxter household even with Celia and her husband busy finding a buyer. Finally, Levi entered an agreement to buy the Champernowne Estate in Kittery Point, Maine.

Four years later, the marriage that for many years had tempered Celia's will and spirit passed with the death of her husband. In death, he found the recognition that so eluded him in life. Thaxter had been the foremost promoter and interpreter in America of the poetry of Robert Browning. Hearing of Thaxter's death, that had come on 31 May 1884, Browning wrote the epitaph for the man he had never met:

Thou whom these eyes saw never
  Say friends true, who say,
  My soul helped onward by my song
 Though all unwillingly has helped thee too?
I gave but of the little that I knew:
  How were the gift requited, while along
  Life's path I pace, couldst thou make
  weakness strong:
Help me with knowledge for Life's old,
  death's new.[8]

Celia Thaxter: portrait in her garden by famous American impressionist Childe Hassam (Dr. John M. Kingsbury Collection)

Celia's garden as it looks today during summer season. A 100-year-old tradition is maintained with ancestral plants from the original garden still there (photo by Ron Titus)

The epitaph is still visible on Thaxter's gravestone in the Kittery Point cemetery.

Celia spent her winters at Champernowne anxiously waiting for spring to breathe life into the land. In June she and Karl would move to Appledore to be with her brothers. Levi and Cedric had provided her with a cottage of her own, located at the west-end of the hotel's piazza. Her parlor continued to be the social gathering place for island guests, who sought intellectual intimacy with the famous poet. On the porch, artists and writers chatted away the summer days as the gentle sea breeze flirted with rail-choking hop vines, wrapped green cables that nearly blocked the daylight from the porch. Their topics were of a different world than that of common folk, and free of conformity or commitment.

Down the cottage front steps, visitors walked a short distance to a thickly vined trellis leading into Celia's garden, a wonderland of colors and intrigue. "Every possible method she could learn about, Celia used in making her garden a 'most breathtaking riot of color.' "[9]

Here, hours were spent exploring, constantly discovering new life, new shades, new tones that beckoned many artists' brushes, but none greater than that of the now famous American impressionist, Childe Hassam.

Her garden was not planted in a formal manner with even rows and small batches of flowers. Rather the flowers grew like the sea that surrounded her ocean home, wild and disheveled, beautiful in their mixture. Today they have changed little from the way they looked when she cultivated them a century ago.

Toward the end of her life, Celia's health began to falter. She did manage to focus her strength for one last book, published in 1894 and entitled *An Island Garden*, a fine work in prose describing the one place where she found tranquility and happiness on earth, her garden. With the writing of the book came her peace with life.

> Celia had not been feeling as well as usual, and on August 25, 1894, Minna Bersten sent for Roland to come to spend Sunday on the island. . . . Roland sat beside her holding her hand as they listened to the music . . . feeling a little tired, she retired early. . . . As the first blush of dawn lightened the sky, Celia asked that the curtains be opened. So she could see the sunrise. When Minna turned from the window Celia was dead![10]

Within five years of Celia's death, brother Cedric passed away while on a business trip to Florida, where he was looking to develop another resort. He had succumbed to typhus on 5 June 1899. Cedric had possessed his father's mind for business and had been admired among his peers:

> He was taller than Oscar. He looked like a handsome Viking. He had a beautiful voice like a bell. He could have been anything. He was the center of conversation among the hotel guests. Surrounded by distinguished men, he dominated the whole group. He was always the life of the party. He made marvelous extemporaneous speeches. Cedric excelled in everything he did.[11]

Unfortunately for the Laighton family, Cedric's passing sealed the fate of their island resort. Oscar became filled with melancholy and shame that he should be the one left to bear the burden of sorrow for his dear family.

Plummeting reservations and spiraling costs were Oscar's inheritance. Before Cedric died, he and Oscar had a brief moment of hope for the hotel's survival. A new market potential had come to their attention and helped for a time to ease their bleak situation.

In the summer of 1896, Thomas Elliott and his wife decided to vacation at Star Island. Mr. Elliott had recently read that the Isles of Shoals' air had therapeutic qualities and could soothe those who suffered respiratory ailments. His wife needed relief from the hot and dusty pollen-filled air found inland. But to vacation on Star meant Elliott would miss the conferences he so enjoyed, held each year at the Weirs on Lake Winnipesaukee. They were meetings he had become interested in after his election as president of the North Middlesex Conference, organized by the Unitarian Church.

After dinner on their first night at Star, Mr. Elliott retired to the piazza and one of the comfortable wicker rocking chairs. A few moments later he was joined by the hotel manager, Mr. Harry Marvin, who queried the Elliotts whether or not they were enjoying themselves. Indeed they were! They were delighted with the facility and service, but, Elliott pondered, "If we only had those [meetings] here I should be as near heaven as possible."[12] Fully aware of the Laighton's desperate situation, Marvin spent the evening suggesting to Elliott that he should bring the conference to the Shoals. He even offered a more than reasonable rate of $10 per person for the week's conference. Mr. Elliott could bearly contain his excitement and countered with his personal guarantee, "to fill them to the ridge poles."[13]

Mr. Marvin went immediately to Appledore and conveyed the good news to Oscar and Cedric. Their initial reaction was less than one would have expected. Oscar remembered,

> "I told him [Marvin] that we must act with caution. 'What is a Unitarian? Are they good people? It wont do to introduce any rough element,'. . . Harry said that he did not know just exactly what a Unitarian was, but, judging from the Elliotts, he would say that they were very nice, harmless people."[14] With little other discussion, the Laightons agreed to "welcome the Unitarians to Star Island."[15]

Thomas Elliott had a mountain of work ahead of him. The "ridgepole" number was 750 people, several times that of the Weirs' conferences! Through the following winter, Elliott contacted key Unitarian leaders throughout New England. With their help, he amassed 610 reservations for the conference. On registration day, 11 July 1897, the Oceanic was without a doubt "filled to the ridgepoles." The overflow of guests was sent to Appledore House.

The week's conference was a huge success. Thirty-five years later, Mr. Elliott would reflect, "the enthusiasm of that first year has never, I think, been quite equaled. . . . I cannot but think that life that season on that

Founders of Religious and Educational Conferences at Star Island. Left to right: Jessie E. Donahue, Oscar Laighton, Millie B. Nichols, Mr & Mrs Thomas Elliott (University of New Hampshire Media Service)

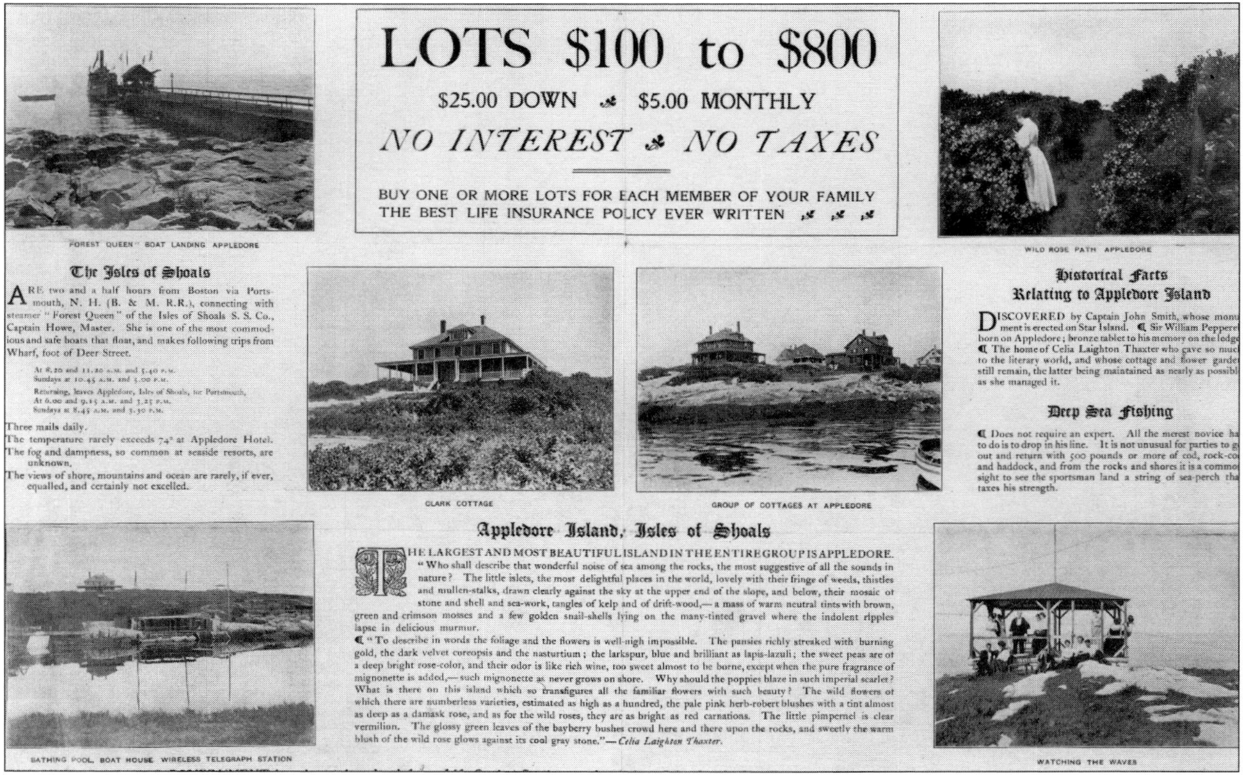

Advertizement to sell house lots. An attempt to raise capital for the ailing Appledore House. Early 1900s (University of New Hampshire Media Service)

sublime island was more like heaven than any other similar experience on this broad earth."[16]

By 1900 Oscar's grave financial situation forced the holding bank to foreclose. Over the next fourteen years, Oscar, his banks and financiers tried several different approaches to save the operation, including the sale of house lots,

> "—585 of them—to be sold at prices ranging from $100 to $500 each; $25 down and $5 monthly; no interest and no taxes. The results of this campaign were negative. The Isles of Shoals Hotel Co. was dissolved, and the 'Appledore Land and Building Co.' was formed in 1909 . . . only 61 of the 585 lots were sold or given away."[17]

From the first Elliott intended to continue the Unitarian meetings on Star Island. He organized a conference and called it the Isles of Shoals Summer Meetings Association, making sure the name would give no particular reference to any one religious group, allowing him to promote the meetings as open to all religious persuasions. With this flexibility Elliott could justify inviting Congregationalists to establish their own series of weekly meetings at Star.

To show their commitment toward a united effort dedicated to preserving the conferences during those difficult times, Reverend Hale, a Unitarian, and Reverend Barton, a Congregationalist, constructed the ecumenical cairn, a pile of stones near Captain John Smith's monument on Star Island, in 1900. They would have to wait another fourteen years for the cairn's prophecy to become reality when the two groups became the beneficiaries of the lost resort era.

The Laighton family holdings on Appledore were lost in 1914. In September the once elegant Appledore House was destroyed by fire, "The last lingering summer guests had gone, leaving only Oscar on Star and the custodian on Appledore, when an explosion of acetylene gas set fire to the great hotel."[18] The local newspaper reported that

> As the smoke and flames from the burning Appledore House at the Isles of Shoals rose into the clear air and sunshine on Saturday afternoon, September 4, and signalled the destruction of one of America's most famous hostelries to thousands of people who lined the beaches and waterfront from York, Maine to Cape Ann [20] miles away, there passed into history a building which has left undying influence on American letters and public life.[19]

The financial collapse became apparent to everyone after the fire. Several people took immediate action to stave off further disaster that might lead to the end of the Isles of Shoals Meeting Association.

Mr. Lewis Parkhurst, a regular guest at Star Island during the early conference days, was a man of means who had access to funds necessary to arrange a deal with the Piscataqua Savings Bank, holder of the mortgage. After several rounds of negotiations in 1915, the sale price of all Laighton interest on Star Island was set at $16,000.

Parkhurst held the note on the island conference center until Unitarian and Congregational leaders could form Star Island Corporation, which they accomplished in 1916. Funds were raised to buy back the island and to conduct much needed hotel repairs. With remaining funds, a steamboat was purchased for the ferry service. Only two years were needed for the organization to raise over $45,000, enough money to pay Parkhurst, dedicate nearly $7,000 for repairs, and $7,250 to form the Star Island Steamboat Company and buy the steamer *Sightseer.*

SS *Sightseer* approaching Star Island pier. Last steam ferry to service the Isles of Shoals (University of New Hampshire Media Service)

As the Star Island Corporation became more comfortable in its new role as owner, it remembered to be thankful and caring toward Oscar Laighton, who was "family" and affectionately known as Uncle Oscar. At first, a room was provided for him during the summer on the third floor of cottage A. Eventually, a first-floor room in cottage C was made available so that he could avoid the steep narrow stairways of A that were typical of island cottages.

Uncle Oscar would spend his final summer days either touring the island waters with guests aboard his run-about *Twilight*, or rocking with a young child on his lap. ". . . he spoke with the same amused sparkle in his eyes recounting a joke at his own expense, and the familiar trace of tears as he talked about his sister."[20] He was forever appalled that God had allowed him not only to outlive his sister, but her three children as well.

Even at ninety-eight, Oscar possessed enough stamina to row among the islands. After long rewarding summers, he would be taken to Portsmouth where he lived the winter longing for his Isles.

Oscar Laighton well on to 90 casting-off for excursion about the Isles of Shoals, *c.* 1930 (University of New Hampshire Media Service)

During the winter of 1939 Uncle Oscar was stricken with pneumonia. The fight had abandoned a body too tired to resist the inevitable eternal sleep any longer. He passed away on 4 April 1939, three months shy of his 100th birthday. His body was returned to Appledore.

A new era was born with the new century. From the Isles of Shoals, rites of passage were finished, a past era gently laid to rest. The future held promise, challenges fresh and exciting. New generations were new keepers of the spirit of the Shoals, and the dreams of Thomas Elliott. For all who pass among the islands, they are as bright and fresh as ever, not to own, but to borrow for a time.

13
YANKEE CLIPPERS ON THE PISCATAQUA

At the time Thomas Laighton moved his family to the Isles of Shoals, Portsmouth still remained second only to Salem, Massachusetts, in importance as a New England seaport.

The trend in world shipping had changed. Merchants were no longer interested in small and relatively slow ships. The need to beat the competition to market created a whole new style of shipbuilding. Great ships—longer, sleeker, possessing tremendous sails aloft—were desired by the merchants to realize greater profits. The era of sail was about to reach its crowning point. For the next five decades Piscataqua River shipwrights would be known worldwide for their fast and timely vessels.

One such respected shipbuilder, William Badger, was known as Master Badger. He was succeeded by his nephew Sam, who would continue to construct fine tallships. But restricted by the size of his yard, Badger was limited from bidding on the construction of the very largest ships, those that would measure over 200 feet. Those vessels were constructed by shipwrights such as Raynes, Fernald, Remick, Littlefield, and Pettigrew.

With each new order came new specifications requiring shipwrights to loft larger and faster ships. It had been common knowledge for sometime among naval architects that a longer waterline meant greater hull speed. Thus the Piscataqua shipyards and other yards downeast were forced to create a whole new breed, a thoroughbred of a ship, the Yankee clipper, possessing a long waterline, fair entry through the water, and slender beam. When heavily laden the fully rigged clippers carried canvas enough to span better than four acres, and flew like the wind! A run of just twenty-four days from New York to Liverpool, England, was not uncommon.

The greatest productivity of this era came from the Raynes yard located on North Mill Pond, Portsmouth. During the twenty years between 1840 and 1860 Raynes constructed over thirty fully rigged ships.

The clipper ship construction industry crested in the 1850s. Ninety-six square riggers were built in that decade, the California gold rush providing the greatest incentive for more and faster ships to transport supplies and people to the west coast. It was inevitable that a construction wave of this magnitude could not sustain itself for long. By 1860, it had all but ended, its life spent in the belch of black coal smoke from the stacks of the overland train. The wave crested over the shoal bottom economy. The power and momentum of the era broke and went out with the tide, never to return.

There were several reasons for the decline of the shipbuilding era, but the most glaring one, which has been inherent in all American desires for great fortune, was thirst for short quick profit at the expense of quality of life.

From the end of the Civil War to World War I the American businessman was so consumed by his own sense of destiny that he could not perceive beyond his days to see a time more sobering and tranquil when he would no longer control the world. After his "boom" had passed, chances are he would not survive. "Unfortunately for him, [the seeker of quick profit] has never known how shallow are the roots of his power, nor has he ever been able to temper his greed. Continual success has led him to believe there can be no failure."[1]

Development of railroad systems throughout America meant competition for cargo. Buyer demands continued pressuring suppliers to move their product to market faster and cheaper, forcing ship architects to develop more reliable means of propulsion, something the ocean winds would never be.

Under pressure, construction yards moved to develop steam-powered ships. Boilers were placed on sailing vessels and connected by shaft to side wheels. Through trial and error, a suitable means of shafting that led from the boiler room through the hull to the end propellers evolved. The die was first cast when, in 1819, the *Savannah* became the first steam-assisted sailing ship to cross the Atlantic. Then in 1838 steam power went into direct competition with sail, when the *Great Western* began the first regular commercial run from England to New York.

Merchants at first relied on the coal-fired boilers only when becalmed, as they were overly concerned about fuel costs. However, in the 1860s compound steam engines were invented that reduced coal consumption by 50 percent. Merchants soon saw the benefits of continuous "steaming," causing their ships to shatter any previous crossing records held by sailing packets. Eastbound passage time went from over twenty days with sail to only eleven days with steam. When efficiency was demonstrated to the buyers there was no stopping them. By the 1880s Britain began shipping more cargo tonnage by steam than sail. The United States merchants, more stubborn in putting up the capital outlay, took another twenty years to have steam power overtake sail. The clippers were able to find a niche only in smaller markets where speed was of no consequence and the cost of steam not yet justified.[2]

As prelude to the Civil War, coastal shipping between northern and southern ports declined in the 1850s, causing the shipyards to struggle. The end to Eliot, Maine's contribution to the clipper era, came in 1852 with the launching of the 151-foot *Judge Shaw* from the Hanscom yard. It was at the same yard just a year earlier that the clipper *Nightingale* had slid from the ways.

The Badgers closed their yard in 1856, with the *Sagamore*, a stately ship, among the largest ever built there at 190 feet. The next major yard closure was that of George Raynes & Sons, the *Shooting Star*, an intermediate clipper being their last in 1859. Though this was the Raynes family's last construction, the yard was taken over for a few more years by William D. Fernald.

The Civil War caused the remaining yards to have trouble keeping a reliable building schedule, since the Portsmouth Naval Shipyard hired the majority of the skilled workforce in the area, much of which had become lifeless in the private sector.

The end of the second great shipbuilding boom on the Piscataqua came at the close of the 1870s. New Hampshire white oak, still considered the finest hard wood in the country for ship construction, was no match for the iron clads which cost an average of 20 percent less per ton to build than one from wood. By blending steam with steel, naval architects created an unbeatable combination.

The great wooden shipbuilding era on the Piscataqua began with the *Falkland* and ended with the *Paul Jones*. It is unlikely that either the builder, William Fernald, or the owner, Charles Mendum, foresaw that the *Jones* would become the last wooden three-masted, full-rigged clipper to be launched on the Piscataqua River in 1877. An example of just how far the region's shipwrights had come since the Revolution is found in a description of the *Paul Jones* which appeared in the *Chronicle* days after the launch:

Typhoon, yankee clipper built at Fernald and Petigrew shipyard, Badger's Island in 1851. Shown here as it appeared off Liverpool after a record-breaking sail across the Atlantic from Portsmouth NH, in 13½ days! (Portsmouth Anthenaeum #PS-746)

> [She stood] 190 feet long on the keel and 200 feet between perpendiculars; Has 39 feet extreme breadth of beam, and 23 feet 6 inches of hold, including 8 feet 3 inches between decks. Her keel is of rock maple, sided 16 and moulded 24 inches with one three-inch shoe. The floor timbers are 20 feet long, and the space of frames from centre to centre is 30 inches. At the gunwales the frames are nine inches. The floor timbers are fastened with yellow metal driven through and riveted on the base of the keel, and are also bolted alternately through the first tier of keelsons. She has three tiers midship keelsons, each 15 inches square, and one tier of assistant keelsons, 16 inches square. Her frame is seasoned white oak [New Hampshire white oak was the best in the world]; the planking, ceiling, deck frames and pointers pitch pine, her hook white oak, and deck knees, of hackmatack. The cabin, which will be the model of comfort and richness, measures 44 feet long and 21 feet wide, finished in mountain ash and black walnut, the panels embellished with choice panel paintings in oil. Her poop is 10 feet abaft the mainmast, and 4 feet high in the clear. The forecastle is 40 feet long and 17 feet wide, containing eight distinct apartments, the ventilation being perfect. Her mainmast is 77 feet, foremast 75 feet, mizzenmast 73 feet, the poles of each being 8 feet; bowsprit 44 feet, jib-boom 30 feet, flying jib-boom 14 feet. Her fore and main yards will be 76 feet, fore and main lower topsails 60 feet, upper topsails 62 feet 6 inches, topgallant yard 50 feet, royals 39 feet. . . . In every respect the *Paul Jones* is a superior ship.[3]

She carried under her bowsprit a full-sized figurehead carving of Jones's likeness. The *Paul Jones* sailed from Portsmouth in November 1877 never to return. Her sailing days were spent in the East India trade. Throughout her career the *Paul Jones* had a knack for running into severe weather. Even on her maiden voyage to Baltimore a storm drove her into Gloucester, Massachusetts. The chronicles of her passages tell tales of typhoons and gales in the far Pacific as well. The *Paul Jones* was lost only nine years after her launching.[4]

Luckily, today there are still farsighted individuals who understand the importance of a time when the world's commerce moved with the breath of the wind across the sea. There are yet those occasional times when the clippers still gather their countless masts dressed with sails that still reach the sky, and glide silently into port. Secured beside one another along the piers their massive web of rigging blends one ship's masts into another, one ship ending, the next beginning, indistinguishably. How could any crewman possibly keep the run of his ship's rigging in order? How could a captain possibly keep straight the orders of command for such a maze looming above him? A bystander at moments feels strangely inept when compared to those sailors of today and those who preceded them a century before.

In the first decades of the twentieth century a person could have walked the once busy docks along a city's waterfront and seen the old abandoned tallships decayed through neglect, tied alongside derelict piers, and could but have wondered what it must have been like there when his forefathers were young. In a few decades what had been considered a common way of life was gone. The last of the proud sailors and captains and shipwrights in their old age had only memories to live by; they, too, were set adrift to become foster children of a new age.

If for just one moment one could take a journey back in time to the Portsmouth wharves, if one could stand on the dock waiting to ship out to sea armed with only a sextant, chronometer, and lead line to sail by. The silence, the absence of engine noise, of thick-smelling fuel, and the creak of the hull under the strain of the sails which longed to turn with the wind and move against the tide would conquer the senses.

"We had the experience but missed the meaning"

Dry Salvages II, l. 93
T.S. Eliot, *Four Quartets*

14
DYNAMITE, PRISONS, AND LIFE BETWEEN THE WARS

By 1877 the civilian employment force at the Portsmouth Naval Shipyard was reduced to seventy-one people. Between then and the turn of the century only one ship was built at the yard, a steam ferry with the ignominious name of #132. This would soon change, however, with the end of the Spanish American War in 1899. By 1903 the workforce was seven times larger than it had been at its low point as the U.S. Navy increased yard activity with repairs. The larger cargo steamships as well as battleships of the "Great White Fleet," coming to the shipyard for repairs, obviously were creating greater demands on Portsmouth harbor pilots when they called on the port. Pilots' skill had to be flawless in calculating the ninety-minute window of slack tide, the only time when such vessels could be moved safely up or downriver.

One particular bend in the river tested to the limits the skill and savvy of pilots responsible for the safe handling of ships. The inside shore of the bend known as Henderson's Point, had gained a more colloquial name over the years, "Pull or Be Damned Point." If a man found himself rowing against an opposing current there he would have to pull on his oars or be damned. It was here that the river currents were at their worst and pilots had zero tolerance for error. There was concern among the pilots that ships of the future might be too large for this passage. If that day came, Portsmouth harbor would die as a major port, choked from world trade and national defense plans. Neither the navy nor private industry wished for that to happen. Moreover, in the process of building a massive stone dry dock between Seavey's and Fernald's Islands the navy realized that Henderson's Point would restrict future ships entering the facility from making a safe approach.

A plan was soon developed for the point to be eliminated. A major excavation project began, complicated by the tidal currents and the discovery of a solid ledge. Deep holes were drilled for placement of explosives as the land was systematically chipped away. When finished 400 feet of the point on Seavey's Island would disappear.

The Massachusetts Contracting Co. began the work in August 1902, taking over three years and using hundreds of men around the clock to reduce the point to an enormous hole. This was rimmed with a thick ledge wall left to hold back the river water with the help of a cofferdam erected against the river side of the ledge so they could weaken the point's rim. More than 500 tons of rock were removed at a total project cost of $749,000.

When no more ledge could be removed safely explosives were used to eliminate the remainder of the point. The *Portsmouth Herald* of 18 July 1905 reported,

> It is now proposed to have the final explosion at Henderson's Point on July 22nd at Four p.m. and while it is not believed that any serious damage will result there from, it is thought advisable that the residents of Portsmouth, New Castle and Kittery should observe the following precautions: brick-a-brack and all small articles that are liable to fall from sudden jar, should be secured. All windows and doors should be opened. . . .[1]

Fifty tons of dynamite went into deep horizontal holes drilled into the bedrock.[2] At the time it was an unheard of amount in the world of demolition.

As the day approached, word was sent across the country. On 21 July 1905 the *Portsmouth Herald* breathlessly reported,

> tomorrow [Saturday] will be a day that will live long in history . . . the electric current will be sent through fifty tons of dynamite imbedded in the solid rock of Henderson's Point. . . . The spectacle will be witnessed by thousands of people. Special trains will bring curious people from all parts of the United States, and engineers from other countries.[3]

Local sources estimated that 20,000 people stood on the river banks perilously close to the site. The wildest predictions concerning effects on the surrounding communities spanned from earthquakes being triggered or tidal waves to massive property damage miles from the explosion.

Once the excavated area was flooded with incoming tidewater the signal to send the charge into the line went out. A Miss Foster had the honor of setting off the charge, which was followed by an explosion that sent water and debris over 200 feet in the air. It was the largest explosion up to that time; not even the massive explosives used at Hell's Gate in New York's East River were comparable.

To the disappointment of those who had all but predicted the end of

Infamous "Pull or Be Damned" a.k.a Henderson's Point, Piscataqua River, *c.* 1900. Site of fierce currents (tidal) (NHHS #A69)

Moment of "Greatest Explosion the world had ever known." Fifty tons of dynamite destroyed what remained of Henderson's Point. Note small boat near rightside of explosion (courtesy of R.E. McDonald, Private Collection)

the earth, remarkably little damage was caused by the explosion. There were a few broken windows in the surrounding neighborhoods and rattled chinaware in the cupboards. The only personal injuries remotely associated with the event occurred when two trolleys collided as they left Market Square in Portsmouth filled with passengers heading home after the explosion. Soon after the debris had settled, Harland S. Fraser, then twenty-two years old, rowed out to the site: "In about twenty minutes I was over there in my rowboat and got a load of fish, and wood for firewood."[4]

Life on the river would take time returning to normal. Engineers needed three more years and several smaller explosions before Henderson's Point was cleared for unrestricted navigation. Today over 100 cargo vessels, some measuring upwards of 750 feet and 50,000 tons, pass where old "Pull or Be Damned Point" once stood. They are moved all year long, day in day out, winter or summer, rain or shine or snow, and now even in fog. Today, over 300,000 tons of cargo enter the port each month as pilots all but bend a ship in half as it is swung through the turn.

In 1905, Portsmouth also gained world attention when President Theodore Roosevelt brought Russian and Japanese diplomats together there in an attempt to negotiate and sign a treaty ending the Russo-Japanese War, an action for which Roosevelt would receive the Nobel Peace Prize.

The war was primarily over issues of neutrality toward Korea and Manchuria. It would presage the Japanese expansion of the 1930s and World War II.

On 8 February 1904 Japanese forces invaded Port Arthur, Manchuria. Eleven months were needed to defeat the Russians and take possession. The war was relatively short-lived but very costly to both sides with several hundred thousand casualties. Within a year both countries were ready for peace with Japan possessing the best bargaining position. President Roosevelt extended his invitation. By June, the two governments had accepted his offer; their delegations arrived in Portsmouth aboard separate U.S. naval ships on 8 August 1905. The negotiating teams were led by Sergius Witte of Russia and Jutaro Komura of Japan. In stature they could not have been more opposite. Witte was massive and barrel-chested standing six feet seven inches; Kumora was petite and demure standing just five feet four inches. Intellectually they were equals, both gifted negotiators, and admirably served the interests of their respective countries.

Serge Witte
АВТОГРАФЪ С. Ю. ВИТТЕ.
С. Ю. ВИТТЕ ПОДПИСЫВАЕТЪ МИРНЫЙ ДОГОВОРЪ.

Sketch of signing Portsmouth Treaty, 1905. Photographers were not allowed in the room (courtesy of the Portsmouth Anthenaeum #Pl-225)

With the coming of September the negotiators were ready to sign a peace accord. The ceremony celebrating the occasion was held at Portsmouth Naval Shipyard in the naval stores building. A plaque placed on the outside of the building reads,

IN THIS BUILDING,
at the invitation of
THEODORE ROOSEVELT,
PRESIDENT OF THE UNITED STATES,
was held the
PEACE CONFERENCE
between the
ENVOYS OF RUSSIA AND JAPAN,
and
SEPTEMBER 5, 1905, AT 3.47 P.M.,
was signed
THE TREATY OF PORTSMOUTH,
which ended the war between the two
empires.[5]

With the major private shipyards gone a new breed of shipwrights engaged in one last great burst of shipbuilding as the United States entered World War I.

Ten days after the United States declared war in April 1917, the United States Shipping Board was created by Congress, giving President Woodrow Wilson emergency powers over shipbuilding in the country. Now that the United States was abandoning its isolation policy to help England and France fight against the Germans, there was a desperate need for merchant ships to transport troops and supplies to Europe.

The federally funded subsidiary, the Emergency Fleet Corporation, was established under the U.S. Shipping Board. Under this program Piscataqua River shipbuilders received an enormous economic boost.

In August 1917 the L.H. Shattuck Co. Yard was founded in Newington, just downriver from the narrows at Dover Point. Twelve building ways were placed on concrete slabs and piling clusters. The first three wooden steamships, 250 to 300 feet long, built to the specifications of the Shipping Board slipped down the greased railways on 4 July 1918. Some 8,000 shipfitters crawled over the vessels, working two long shifts, from 7:00 A.M. to 5:00 P.M., and from 5:00 P.M. to 3:00 A.M. A large hotel not far from the yard accommodated up to 800 workers for dinner at one time.[6]

Elmer Brooks, then twenty years old, recalled some fifty years later his days at the yard:

> "They [the ships] were all completed at the dock except the power. They towed 'em from there to Portland to put the power to 'em. . . . Took about six months to construct one ship. . . . They used to steam them planks and bend 'em in front of every boat. They was southern pine. . . . There was lumber enough down here to rebuild the City of Portsmouth. . . . I been on then hammers nights with six guys. Air hammers. Drivin' pins down in 'em. Two foot pins. . . . Round about daylight everyone near exhaustion. The last guy that's holdin' the hammer, it would put him right up in the air, that plunger would shoot out across there. Done it time and again."[7]

While workers at the Shattuck Yard were hard pressed to build their ships piece by piece with any amount of speed, the government was figuring ways to produce more vessels in less time. The Shipping Board hired Theodore Ferris as naval architect to design not only the ships coming out of the Shattuck Yard, but also to revolutionize shipbuilding technology. Ferris developed a design and construction idea ahead of its

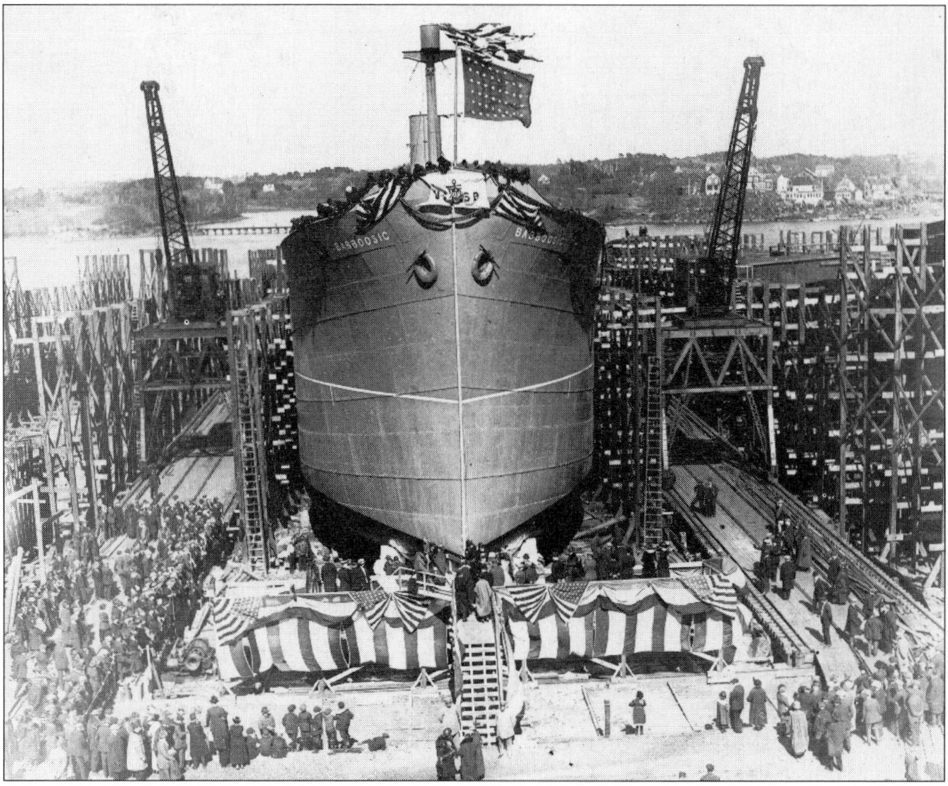

Launching of transport ship *Babboosic* during World War I from Atlantic Shipyard, Portsmouth (courtesy of Strawbery Banke, Patch Collection #1338–77)

time. Steel-clad vessels 440 feet long would be mass produced in assembly line fashion. Ironically, while the government was allocating funds to the Shattuck Yard, which used 200-year-old building techniques, similar funding went into the new Atlantic Corporation Shipyard just two miles downriver near Freeman's Point in Portsmouth, where steel ships 440 feet long were to be constructed.

In September 1917 the Atlantic Corporation proposed to build fourteen of these prefabricated ships. Railways were set up in the traditional fashion, but long and very large buildings were erected ahead of the rails where ship sections were fabricated. All fourteen vessels were to be identical, have a reciprocal engine, and be registered at 8,800 tons. Once the yard was up and running its owners planned to produce two ships per month until the order was filled. The first came down the ways

Dinosaurs of the last great shipbuilding in private yards on the Piscataqua. Two hulls never finished at Shattuck Shipyard. Photo taken 1939, twenty years after yard closed. Today, the collapsed remains of these ships can still be seen (courtesy of Andy Mantis, Private Collection)

in January 1919, several months behind target date and after war demands for transport ships had passed.

With the end of World War I the flow of funds was cut so abruptly that partially constructed ships at the Shattuck Yard were abandoned to rot on the ways. The remains can still be seen along the shore in Newington, looking like dinosaur skeletons, with no real shape left to them, giving no clues as to what they were to have been. The Atlantic Yard folded as much from mismanagement as from the cutting of government funds. Today, one can cruise along the river at low tide and see the clusters of piling tops used to support the last great ships of Piscataqua's upriver yards.

During the Spanish American War the undeveloped Seavey's Island property located just downriver from Henderson's Point had become the site for Camp Long, a temporary detention facility. A group of 1,600 captured Spanish soldiers from Cuba was kept in bivouacs there until war's end. The prisoners had arrived by U.S. troop ship and were kept under guard until eventual repatriation to their homeland.

This was followed in 1905 by the construction of a naval prison just downriver from Henderson's Point to replace the prison ship *Southery* as a permanent detention facility. The ship was moored at the yard's back channel docks and used for handling "the overflow of general court martial prisoners at the Boston Navy Yard."[8]

The building was located close to the river's high embankment, eventually giving those military prisoners, who had a window in their cells, a spectacular view of life on the river and a nice prospect of the rear façade of Wentworth-by-the-Sea Hotel resort off to the south. The site was near where Thomas Fernald had built one of the island's first settlement homes in 1650. The Fernald family cemetery sits to this day in the shadow of the prison walls. Upon the prison's completion, the *Southery* became a unit to retain new arriving prisoners as well as a training facility to assist in prisoner rehabilitation before their term was over. The prisoners operated a pig slaughterhouse on board the ship, creating much ill will among back channel property owners.

The original prison structure, the nave, was designed to look like a castle with watchtower turrets. Its design and that of the section later added on during World War II, legend says, inspired Walt Disney in developing a design for Magic Kingdom. On 11 April 1908 the prison was opened for service. It provided 320 cells for military inmates and was staffed by forty-two Marine guards, whose zealous demands for discipline among the inmates became infamous throughout the military. A life of hard work, little recreation, and pale food soon became the daily routine. However, from the start prison policy did incorporate plans to make an honest attempt to rehabilitate the men, which at the time represented a radical change in the military penal system. Redemption and reinstatement became a reality for many prisoners upon completing their term.

In 1916 the prison command instituted more reform measures for the prisoners by establishing a school to which any prisoner lacking a grammar school education was required to attend. By 1917, prison chief Commander Osborne continued to press for even stronger reforms within the prison walls. Disgusted by the very nature and ills of normal prison life, he set forth an internal self-governing system whereby the fundamentally "healed" prisoners took charge of running daily life inside. All Marine guards were removed to outside grounds duty. Those prisoners who qualified were also assigned to job detail in navy yard workshops; others worked in single-story buildings erected near the prison, where they repaired shoes and operated a printing press. Inmates cultivated their own vegetable gardens simply to put color on their plates at mealtime. The new policy paid dividends the first year: 743 inmates were restored to military service, followed the next year by 1,563.

World War I brought inmate population up from 350 to 2,295 in one year, a figure far exceeding the prison's anticipated capacity. During the next few years some clever inmates were able to manipulate the internal governing structure and became abusive with their power, often carrying out discipline far beyond what was deemed necessary. From this period rose rumors that persist to this day of acts of brutality and violence.

A new commander saw this abuse for what it was and abolished the policy of prisoner self-governance, but kept the main directive of restoring the men to duty. In 1925 a new shop was established next to the prison where the men made clothing for those who were "getting out." The prison served as a model disciplinary facility, gaining recognition throughout the world. In 1934 a delegation from Japan paid the prison a visit and saw at first hand how the system worked. It became the basis for the Japanese Navy Penal System.

With World War II came construction of the center tower and northeast section, attached to the main prison in November of 1942. These additions gave the facility even more of a castle-like appearance and would serve as new living quarters for the Marine guards.

Job duties for the inmates were expanded during this time to include manufacturing thousands of camouflage nets along with their expanded clothing production, which grew to 70,000 units per year.[9] In 1943, an eight-story "box" was attached to the prison's southwest end, standing just a few feet back from the sheer cliff of the riverbank. This final addition brought prison capacity to 3,000, a figure actually exceeded in 1945 when the inmate population rose to 3,088—the highest count the prison would ever see. This new wing also housed a mess hall, tailor shop, printing shop, book bindery, and a shoe repair shop, along with medical and dental facilities. The seventh-floor amenities included an auditorium for movies and church services.

The "castle" as it appears today. Portsmouth Naval Prison. Center tower reportedly inspired Walt Disney for his Magic Kingdom at Disneyland, Anaheim, Ca (photo by Geo A. Sylvester)

During World War II prison command continued with the rehabilitation program and was successfully returning more men back to duty than those who were receiving dishonorable discharges. "An 'Honor Company' was established in 1944 . . . these men worked in the navy yard without supervision."[10]

The honor company kept the grounds outside the prison manicured to perfection, built a dock and boathouse nearby, and constructed two dozen Quonset huts to house schools and more workshops. A tall fence capped with rolled barbed wire fully enclosed the grounds and the prison. Watchtowers were placed every few hundred feet along the fence where guards stood watch year round with rifle in hand, cartridge in chamber. In 1947 prisoners were allowed to publish their own newspaper, The *Castle Courier*, which remained in circulation to the last active days of the prison.

During the 1950s the prison went through several name changes while command kept the initial resolve to restore inmates to service or society accordingly. Retraining facilities were expanded to include Camp Langdon, a former army war camp in Newcastle. Camp Langdon graduated an impressive 86 percent of its retrainees.

The Vietnam War brought inmate population back to 1,288 in 1969, but by the war's end only a few hundred were left. Defense Department austerity programs called for the exemplary prison to be closed in 1974. For the next ten years the "castle" sat empty and exposed to the weather, until 1984 when all of the building's windows were boarded close. This was seen as far more cost effective than spending millions to raze the building. Today only a small portion is used for storage.

A look upriver beyond the navy yard between World Wars I and II would have revealed along the Piscataqua's waterfront a diversity of maritime activity. Just up from Ceres Street in Portsmouth coal docks were still busy importing an estimated 500,000 tons of West Virginia coal each year. Dover's port was quiet by comparison to the years before the great flood of 1896. The once numerous ferryboats that plied the entire Piscataqua tidal basin were less active. Gundalows became little more than shadows upon the river, products of an earlier time, looking out of place, irrelevant next to the modern ships with which they shared the river.

Major commercial activity was involved in cross-river ferry service, especially at the lower end. The electric car ferries worked a shuttle between Portsmouth and Badger's Island for both train cars and passengers. This trolley was established on narrow guage rail and networked a transportation service throughout the local communities including the Yorks of Maine. Ferries from Portsmouth hustled workers back and forth to the navy yard until the Memorial Bridge was completed in 1923, a time when virtually all downriver cross-ferry service ceased to exist.

During the winter of 1918 an exceptionally deep and extended cold snap was preceded by a January thaw resulting in the complete halt of vessel traffic on the river's lower end. The quick "thaw" caused massive sheets of ice in Great Bay to break free from the shore and move downriver on the outgoing tide. When the ice arrived off the navy yard its leading edge became jammed between Henderson's Point and Pierce Island. By mid-February the fractured ice had frozen solid, trapping cross-river ferries in mid-stream. The passengers would actually make the rest of the trip on foot. Some daring people went as far as attempting to drive vehicles across the ice from shore to shore. Waterfront pilings were wrapped with thick rime ice. No time since has the river been frozen as it was in 1918.

Continuing upriver on the way to Durham and Exeter, heading past Dover Point, the channel is squeezed between Fox Point, Newington, and Goat Island. Since the 1870s the island had been home to a man who lived in solitude among his sheep, dogs, and his lobstering and fishing and occasional farming. Jim Murtaugh had left his home and saloon business in Dover after his wife had walked out on him. The following are excerpts taken from the first-person account of Richard Pinkam, who, as a boy, had befriended Mr. Murtaugh:

> "Now the old hermit, Jimmy Murdock. We called him Murdock . . . came here when the schooners used to come up from Boston, going to Newmarket and to Exeter, and he passed this island many times . . . he was a hermit. . . . In the winter he built a houseboat out of old planking and he had his bunk and stove and everything in there to live with . . . mornings he'd just open a window and start shooting duck or geese. . . . In the summer he dug into the banking above the high water mark and dug this big room and he closed the sides and ceiling and the back of it in with these old planking of driftwood. Had an old sail across the front. . . .
>
> "We had picnickers there put a flagpole up one time for 'im in case of emergencies. . . . One afternoon . . . my mother was goin' out to the hen house and she happened to look up river and she saw the piece of cloth atop the flagpole and hollered to me. . . . She said Jim Murtaugh's in trouble! . . . So I jumped right in the boat and headed for the island. I got over there. . . . Didn't hear anything. And I got out, run up the bank, and he was lying up on the bank rolling back and forth on his belly. . . . He said, 'I'm dyin'.' I said, 'What's the matter?' 'The pain.' He said, 'I never had such pains in my stomach in all my life, I'm dyin'.' '. . . I'll tell you what I want. I want some castor oil, and I want a lot of it.' "

When Pinkham returned with the castor oil and Murtaugh had swigged it down in one gulp, he explained to Pinkham that,

> "He'd been to the store in Dover the day before he was sick, and he bought a lot of groceries, and among other things he bought was the one thing he loved . . . cheese. He bought five pounds off a wheel of that cheese and was hungry when he got home . . . and he eat that five pounds of cheese that afternoon and that evening. . . . It never hurt him before, but he'd never do it again. But he was quite a character, a man you had to like, if you knew him you had to like him."[11]

Hjordis Parker offered the following remembrance of Jim Murtaugh's last days:

> "I heard that he died of the flu. He was taken to Dover Hospital, and of course the first thing they did was to give him a bath. When he got through, he said 'By golly, that was good. I wish I'd done it before.'"[12]

Back down the river, Portsmouth's waterfront had fallen on hard times between the wars. The old warehouses were all but abandoned. Portsmouth harbor tugs were using the once active shipping docks, the ferry *Sightseer* still provided summer service to Star Island Conference Center, and indigents were finding a new home there.

15
PORTSMOUTH AND THE SUBMARINE

It is not generally understood how extensive submarine research was in America prior to World War II. Historically, submersible vessel designs date back centuries, but it was not until the Department of the Navy had received the go-ahead to pursue submarine technology early in the twentieth century that submarines would go on to become dominating weapons of war.

The first American submersible to see combat, the *Turtle*, had no direct influence on the outcome of the Revolution. The Civil War's *Monitor* and the *Merrimac*, though not submersibles, looked as if their architects had intended them to be diving ships but had lacked the knowledge of how to engineer it. Of the two submarines constructed during the Civil War, only the Confederate's *Hunley* saw action. It became the first submarine in history to sink an enemy ship with a torpedo. In fact, when the Union vessel *Housatonic* was hit, the explosion sank not only that ship but the *Hunley* as well. The early stages of submarine development were carried out exclusively at private shipyards until 1914. However, the government had earlier purchased its first torpedo-firing submarine from John P. Holland:

> This craft was launched in 1897 and was powered on the surface by a gasoline engine and, while submerged, by battery-fed electric motors. The navy purchased this submarine on April 11, 1900, a date now observed as the official birthday of the submarine service. On October 12, 1900, the navy commissioned the sub as USS *Holland*.[1]

The Electric Boat Company of Quincy, Massachusetts led the efforts in persuading the navy to issue submarine contracts. For a number of years this gave Electric Boat a nice monopoly on the industry. The dominance of private yards in submarine production continued until complaints from submarine officers made it apparent that general dissatisfaction toward privately built submarines over vessel safety and quality was widespread.

A Portsmouth delegation led by local newspaper owner F.W. Hartford went to Washington DC in 1914 to lobby for the soon to be issued contract which called for design and construction of the *L-8* submarine.

Secretary of the Navy Josephus Daniels had authorized bids on the $525,000 project to be submitted from government yards.

> The old method of having the Navy purchase submarines alarmed Daniels. "I thought that the only way to compel the two private submarine builders [the other being Lake Torpedo Company, Bridgeport, Conn.] to make the best submarines at a reasonable price," Daniels wrote, "was to demonstrate that they could be built in a navy yard."[2]

The argument the delegation made for the Portsmouth yard was simple and to the point: "'There would be practically no outlay to get ready for this work,' and that the, 'yard had the lowest overhead charges of any yard in the country.'"[3] Daniels accepted the Portsmouth bid thus beginning a construction program at Portsmouth Naval Shipyard which would continue for fifty years.

Not until the 1960s would private shipyards convince the government to close its construction facilities. Today, all seven government yards are issued exclusive contracts for repair, overhaul, and refueling of naval vessels, while private yards handle new construction and some repairs as well.

Construction began on the *L-8* late in 1914, and was performed under tight security in the Franklin Building, at the time the largest wood-framed structure in America.[4] The submarine's round hull was fashioned with a bulbous nose, a design naval architects would abandon for the more sleek and traditional ship's hull typical of World War II submarines, as surface patrol was considered a mission necessity. Naval architects would return to the now familiar whale-shaped hulls in 1952.

The L-class submarines were highly sophisticated vessels for their day and

> were 165-foot, 456-ton submarines with diesel engines for surface propulsion. For armament, the L-boats had four torpedo tubes in the bow. A single 3-inch, 23-caliber gun was mounted on the deck for attacking small surface ships. The speed of the L-boats was relatively high, cruising at 14 knots on the surface with diesels and operating on electric motors at 10-1/2 knots while submerged. Her crew compliment was twenty-eight.[5]

Portsmouth Naval Shipyard would gain valuable support from the Department of the Navy when $122,000 of the original contract price for the *L-8* went unspent. The Portsmouth-built *L-8* became the first submarine to be constructed in a government shipyard and the only American submarine to see action in World War I.

Launching of the *L–8* submarine, 1917, Portsmouth Naval Shipyard, from a period postcard (courtesy of the Portsmouth Anthenaeum #Pl–1731)

Twenty-six submarines were built at Portsmouth before World War II. A major boost over other yards came in 1919 when a captured German U-boat was sent to Portsmouth. Naval architects were already aware of the U-boat's technical superiority. What they learned was incorporated into the next generation of American submarines, the S-class, advancing the fleet into the 1930s.

S-boats were transitional submarines, field-testing laboratories at best. However, they helped advance more efficient submarine technology:

> The S-Class submarines were still plagued with many problems. Designed during the war to attack enemy warships, they could not do so. More than 200 feet in length, the S-Boats carried four torpedo tubes and averaged fifteen knots on the surface and eleven knots submerged. They were too slow and fragile for extended fleet operations. Several sank during the 1920s, including two built at the yard.[6]

The *S-5* went down off the coast of Delaware in September 1920. After the crew had carried out the captain's orders to blow aft ballast and fuel tanks, the submarine rocketed to the surface from nearly 200 feet down. There she bobbed stern up 20 feet in the air. Her crew managed after a day and a half to cut one small hole in the hull. A cargo ship passing nearby saw the distressed vessel and went over to lend a hand. The following conversation was conducted between the men from the ship in their lifeboat and the officer talking from behind the little hole in the submarine's hull: "'What ship?', '*S-5*.' 'What nationality?' 'American.' 'Where bound?'" 'Hell by compass.'"[7] All men were saved after spending over two days bobbing tail high in the ocean.

The offspring of the ill-fated S-boats were the V-class submarines which were far more sophisticated in battle. These new submarines were

> designed and fitted to accompany an American fleet under all conditions. . . . The first three V-Boats, better known as the *Barracuda*, the *Bass*, and the *Bonita*, were launched [at Portsmouth] during 1924 and 1925. Each cost about $7 million. These V-boats were 341 feet long with an operating depth of 200 feet . . .Workmen installed into most submarines a refrigerating plant, cold storage space and an air-conditioning plant.[8]

In the 1930s, the Portsmouth-built *Dolphin* was developed from the V-class as an experimental submarine. Her technology moved the United States directly to the submarines used in the World War II service.

In 1924 the Department of the Navy instituted the assignment of fish names to submarines in addition to their official class number. This became a one-man job carried out by William F. Calkins, a naval officer stationed in Washington, D.C. He spent his day finding names for all new submarines. This became a difficult task when the number of active submarines rose to over 500. Calkins wrote:

> There are not as many fish as you think. . . . I was reduced . . . to scrambling around for names like *Spinex*, *Irex*, *Mero*, and *Sirago*. You wouldn't want to call a naval vessel the USS *Big-Eyed Scad* . . . there were the *Chub* and the *Hardhead* . . . both minnows, but we couldn't name a fighting ship the USS *Minnow*. We decided we could not put the sardine on the navy list, but we named the USS *Sarda* – same fish.[9]

During the submarine construction period at Portsmouth, yard workers took pride in being among the leading innovators of submarine technology. In 1937 they launched the first all-welded hull, the USS *Snapper*. A welded hull section had superior test results during underwater explosion experiments. Comparable riveted hulls failed the same test, with all rivets popping. This new hull also allowed submarines to attain depths greater than 300 feet. From the *Snapper* to the nuclear age, all hulls were not only welded but also equipped with escape hatches allowing personnel evacuation from their sunken submarine. By the late 1930s submarine technology had progressed to the point where the McCann Rescue Chamber and the Momsen Lung were perfected as rescue devices to allow removal of sailors from their sunken vessels.

Prior to World War II the Portsmouth Naval Shipyard's workforce had grown to 3,968, up from the 1,150 figure attained during World War I. In 1939 the yard was assigned two construction contracts, the sister ships *Sculpin* and the *Squalus*, representing a "new" S-class boat.

After her launching, the *Squalus* was put through a series of exhaustive tests. After completing eighteen successful emergency fast dives off the Isles of Shoals, the *Squalus*, on the morning of 23 May 1939 at 0840 hours went into her nineteenth test dive. During the dive all lights in the control room were showing green. Not one light gave hint as to what was happening in the after compartment, where a fresh air induction valve had jammed in the open position without the light turning red. When the captain finally became aware of the error the *Squalus* was in a slow steep-angled descent, stern first to the bottom. "She sank in 243 feet of water. Despite [captain] Naquin's order, 'BLOW MAIN BALLAST!,' the *Squalus* failed to rise."[10]

Just as the *Squalus* was sinking, her sister ship the *Sculpin* was setting sail from Portsmouth at 1130 hours. By the greatest stroke of luck for the crew of the downed submarine, the *Sculpin* sailed over the *Squalus*. Crewmen on watch on the *Sculpin*'s bridge sighted the bobbing telephone buoy of their sister vessel. The time was 1241 hours.

William Isaacs, the ship's cook, gave his chilling account of those first minutes aboard the *Squalus*, recounted by Nat Barrows in his book, *Blow All Ballast!*:

> In the after battery room . . . William Isaacs, had just come back [to] the galley. . . . At that moment, the boat took a downward pitch towards the stern and strange noises filled the battery compartment. . . . Isaacs thrust his head out of the galley door. . . . A sheet of water hit Isaacs in the head and nearly knocked him down. . . . He jumped out of the galley and into the little air-lock corridor that led aft, a passageway large enough for only one man at a time. Water cascaded down his back as he leaped. . . . Isaacs bent over to look through the glass port in the door . . . the engine room was half full of water and a great fall roared down through the main engine induction outlet. . . . He moved away from the door – the only living man to have seen that terrible waterfall – and worked over to the bulkhead stops in the ventilation line. Water was pouring out there in a rushing stream. He tried in vain to close these flappers . . . [then] headed uphill toward his only hope for safety – the control room. Already the water in the battery room was at his knees, and

> rising. . . . He knew also that once the water hit the batteries under the compartment flooring deadly streams of chlorine gas would finish any man forced to breathe them. . . . Past the crew's mess tables, through the crew's sleeping quarters, he stumbled desperately. . . . Up at the top of the slope in the battery room, a man was trying to pull the door shut. "HOLD IT! HOLD IT!" Isaacs screamed. . . . He jumped into the control room. For a moment he stood just inside the door. . . . He watched the door come shut, sealing the control room. It was too late for any others to make an escape forward; . . . Isaacs thought of the other men back aft and a chill went through him. "May their souls rest in peace," he muttered.[11]

By 1223 hours on 25 May, two days later, all thirty-three surviving crewmen were brought up in the McCann Rescue Chamber. Four historic trips were made literally from beyond the grave. It marked the first time in modern history that men who had gone down with their ship lived to tell their story. Sadly, twenty-six shipmates of the survivors had died that day the *Squalus* went down.

After several failed attempts to raise the submarine, salvage teams were successful on 13 September and towed her back to Portsmouth. She was rebuilt, then recommissioned as the USS *Sailfish* only one year after her fatal dive. The *Sailfish* was among the finest submarines to see action in World War II, distinguishing herself with an excellent war record. Her bridge and conning tower are today located in the grounds of the shipyard and serve as a memorial to the men who had sacrificed their lives aboard the *Squalus*, and to all of the men of the United States submarine force.

In World War II the government spared no expense in the naval buildup. The Portsmouth yard continued its leadership role at the time. By 1943 general employment rose to 20,466 employees, working on three split shifts twenty-four hours a day, seven days a week. A large percentage of the workforce was comprised of women from the surrounding communities of Maine, New Hampshire, and Massachusetts. Congress, meanwhile, went from authorizing 21,000 tons of submarines in June of 1940 to 70,000 tons one month later. From 1939 to the end of the war in 1945, the Portsmouth yard commissioned eighty-eight submarines, making it the most active naval construction yard on the east coast. "A total of 32 submarines were completed during 1944 and on January 27th, four submarines were launched on the same day. Building time per submarine was reduced from 469 calendar days in 1941 to 173 days in 1944."[12]

Three submarines ready for launch on 27 January 1944. Left to right: *Razorbill*, *Redfish*, *Ronquil*. Located dry dock#1, PNSY (University of New Hampshire Media Service)

The term "Portsmouth-built" was synonymous with quality, with the best. This becomes evident when former World War II submarine crewmen tell of how, when they stepped aboard a new submarine, they would ask, "Where was she built?"[13] A sigh of relief came if they had heard, "Portsmouth," if for no other reason than consideration for their comfort while on long patrols. Portsmouth submarines were equipped with the most advanced air conditioning and heating systems in the fleet.

The Portsmouth submarines became distinguished by collecting one exceptional war record after another. The *Sailfish* received the Navy Cross after conducting one of the most productive submarine patrols of the war. She scored the first sinking of a Japanese aircraft carrier, a tragic twist of fate, drawing the *Sailfish* back to the day she had gone down as the *Squalus* and the *Sculpin*'s crew had found her on 23 May 1939. Captain Ward "had sunk the 20,000-ton *Chuyo*, . . . unknown at the time to Ward and his men, the *Chuyo* was carrying aboard twenty-one American prisoners of war, . . . survivors of the USS *Sculpin*. After [she] was scuttled and sunk in mid-November."[14] By sinking the carrier *Chuyo* the *Sailfish* killed all but one of the survivors of the *Sculpin*.

The *Archerfish* scored the greatest strike of the war by sinking the newly commissioned Japanese carrier, *Shinano*. At 70,000 tons, the carrier became the largest warship ever sunk in any war to this day. The USS *Pollack* gained distinction by scoring the Pacific War's first kill—a cargo ship, the *Cravellis*, at the time the largest Japanese tanker. The *Redfish* was responsible for torpedoing the new 18,500-ton carrier *Unryu*.

Though the majority of all submarine missions were directed at "killing" enemy ships, other patrols such as sea rescues of downed pilots, reconnaissance, and secret missions were also given priority status. One of the most bizarre non-combative duties of the war involved the Portsmouth-built *Trout*. She had just delivered supplies and 3,500 rounds of anti-aircraft shells to U.S. personnel on Corregidor in February 1942. Before returning to sea the captain put in a request for ballast, preferably sandbags to replace the lost cargo weight. The sandbags, considered too valuable to the forces on Corregidor, could not be spared.

The ballast that was eventually found came up the gangway in the form of gold bullion: 583 bars, each one weighing 40 lb and placed in the *Trout*'s bilge. The precious cargo of gold and the additional silver and securities also stowed aboard were taken from the Philippines to the United States for safekeeping. A month after the *Trout* had left Corregidor its precious cargo was unloaded in Pearl Harbor, each bar inventoried as it left the ship; 582 bars were counted; one bar was missing, "a $14,500.00 ingot. An inch-by-inch search of the *Trout* finally located the missing bar. The gold ingot was in the galley; one of the cooks was using it as a paperweight."[15]

United States submarines were responsible for enemy losses totaling 1,334 vessels amounting to over five million tons, devastating losses from which no power, no matter what their resources, could ever expect to recover. This impressive total did not come without a price. Fifty-two American submarines were lost with nearly 4,000 sailors. Thirteen Portsmouth-built submarines never came back to their home port.

Shortly after World War II ended, American naval forces searched the Atlantic for stray German U-boats. Portsmouth Naval Shipyard, being the largest on the east coast, was awarded many of the surrendered submarines:

> U-Boats *U-805*, *U-873*, *U-1228*, *U-234*, [and *U-505*] among others, were towed into the yard for extensive study and were eventually disposed of. The crews of the submarines were held at the naval prison . . . while prisoners were here they were required to work on the captured submarines and explain various systems to the naval authorities.[16]

In September 1945 the *U-3008* arrived in Portsmouth harbor. She was "the world's most advanced sub. . . ."[17] Every facet was gone over by yard engineers in search of new information that would help their own submarine force still engaged in the Pacific War. Among the most significant findings was the submarine's exhaust snorkel, which allowed the vessel to remain submerged while recharging batteries with diesel-powered generators. The *U-3008* was eventually commissioned by the U.S. Navy and served until 1951.

One German U-boat, the *U-505*, was brought to the navy yard from

Captured at the end of World War II, German U-Boat *U-505* swings on sub-mooring in Portsmouth harbor entrance, awaiting tow upriver to shipyard. Now located at Museum of Science and Industry, Chicago (Portsmouth Naval Shipyard Museum)

Bermuda after the war and sat for ten years without care. She was to have been taken far offshore and sunk, but for unknown reasons that plan was never carried out. Instead, the boat just sat at the yard, until Admiral Gallery, the commander of a naval air reserve training base outside Chicago, convinced the navy and Congress to give the submarine to the Museum of Science and Industry in Chicago, where it remains to this day.[18]

This enemy submarine program, the yard's commissioning of four submarines before 1950, and a handful of construction contracts for small surface utility vessels were not enough to justify maintaining wartime employment levels. From the high figure of 1943, the number of employees plummeted to 5,542 in 1946. Since then only the Korean War years brought employment to over 10,000, with most years fluctuating between 5,000 and 9,500 to the present.

Old submarines such as the *Sailfish*, which no longer met the needs of the navy, were dismantled. Other submarines were taken offshore and used as targets for bombing practice. The others were either sold to foreign countries or upgraded in the GUPPY program which became part of the expanded operations at Portsmouth. GUPPY is an acronym for Greater Underwater Propulsion Power. The "Y" had no meaning other than turning the acronym into a fish. These World War II submarines were given more powerful diesels, and their battery capacity improved, "thereby increasing underwater speed and endurance."[19]

Portsmouth Naval Shipyard became responsible for the GUPPY program's development, and delivered the first conversion, the ODAX, in 1947. Besides having greatly improved interiors, these submarines' outside hulls were stripped of all unnecessary gear and the bow changed to a bulb shape. All of these changes reduced friction or drag through the water. The bulbous bow was a look into the future of hull designs. Twenty such conversions were completed at the yard, as well as the installation of new exhaust snorkels, enabling the submarines to extend time submerged for as long as the captain needed. The GUPPY-snorkeled submarines continued in service until the 1970s.

The 1950s brought an entirely new look to American submarine technology. A new breed of submarine burst on to the scene in the winter of 1953 from the Portsmouth yard with the launching of the USS *Albacore*. Naval architects seemed to have dusted off the old blueprints of the *L-8* and found that her hull design had been right from the start. The

USS *Albacore*, setting out from Portsmouth, set the standards for the future U.S. nuclear submarine fleet (Portsmouth Naval Shipyard Museum)

bulbous, round, tear-drop shape had proved, through extensive tank testing, to be the best hydrodynamic design needed to create a craft which was intended to spend its entire patrol far below the ocean surface. The *Albacore* became the first modern navy submarine designed with the now familiar whale-shape hull. "She was intended to be, in the words of the naval designer Eugene Allmendinger who worked on her throughout her career, 'a full-scale floating hydrodynamics laboratory.' "[20]

The *Albacore* pushed back the limitations of past designs, giving its architects the feeling that there were virtually no limits to her speed and maneuverability. They had finally discovered how to make the submarine literally "fly" underwater. With the help of the *Albacore*, future navy submarines would become true pelagic, deepwater ships, capable of speeds greater than fifty knots and of extremely deep dives. Each steel section was subjected to pressure-tank tests before being fitted into the ship's hull. As a result, submarines were capable of going on deepwater patrols for months at a time. New hull fabrics, silent machinery, and quiet props have today made the navy submarines virtually invisible to sonar tracking devices.

During her career the *Albacore* set world speed records that are still classified today, though the ship has been decommissioned since 1972. The *Albacore* also established many high-level performance standards with her conventional diesel-electric power coupled to a revolutionary propeller system. Her leading technology launched America's nuclear submarine fleet into the twenty-first century.

Nuclear power research for submarines was initiated in 1939. World War II suspended this development. It would regain atomic power development which would regain the interest of naval engineers in the early 1950s. Portsmouth shipyard's closest competitor in the private sector continued to be Electric Boat Co. which had built the world's first three nuclear-powered submarines in the early 1950s. However, in 1956, "the Portsmouth Shipyard joined the nuclear club by laying the keel for the *Swordfish*, the first atomic-powered submarine constructed in a government yard."[21]

Admiral Rickover, father of the nuclear submarine fleet, made frequent visits to the yard for personal inspections of his ships, making a point to be aboard for the first of a long series of sea trials and test dives that had to be conducted on each submarine before it was ready for active duty. The admiral demanded high standards of performance not only from the crewmen, but all construction workers—nuclear inspectors to shipfitters.

On one such test run, the admiral allowed himself a rare public display of humor. He was aboard Portsmouth's *Seadragon*, the second nuclear submarine built at the yard. During a shakedown run the submarine struck a whale, badly bending its propeller. No apparent report was made available on the condition of the whale. The submarine's radio man called back to the yard and reported, "Whacked whale, warped wheel." Upon returning to the yard, Admiral Rickover came over the vessel's intercom system and said, "I think you have a whale of a vessel."[22]

The Cold War era at the yard had its share of tragedy. On 10 April 1963 a newly constructed submarine, the USS *Thresher*, sank 220 miles east of Cape Cod in 8,400 feet of water with the loss of all 129 men on board, including a number of shipyard workers. The *Thresher* went into a steep test dive from which she never recovered. She had been the lead boat for a new class of submarine, the SSN-593s or *Thresher* class.

For its day the *Thresher* was the most advanced submarine in the free world. Her hull was a product of the new "invisible" technology, "'Comparing the noise made by the *Thresher* against the *Skipkacks* [older nuclear boats],' said one submariner, 'is like comparing a new Cadillac to an old Model-A Ford.'"[23] Today, the bells toll daily from the *Thresher* Memorial Chapel at the shipyard for the men who died. A bronze plaque by the door of the chapel reads, "In memory of our departed shipmates who still sail a mighty ship USS *Thresher* SSN593 3 August 1961–10 April 1963."[24]

At the time of the *Thresher* tragedy the major portion of submarine contracts were for nuclear attack class. However, in 1961 the *Abraham Lincoln* became the first Polaris missile submarine built at Portsmouth. Five more submarines were built after the *Lincoln* before the last contract for new

Bow-first launching of USS *Sand Lance*. Last submarine built at PNSY, 1969, closing a nearly 200-year tradition of shipbuilding (Peabody and Essex Museum #23,095)

construction was issued for the *Sand Lance*, an attack-class submarine. Future contracts for the yard were held back when Secretary of Defense Robert S. McNamara, in 1964, announced that the navy would close its government operations at the Portsmouth yard in 1974. The *Sand Lance* would be the last submarine the yard would ever build. On 25 September 1971 the *Sand Lance*, the SSN–660, was commissioned, ending another great era of shipbuilding on the Piscataqua River.

With the *Sand Lance* closing out the construction phase of the yard's operations, workers could stop for a moment and reflect on their career and feel proud of their accomplishments and the records set by Portsmouth-built submarine ships:

> First government-built submarine, 1914
> Only U.S. submarine to serve in World War I
> First submarine to circumnavigate the world
> First submarine to sail around Cape Horn, South America
> First submarine to sink a Japanese vessel in World War II
> First submarine to sink a Japanese aircraft carrier
> Longest submerged run for a diesel electric submarine
> First all-welded hull
> First torpedo bubble eliminator
> First submarine air conditioning
> First modern whale-shape hull design, post World War II
> Fastest submarine in the world
> First government-built nuclear submarine
> First nuclear submarine to sail into western Pacific. . . .

The end of the construction era brought new challenges for yard workers and a flurry of contracts to repair and overhaul already commissioned submarines. In 1964, Robert McNamara stated that he would need "first hand evidence,"[25] in order to consider keeping the yard open. The proof was found years after McNamara had left government service.

Facing sure layoffs, the workers never lost their pride in their work. Soon the Portsmouth yard became known as the most efficient repair and overhaul yard in the country. The workers' determination to survive, their longstanding love affair with pride and excellence, coupled with a performance record second to none, gave New Hampshire

Representative Louis Wyman and Senator Norris Cotton, along with Maine senators Margaret Chase Smith and Edmond Muskie, the "first hand evidence" needed to convince the only man in America who could overrule the closure order, President Richard M. Nixon,

> On March 24, 1971, the yard received its reprieve and extension of life. In Washington, D.C., [the legislators] received identical hand-delivered letters from couriers from President Nixon. The letter on White House stationery initialed by Nixon stated: "I have delayed answering your questions on the future of the Portsmouth Naval Shipyard until the review I requested was completed. Now, on the basis of that review and the recommendations made to me, I am pleased to inform you that the McNamara order closing the yard in 1974 will be rescinded."[26]

Today the yard faces new challenges and a most uncertain future as America stands on the threshold of a new world order bereft of a comparable power against which its armed forces will be measured. The workers stand today against the odds, maintaining their leadership position in the field of repair, overhaul, and refueling. They continue to provide shipyards throughout the United States with skilled personnel found nowhere else. Their proud motto reads, "Sails to Atoms". Their record speaks for itself. In 190 years, 176 naval ships have been built, from the 74-gun ship of the line *Washington* to the nuclear submarine *Sand Lance*. Of these ships, 134 were submarines. "Portsmouth-built" will always be synonymous with leadership, pride, and quality.

16
THE CONFERENCE YEARS AND A NATURAL HISTORY SAVED

Between the war years, life at the Isles of Shoals was filled with summer conferences, fishermen, lobstermen, and the Coast Guardsmen on Appledore and lighthouse servicemen on White Island. A life apart from the mainland still existed. The Star Island Religious and Educational Conference Center continued to operate despite occasional setbacks such as the one in 1902, when Oceanic Hotel employees—twelve waitresses and two men—had drowned during an innocent afternoon excursion when their small sailboat had suddenly capsized in a squall near Appledore's southwest point.

During World War I the Shoals were placed off limits to most civilians for security reasons. Conferences for those two summers were held at the Wentworth-by-the-Sea. They resumed on Star after the war and would not be disturbed again until World War II.

In the 1920s Star Island Corporation embarked on an ambitious project to rebuild a likeness of old Gosport village. The stone dwellings were clustered below the southside of the chapel creating a beautiful and quaint setting. While this project was underway on Star Island, the corporation began a systematic buy-out of as much of Appledore's property as possible. In 1924 they purchased seven and a half acres, followed by the acquisition of better than 95 percent of the island property. Later, they added Duck Island to their holdings.

Each succeeding summer brought more guests to Star Island, more youths, elders, and families alike. The times also brought the arrival of Frederick McGill and Virginia Frederick in 1922. They were involved with Unitarian young people's conferences, met there, fell in love, married, and raised a family.

Guests and friends sat with Fred and listened to his warm stories of life on Star spanning six decades. Even folk who were returning after a fifty year absence could ease into a nostalgic conversation with Fred as if they had only been gone since yesterday.

Looking north from Smith monument, Star Island, looking much as it does today (Star Island Corporation Private Collection. Photo by Bill Finney 1977)

Fred's wake-up calls were legendary. For many years he went about the hotel hallways and bellowed in perfect tune, "GooOOood Morning. . . ," which echoed to the uppermost floors. Having gained the guests' attention, Fred followed with a weather report, breakfast menu highlights, and whatever bulletins that were pertinent to the new day's schedule. Fred still returns to Star each summer and strolls the island with a crisp walk, and with an eye to the future, while remembering all of his days on the island in the sea.

A unique characteristic of these conferences has remained. Despite their affiliation with the Unitarian-Universalists and United Church of Christ, they are still non-denominational by practice. Their leaders to this day will not refuse a person registration because of religious convictions or the lack thereof. Today the Star Island Corporation, the hotel operators, enjoy near capacity seasons.

It has not always been that way, though. During post-World War II years, the corporation's funds were desperately low, and conference attendance was far below expectations. Further complicating the situation was the hotel's physical health. Collectively, all systems needed repairs, replacement, or upgrading. From the basement to the attic, from the utility shed to the boat dock, it all needed immediate attention.

Prior to World War II a general, unspoken feeling existed among the hotel management that an uncertain future coupled with the lack of growth in the conference programs made long-term maintenance investment a neglected item. During the war army and navy camps were established at the Shoals with the islands off limits to most civilians. With no essential upkeep during those years, the hotel had fallen into a near derelict state when the facility was returned to the owners in 1946.

Following the war one individual, who realized that action not words would rescue the hotel and its longstanding tradition, took the lead to revive the spirit of the islands. Lyman Rutledge, a man of the cloth, rekindled the hope of the "Old Shoalers," while inspiring a new generation.

Rutledge went to work alongside contractors such as Dick Soule, Harry Sullivan, and Bobby Wharem, when fundraising monies were made available. Together they orchestrated the revival. With no large or sophisticated equipment, they took on the impossible task of fixing the 1873 stone pier, damaged by storm waves. The team moved rocks of several tons back into place with block and tackle and small tractor. Rutledge oversaw every aspect of the restoration as he guided workers through impossible head-knocking difficulties. Not once did he allow questions to shake their conviction. In time all doubt vanished.

Through the critical 1940s and 1950s momentum was turning the tide of doubt into a clear vision and commitment toward the future. The hotel would survive for at least one more generation. Through his unselfish commitment to the spirit of the Isles of Shoals Rutledge managed not only to help save the hotel, but also to compile an incomparable series of books on the history of the islands, each one written with the same love and dedication shown earlier by Brock, Tucke, and Celia Thaxter.

Even in old age, away from the daily chores of the past, Rutledge could be found on the island sitting with children by a crackling fire under a canopy of stars with an ink-black sea surrounding them, as he hitched their dreams to a long-ago tale of pirates, or sea captains, and sailors. A light breeze would brush gently over their cheeks, or was it the

Lyman Rutledge hitching dreams to long-ago heros (Star Island Corporation Private Collection)

breath of a distant hero? Rutledge knew. He willed the dreams on, and the children happily followed.

In 1962 Harry Lent was hired as hotel manager to carry on with the project set forth by Lyman Rutledge and concerned members of Star Island Corporation. A teacher from Newton, Massachusetts, Lent used his exceptional leadership and organizational skills to take the hotel operation to new levels of efficiency. With these qualities and the guidance from a dedicated Star Island Board of Directors, Lent brought the facilities up to modern standards as best he could. This was accomplished without the loss of the unique nineteenth-century feel and ambiance which the island had always possessed.

Today, though Lent is retired from the conference center operation, signs of his accomplishments are plain to see. The upbeat spirit and pride in the hotel continues with a new generation of board members and new management dedicated to preserving the island life. They are preparing the conference center for the twenty-first century when there might be fewer places left for someone to go and, if only for a moment, leave the troubles of their daily life behind; a place where they may go to reflect, rebuild, and fulfill their spiritual needs with neighbors from around the world. It is a spirit Virginia McGill so aptly sensed when she wrote, "There is a light you bring and a light you take away."

After World War I, while activity at the Isles of Shoals was dominated by Star Island conferences, a separate and independent life continued among the other islands. Fishermen continued to fish, a few vacationers came to the handful of private cottages, and yachtsmen found more than ever that Gosport harbor was a fine nook along the coast to anchor up for a day or maybe two. The winter population was for the most part limited to Coast Guardsmen on Appledore, lighthouse servicemen on White Island, and a caretaker on Star. Few fishermen, if any, would bother with the harsh weather at the Shoals when a comfortable home waited for them on the mainland.

For several generations Cedar Island lobstermen would move out to their island in the spring, fish all summer, and leave in the fall, a habit still carried on by their descendants. Reverend Frank Crandall of Salem, Massachusetts, acquired the deed to Lunging Island in December 1927 from Albert and Emily Staples. The reverend made a fine summer home out of the nineteenth-century cottage on Lunging. Miss Rosamond Thaxter, Celia's granddaughter, along with her family made sure that Smuttynose would remain accessible to sea scouts and campers.

During prohibition, rum-runners plied the waters of the Shoals at night as they returned from Nova Scotia with a boat load of illegal liquor. Smuggling became such a problem that the Coast Guard had to spend much of their time patrolling the Isles of Shoals from their new station built on Appledore in 1920. If they were lucky on those dark nights they might have caught the rum-runner whose boat glided ever so quietly through Gosport harbor, or pulled into a little cove before moving on to the coast.

The human history of the Isles of Shoals is matched in diversity and importance by the islands' extraordinary natural history, pristine environment, and endless abundance of marine life. A marine zoological laboratory and summer camp was established on Appledore in 1928 by University of New Hampshire professor C. Floyd Jackson. He secured a ten-year lease for three buildings from Star Island Corporation and purchased a fourth to house staff, students, and the science operation. Due to the impending war, another long-term lease was not renewed. In 1938, however, Dr. Jackson was allowed to continue operations for three more seasons until the government declared the Shoals off limits.

The idea of someday returning to the Isles of Shoals for marine research and field studies did not die with the war. The University of New Hampshire had shown an interest, but due to funding problems and the inherent access difficulties in getting to Appledore, the idea was abandoned.

World War II brought the army and navy to the Shoals. Soldiers established camps on Appledore and Star, as they maintained a vigilant watch over the entrance to Portsmouth harbor against German U-boats. Navy specialists in the field of sonar detection established a network of surveillance cables strung through the Isles of Shoals waters. Any monitoring of an unidentifiable submarine within the search area set into motion a series of quick response actions. An immediate telegraph alert was sent to harbor defense command center at Fort Stark, Jaffery Point,

U.S. submarine entering Portsmouth harbor during World War II. Note floatation in front of sub suspending anti-German submarine net. Kittery Point, Me, in background (Portsmouth Naval Shipyard Museum)

New Castle. Word was then relayed to Camp Langdon, deeper in the harbor on Great Island, where a team of men activated a giant winch on a ledge outcropping near the beach. A net was then drawn across the entire width of the shipping channel between Wood Island on the east-side and Camp Langdon on the west side. Anti-submarine caissons were built like stepping stones between Wood and Garrish Islands to complete the barricade.

During non-alert periods, which was most of the time, the cable net between Camp Langdon and Wood Island was drawn back from the camp part way, leaving half the shipping channel open to traffic. However, any friendly ship entering the port was required to have a navy pilot on board to insure safe passage through the radio-activated mines.

On dark, quiet nights local residents who walked down to the beaches as part of a foot patrol guarding against German landing teams could actually hear the rumbling exhausts of the U-boats which were recharging batteries within a mile or two of shore. Evidence remains today revealing just how close the Germans had been to this coast. A U-boat reportedly sits at the bottom of the ocean and serves as a sailor's tomb one mile off Hampton Beach, New Hampshire; two others were sunk a few miles east of Duck Island, Isles of Shoals.

Toward the war's end army engineers and construction workers erected an observation tower on the high ground of Appledore, seventy feet above sea level where the square building rose another 132.5 feet. They fastened, on its flat roof, a 51-ft steel-framed tower supporting an 11-ft high wooden-stayed tank that housed a radar antenna. In total, the structure rose 264.5 feet above sea level. From the top floor observers could see a full 360 degree view of the horizon while monitoring all surface vessel movement from Cape Ann to Cape Porpoise, including Portsmouth harbor entrance, as well as twenty miles to seaward. Following the war, the tank and its support structure were dismantled, leaving to this day the concrete tower, standing along with many other such towers on the immediate coast as reminders of the war. The tank went to Star Island to house a noisy generator set at the caretaker's cottage.

The 1950s brought an end to the Coast Guard's line-of-sight network along the coast of New England. Every square inch of coastal waters had been within sight of at least one lifeboat station. They sat like Monopoly game pieces up and down the coast.

Radar developed during the war, along with high-speed diesel-powered search and rescue vessels, instantly made traditional lifeboat stations and their surf boats obsolete after the war. The order of the day from Coast Guard headquarters in Washington, D.C. was to consolidate operations. One by one, each lifeboat station was abandoned, including Appledore and Wood Island in Portsmouth harbor, where over thirty men were stationed at one time during World War II.

In their place the Coast Guard installed a major facility at Fort Point, New Castle, and supplied the station with several small rescue vessels, powered surf boats and two large oceangoing ships. Helicopters were also pressed into service. The modern Coast Guard with fewer stations could provide not only better service along the immediate coast, but also reach far out to sea where before the war a distressed ship had only a remote chance of being rescued.

After the war Appledore's north and westends were abandoned. With no one to care for or protect the cluster of old cottages vandals soon appeared on the island. They partied and destroyed priceless features of the cottages, such as dark-grained hand-carved fireplace mantles. In one thoughtless moment they had also torched the Coast Guard boathouse in Babb's Cove. They all but removed the signs that a cultured people had once lived there. Many roads and walkways were soon lost, no longer traceable, as ground cover crept over the island, rising up into an

Historic Fort Constitution, site of fortification since 1632, where Coast Guard established a major station in the 1950s (photo by Geo. A. Sylvester)

impenetrable alder jungle. Some cottages decayed so badly from years of neglect that they fell under their own weight; others waited patiently for the revival and salvation that was to come.

Ninety-five percent of Appledore lay dormant during the 1950s and 1960s. However, on Star Island a man was exciting a renewed interest for another natural science center at the Shoals. In 1964, Dr. John M. Kingsbury, a Cornell University professor, accepted an invitation to attend that summer's Life On A Star Conference as guest lecturer. He "was persuaded . . . to bring his wife and little girl to a family conference. Dr. John M. Kingsbury would conduct a week long program in marine biology . . . his field was plant science, and his specialty marine algae."[1]

That summer of 1964 a seed was planted and from it grew a dream. A dream which once fulfilled would not only be self-enriching, but provide a unique educational experience for young marine biologists, researchers, and teachers from all over the world.

By June of 1966 Dr. Kingsbury had persuaded Star Island Board of Directors to grant access to their hotel. All that was needed to start his classes were a small southeast room in the hotel known as Lawrence Hall, and the first two weeks of June, before the Oceanic Hotel season began. Kingsbury organized a team of specialists who also served as advisors, confidants, and instructors. Together they played their part in this developing dream, which led eventually to a move to Appledore in 1973, where Shoals Marine Laboratory (SML) could realize its fullest potential. "The members who pioneered this project were . . . John M. Anderson, invertebrate zoologist; Oliver Hewitt, ornithology and marine wildlife; Perry W. Gilbert, ichthyology and marine mammals; Jon P. Barlow, oceanography and marine ecology; and Edward Raney, ichthyology."[2]

The University of New Hampshire's Marine Studies Program coordinators participated in Kingsbury's project to the extent that state funds would allow. Today, SML studies have expanded to reach from the entire Gulf of Maine to Mount Washington in the White Mountains of New Hampshire.

A man possessed by a dream is a man not to be denied. Kingsbury was not only a brilliant educator, but showed he had equal talent as a promoter, ceaselessly publicizing SML. Across the country he went raising pledges and funds needed to build new facilities as well as repairing old cottages on Appledore. Grantsmanship and bartering became his tools. The intensity, the singularity of mind and purpose by which Kingsbury accomplished his goals would inspire a legion of supporters.[3]

There were days when Kingsbury returned to the Shoals from one of his many head-knocking campaigns, the weight of his responsibilities and its reality showing clearly on his brow. He would share the many stories of wins and losses, frustrations and breakthroughs, but always end with, "We're getting there. It's tough. But, we'll make it."

> The physical facilities today include nine buildings and six boats. The Palmer-Kinne Laboratory (at the base of the tower), opened in 1975, has bench space for sixty people. Students are housed in three new dormitories, while renovated structures accommodate the academic and operating staffs, the library, infirmary, and office.[4]

The cottage left by the Coast Guard in the 1950s has become SML's staff quarters.

With little difficulty, it can be readily imagined just how Kingsbury's project and the local environs would have been affected if Aristotle Onassis had accomplished his dream of building an oil refinery in

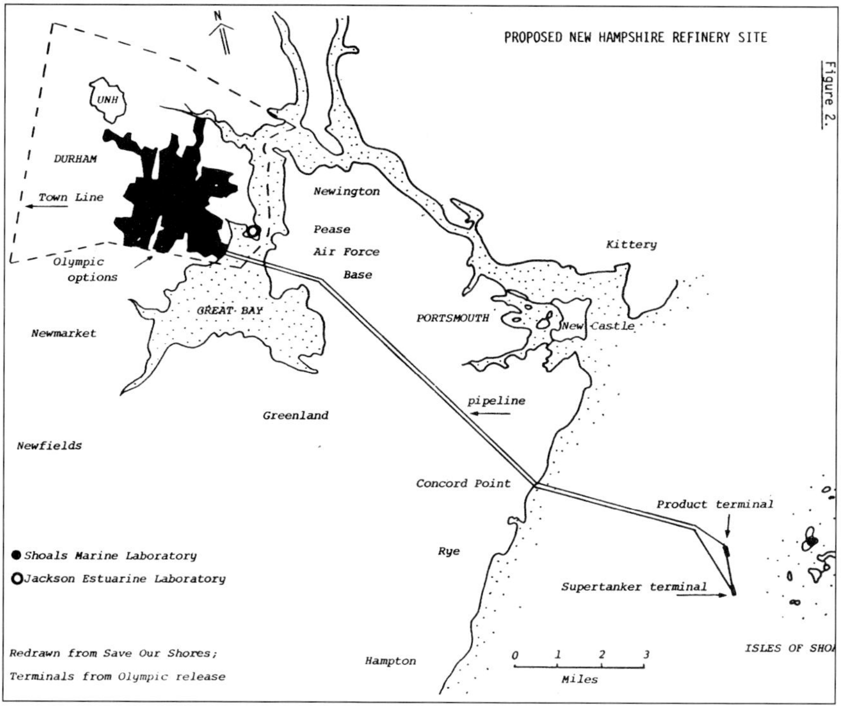

Proposed New Hampshire refinery site by Olympic Oil Co. owned by A. Onassis (Dr. John M. Kingsbury, Private Collection)

Durham, New Hampshire, in 1974. It was a relatively simple project for someone who at the time was considered the world's wealthiest man. It was simple for his people, controlling Olympic Refineries, to attempt to exploit the vulnerable and quiet village. With $2 million of "public relations" money, they tried to blend the project into the townfolks' everyday life. They used the power of speculation when promising Governor Meldrim Thompson great wealth and prosperity for his state. The governor, wanting such economic strength for his state, bought into the idea. Backed by the *Manchester Union Leader*, Thompson was able to mount a formidable campaign across the state, to bring to "Durham the largest [oil] refinery ever started from scratch anywhere in the world."[5]

Through use of soft-sell deception, Olympic-led men went quietly about Durham selling the idea to landowners that a man of substantial means wished to buy options on land for a future wildlife preserve, just weeks before the $600 million project was made public. Purchase options on 3,500 acres, representing 20 percent of Durham land, were secured in the area of Little Bay, at a projected price of $6 million.

Options were placed on 700 acres, or 8 percent of Portsmouth's land. Rye was another town marked for the project, across which nine pipelines and a number of truck terminals would be placed. Two forty-eight inch pipelines would bring Saudi Arabian crude oil in from off-shore monobuoys located just inside the lee of the Isles of Shoals. The other smaller lines would move a variety of liquids to the refinery, including several thousand gallons of water each minute of plant operation.

The owners of Lunging Island were unfairly put between a rock and a hard place when the town of Rye had just raised their taxes 1,000 percent. At the time they were facing possible loss of their precious island to eminent domain. Olympic Refinery representatives soon offered a handsome price for the island with a guarantee that the owners would have continuous access to the island for as long as they wished, an option not available to them if the town had taken the island. They signed the papers of intent while deep inside they prayed for the project's failure.

The refinery's "output would have been approximately equivalent to the output of all the refineries in New Jersey (400,000-barrels per day), and it could have met 25 per cent of total New England demand for petroleum products."[6] One thousand-foot supertankers would have replaced the Isles of Shoals as the most prominent feature on the horizon.

Several key factors played a role in the project's eventual demise. Private individuals dug in, in opposition, immediately upon hearing Governor Thompson's official endorsement of Onassis's plans. Landowners claimed they were duped into the option on their land and vowed not to honor the agreements. Prominent citizens spoke up against it. Dr. Kingsbury led the fight to educate the state and Durham voters to the irreversible damages that an oil spill would cause to the region's rich marine life and ecosystem. The Maine side of the Isles of Shoals was simultaneously declared a National Historic site in 1974, adding mountains of red tape to the permitting process. Legislators passed NH House Bill 18, requiring local town approval of site plans for oil refineries.

Home rule faced its greatest test when, on 6 March 1974, a vote was conducted in the town of Durham where 90 percent of those voting were in favor of defeating the proposal. The next day the true test of House Bill 18's strength came as legislators had to choose between home rule and state rule. The wishes of Durham were upheld. The next day, Olympic Refinery representatives retreated to New York and the discussion of an oil refinery in the area has not been raised since.

A television biography of Onassis's life claimed this defeat—the first major one of his career—had contributed to the rapid decline in his health. Within a few months of the historic town vote in Durham, Onassis was dead.

Kingsbury would finally remove himself from the hands-on control of SML by the end of 1977. The directorship was passed on to Dr. John B. Heiser, a former student of Kingsbury's at Star Island in 1967. Heiser, a man of great stature and persuasion, went on to establish his own effective methods of operation for SML while seeing to it, as Kingsbury had, that SML survived and prospered in an uncertain academic world.

In the years following his retirement as SML director, Dr. John Kingsbury has remained active in fundraising campaigns and lobbying for goals set forth by the laboratory, but today his vibrant face is seldom seen down on the docks in Portsmouth. Once or twice a year he might show up, usually for one special event or another. It can be said, though, with a certain amount of surety that if one day SML found itself faced with another life-threatening problem, Kingsbury would be there to help lead the way. His commitment to his dream is for life.

17 GENERATIONS

When I completed the previous chapter the book was, for all practical purposes, finished. But then, I thought, there was one part of this history which may have been left out. My own forty years in the region might help those readers who were part of these times to relive an important moment in recent history. Over time my own memories had been trapped on a dark ocean floor. A snare tripped loose those times of my past which were long forgotten. Some rose to the light, some would not. What may appear as selective memory, in most cases, is no more than the stubborn darkness and a will not to dwell too long.

My father, Arnold Whittaker, was born in Winchester, Massachusetts, on 25 August 1917, the son of an English immigrant from the suburbs of London. In his early life, he dreamed of little else than the outdoors, and playing hockey, and taking care of his selection of farm animals. On his first day at school he firmly told his teacher, "I don't need to go to school . . . I'm going to work on a farm and raise animals." Throughout his school years, he kept a stubborn hold on that promise. Picking up skills in math and science helped Dad prepare for the day when he would leave college and buy that farm.

After high school he spent just one year at the University of Massachusetts. During those years, his family spent summer vacations at the seacoast of New Hampshire and were friends with Carl Gage, who owned an estate on Odiorne Point in Rye. Dad approached Gage one day and asked if he could use an area of the estate to raise chickens for breeding. With permission, Dad was soon hard at work on the ancient lands of David Thomson. His farming would span twenty years.

Through World War II, Whittaker Farms of Stratham, New Hampshire, sent thousands of hatching eggs and day-old chicks to countries around the world. In the 1950s Dad's energy was focused on genetic breeding. Soon he was producing worldwide prize winning "broilers."

Five-year-old Robert shadows his father, Arnold Whittaker, around their poultry farm in Greenland. Mr Whittaker got his start raising chickens after school in the 1940s (author's private collection)

Summer vacations found him pursuing his next love in life, sailing. For the month of July we would stow our belongings on his thirty-foot cutter, the *Robynlee*, named for his three oldest children, Robert, Lynn, and Lee (brother Larry had not been born yet) and spend the time cruising downeast. Dad soon developed a reputation among other coastal sailors as a fine dead-reckoning navigator.

In 1958 Dad's entire inventory of breeder chickens contracted a highly contagious blood disease. Within two weeks the call came in from his other two farms. All chicks tested positive. There was nothing to do but destroy the birds. It was over.

Overnight, Dad fell from a place of prosperity to poverty. In the spring of 1959 we moved to Little John Island, Yarmouth, Maine, where we stayed in a summer cottage Mom had owned with her brother Bill. The house was never intended for cold-weather use. Daylight came streaming in through cracks between the clapboards. In the fall, I remember most the cold, and how Mom and Dad worked so hard each morning to get us up and ready for school, stealing us from the warmth of our beds.

Dad never wallowed in self-pity. We never heard our parents complain.

They saw our family's new life as an adventure, not to be feared but accepted. Dad got his captain's license and started piloting a charter fishing boat from Cousins Island. I served as his deckhand. In the fall he worked night shift at Shaw's original Preble Street store market in Portland to provide the necessaries for his family. For three years Dad struggled to provide for us. We children never knew we were poor. It never showed in our parents' faces.

In early winter of 1961, Dad received a telephone call. After he put the telephone down his face was shadowed with disbelief. We could see the old fire and gleam slowly rise in his eyes. "I've been offered the contract for the ferry service to Star Island at the Isles of Shoals. If I'm interested."

"IF you're interested!" we all cried. There was one sobering condition, Dad would have to find his own boat, one that carried 100 people.

I flashed back to those days on the Piscataqua River and the Portsmouth Yacht Club, where Dad had kept the *Robynlee*, and remembered how I used to watch the *Kiboko* cruise by with its passengers for the Shoals. I always wondered who those people were and what was going on there at Star Island. We all spent the next hour huddled around Dad as he explained the telephone call. Harry Lent, the newly appointed Star Island hotel manager, had been instructed by Star Island Corporation Board of Directors to find a new operator for the ferry service. Harry had called Dad and told him that it was a time for change at Star Island. The board felt a new operator would better fill their needs and general philosophy.

Harry was unfamiliar with the Portsmouth waterfront and its people. His inquiries led him to John Sybolt, then owner of the Portsmouth tugboats. Sybolt recommended, without second thoughts, Arnold Whittaker as a man who had achieved a reputation throughout the region for his exceptional boat handling, sailing and navigational skills.

It was the slowest winter on record in the Whittaker household. Never in my life have I so wished for winter to end. Late in the season Dad bought a boat in Montauk, Long Island, with the help of relatives. In April Dad and I went to Montauk to bring the boat back home. I was fourteen the first time I went aboard the *Viking*. She was twenty-five years old, but to me she was the neatest boat in the world.

In April nightfall still came early as we headed into Massachusetts Bay. Off on the far western horizon, the lights of Boston sparkled against the red sunset. Ahead toward the east we saw the lights of the south shore of Cape Ann, and the flash of Thatcher's Light. After rounding Cape Ann, Dad set his course for the Isles of Shoals some twenty miles away.

We moved slowly out from Thatcher's into the night. Clouds quietly drew the darkness in over head. I searched, but soon lost hope of finding the horizon. I would come to know the uneasiness I felt at the time as melancholy. It has happened to me many times while out at sea as night descends over the ocean. For a moment, and only a moment during twilight, this feeling remains until I snap to, flick it away, and move on with my worldly duties.

Late that night, we pulled into Gosport harbor and made up to the stone pier on Star Island. It felt good to be secure in the harbor. The task of the day's trip had tired us; sleep came as a welcome relief.

At first light we heard a man yelling down from the pier. As we emerged from the cabin, he introduced himself as Bobby Wharem, the island caretaker.

"I remember them saying something about a new boat was going to be running this summer," Wharem said, as he invited us up to the bunkhouse where his wife Joanie was cooking breakfast. He was not a big man but stood straight-backed with an odd forward lean to his walk, a mannerism, I would learn years later, which has been noted in Shoalers since recorded time. Every bit of the small island's terrain slopes either up or down.

On the walk down to his house Bobby shared with us things about the island and the *Kiboko*, the ferryboat we were replacing, and her owner Dick Johns. "It's a beautiful boat, like a yacht. Dick keeps it up in perfect condition." I felt myself getting defensive. The *Viking* was a lot of things, a yacht was not one of them. Her finish, though clean and neat, was rough, but she was ours and I was proud of her. I kept quiet as they talked.

The Wharem's home was little more than a shack. It had been built by the Coast Guard and sold to Star Island Corporation in 1946, the year Wharem became caretaker. As we stepped inside, I was impressed by the warmth that flared on my cheeks from the potbellied coal stove in the far corner, despite the obvious lack of insulation in the walls. This was their home year round, but they were alone on the island for the six cold-weather months of the year. Electricity was provided from a small generator in a shed behind the bunkhouse. Bobby had moved

Crew aboard *Viking*, second vessel to serve Isles of Shoals by that name, 1962. Left to right: Joanie Wharem, Harry Lent, author, Bobby Wharem. Captain Arnold Whittaker is in the pilot house (courtesy of Bobby Wharem)

there when only seventeen years old, spending his entire adult life on Star.

At thirty-four years old, Wharem had recently married a woman who thought she could love her husband no matter where they lived. Joanie soon found life on the island far too remote. They would leave the island the next year. Four years later in the late 1960s and still in my teens, I spent the month of March alone in the Wharem's bunkhouse. On very cold nights I would bank up the coal stove and move my bunk in closer. I would lie on my side facing the stove and felt warm as toast; when the coals died my backside became cold as death.

Over the years, I came to realize that Bobby had become somewhat of a living legend. When, in the early 1960s, a Coast Guardsman drowned on his way from White Island to Star to see his wife and child who were arriving from Portsmouth on the noon ferry, it was Wharem who told the search parties that the body could be found in the area of Appledore Island below Sullivan's cottage, in the old quarry. Hours later the body was just where he had said.

Among his feats was the rescue of a young man who had slipped into the surf on the far side of the island. The man,

> being plump enough to enjoy natural buoyancy, he kept afloat for at least a half-hour while our courageous engineer [caretaker], Bob Wharem, went into the water himself, crawling over barnacles-encrusted rocks and swimming to the rescue while bearing a life-preserver for the young man to grab. The two finally came ashore after a struggle with the currents and with the sharp and slippery rocks. They were both severely scratched, but safe. For this feat, Bob would later receive a Carnegie Medal.[1]

After finishing a wonderful breakfast, we said our thanks and good-bys to Joanie, as Bobby offered to walk back to the *Viking* and help with the dock lines. As we turned out of Gosport harbor, through Malaga Gut, Dad set course for downeast. We both agreed that we were looking forward to working with the Wharems. The rest of that spring found Dad laboring over the *Viking* every spare moment. So much had to be done before summer.

With thirty years now serving to protect me from that first season, I find it all but impossible to sharpen my story with day-to-day detail. Time has brushed my memory into soft-hued images blended one among the other with no real definition. When I step back, the picture I get is warm, and the chill of bad memories fades.

I do remember how impossibly cramped our docking area appeared. John Sybolt had offered Dad a small part of the Portsmouth Navigation Co. pier behind the harbor tugs. Dad practiced docking the single-engined *Viking* into that pigeon hole of a spot, between Newick's lobster pound, that old shack standing painfully atop craggy pilings in the little crease along the waterfront which today is Jane Blalock's Ferry Landing Restaurant, and the tugs.

The waterfront along Ceres Street was in pitiful shape. The town was a sleepy backwater navy port, with its beer joints and wild women, living day to day on the whim of government spending at the shipyard. Just back from our location, standing up from the docks, was a tall row of old brick warehouses casting shadows over the street virtually all afternoon, adding to the dismal feel the area possessed. Up around the corner on Bow Street was George's Cafe. There waterfront locals called on George, the barkeeper, to curse the world while fortifying themselves. Across the street from the corner, the Simpson Brothers' little store supplied us with the rain gear, watch caps, and flannel shirts we needed. Around the other corner from George's, on to Market Street, sunlight bathed the row of warehouses and a few store fronts. I remember Mario's Meat Market, the Christian Science Reading Room, and Jackson's Marine Hardware store, where I would go every spring to buy boat supplies.

At Jackson's, Clarence would help fill the order, as he led me through rows of heavily stocked shelves. Marine gear hung from the ceiling like clumps of bananas. I still wonder how he could find what he was searching for. The smell is what I remember most, the fresh intoxicating smell of hemp mixed with the aroma of ancient wood and red lead paint.

Upriver from the tugs, Tom Shepard and his Dad had their family home, where they lived upstairs, while on the ground floor Mrs. Shepard had a place to sell seafood. For 50 cents we bought lobster rolls that bulged with mountains of fresh meat. Beside the store, Tom carried on a lobster boat building trade with his dad while spending the early morning hours hauling lobster traps in the river, as his son Timmy learned the trade or played with his dog and friends along the wharf.

Still further upriver, back from the waterfront, on Market Street, an old cluster of run-down homes represented the last of the Italian immigrant section of town. In front of them, on the waterfront, where coal ships once berthed, Dave Mahoney was starting a new salt import trade. Today, ships 700 feet long bring over 20,000 tons of salt each for use on highways during winter.

In summer there are more nice sunny mornings than not, somewhere. On the seacoast good weather does not happen with any regularity. One August we were blessed with twenty-one straight days of fog! There were mornings when a simple walk to the front porch would reveal nothing but a dense, damp curtain of gray wetness thick enough to seep through my clothing. It was impossible to see the *Viking* down at the dock only 200 yards away. Some days, not even the near end of the long pier was visible. Fog was a fact of life. For the first six years of operation the *Viking* had no radar. Dad's navigational aids were the same as those used by mariners for hundreds of years: a time piece, a compass, and a depth sounder, with crew serving as his eyes and ears on bow watch.

In the morning on the waterfront I cleaned the dock area, that was among other things a filthy, dingy street. Drifters, "winos," once good people cut loose from society's mainstream, eventually washed up along Ceres Street, their home during the summer. They were found in the

Young voyagers waiting for the *Viking* at Ceres Street dock, Portsmouth, 1963 (Star Island Corporation Private Collection)

cool shade of abandoned garages at the other end of the street. Hot nights some slept on discarded mattresses under lilac bushes alongside what is now Carter's Antique store.

As morning warmed into midday, these residents began making their way toward our dock. Somehow they were aware of the time and knew it must be close to when tourists would begin to arrive for the boat ride. This meant money for bottles of muscatel or canned Sterno. With money of my own I would coax them back down to the far end of the street when they became too overbearing with our customers.

They all vanished, in time, along with the rest of the old backwater character, as the city slowly found itself caught up in the revival of its old abandoned marketplace. The rough edge of character was slowly being polished smooth by a new commercial style. Waterfronts from the Olde Port Exchange of Portland, Maine to Norfolk, Virginia, once abandoned, were being revitalized into new, different, sanitized centers of commerce.

At 10:30 A.M., Dad began selling tickets from his small portable one-drawer table for the 11:00 A.M. departure. That table stayed with him for fifteen years until weaned from it for a ticket booth. By five minutes to eleven, we would have everyone on board for their day trip to Star Island.

At Star Island the kitchen staff offered these people a wonderful family-style lunch served in the hotel dining room, where a section was set apart from the regular conference guests, usually by the porch windows. We had no direct means of letting the chef, Lenny Reed, know how many lunch guests to expect. There was no reliable telephone, C.B., or shortwave radio service. The island was isolated from the outside world, almost.

With five minutes left before departure an island messenger brought from the pilot house a small gray box holding two carrier pigeons. Little capsules with strips of paper inside were attached to one leg of each bird. The messenger wrote on the paper the number of daytrippers who had signed up for lunch and any special dietary requests. Then we tossed the pigeons gently into the air, where their wings quickly unfolded. They spiraled high over head, above the rooftops of Portsmouth, and disappeared beyond the buildings.

Our trip on the *Viking* took one hour and ten minutes, while the pigeons took only half an hour. They were circling the hotel flagpole two or three times before we had cleared Portsmouth harbor. Then they flew into an open fourth-floor window located at the hotel's westend where chef Lenny was waiting. The thirty-minute lead time was all that Lenny and his assistant Patrick Russell would need to prepare tables and meals for their noon guests.

Patrick was a tall man with rolled shoulders and a shock of white hair that stood high atop his forehead. His huge toothless jaw protruded and flapped like a puppet when he talked. Old Patrick had his thick Irish brogue. I soon gave up trying to understand most everything Patrick uttered.

On days off a friend or two would join me on expeditions to other islands such as Smuttynose or Appledore; or we would go over and see the Foyes on Cedar, or venture way to the northeast to Duck Island, when the naval air reserve was not dropping bombs on it.

Norm Foye and his wife Mary also left the mainland each summer to live on Cedar Island for a season of lobster fishing. They brought with

Star Island chef Lenny Reed on right and assistant Patrick Russell on left with crew (Star Island Corporation Private Collection)

them their children, George, Eddie, and Bobby. George was the oldest, Eddie was my age, and Bobby my brother Larry's age. It took little time for us to become good friends in work and play.

Normy, a big barrel-chested man with thick strong hands, had a voice unlike anyone's I had ever heard. It seemed electrified in its character and volume. In his day, Norm Foye was respected throughout the Shoals not only as a family man but as a lobsterman as well. When time allowed he was often found on Star or Appledore giving a lecture to island guests and students.

Normy sat watch over his world each afternoon from his front porch chair. Mary was always near by. Their place in life was more secure and solid than anyone else's I had known at the Shoals. Normy's enormous laugh could be heard clear across Gosport harbor even in a gale. He was a friend to all good people who visited the isles, to all who came without pretense or want for what was his.

All Foyes who helped with the lobster business were up and hauling traps by daybreak. By mid-afternoon, their work completed, time could then be spent preparing their gear for the next day. Or, for the kids, free time meant going over to Star and playing football or softball or just to get an ice cream at the hotel snack bar.

Today son George and his wife Diane with their children carry on the family tradition on Cedar; brother Eddie died accidentally soon after high school, way too young, way before he ever had a chance to meet his unlimited potential; Bobby made a new life for himself and his family on the mainland. The last time I saw Normy was during his final summer at Cedar. I had learned from Dad, Normy had been sick.

My wife, Robin and I were at Star visiting one afternoon. We had some extra time so I took her for a row around the harbor and over to Cedar; I told Robin that this was one of my great pleasures in life especially on weekends when boats from all over the east coast packed the harbor. We rowed in among them and eventually made our way to the island. I could see George down on their dock. I shouted a "Hell-O" from a distance. After all those years, respect dictated a proper approach. I asked if his dad and mom were on the island. George took a few seconds before he recognized me, then waved us in. No one approaches or steps foot on Cedar Island unless they are acknowledged by one of the Foyes.

Normy and Mary were where they always were that time of day, in their favorite chairs on the screened porch. They offered us a drink of Normy's special stuff and we sat with them for a good hour or so as we took turns talking and listening and watching the gulls float on the light warm air brushing across the islands. I was struck by how strong and healthy he looked as we reflected on how life had been in the world years ago and how a change had come to the Shoals, a change Normy was not too sure about. "No Bob, it's not the same anymore," he said. "I just as soon have lived when I did."

He did make a brief comment on his health. He felt great and was sorry that through the many years of fishing under the hot summer sun he had not known to bother with protecting his arms and hands.

We left them that day with both making sure we'd come back again. I had no feeling it would be my last good-by to Normy. I'm only thankful Robin had her chance to meet him. Early that winter Normy closed his eyes while sitting in his chair at home in Kittery and went to sleep for the last time.

The late trip out from Portsmouth on the *Viking* was always the best time of day, especially if things had gone smoothly. Dad and I talked about the day or about a project for the boat, or how in the world he was going to be able to afford 13 cents a gallon for diesel fuel. Many times I would just lay on the cabin top and let the sound of the diesel coax me into a nap.

At Star we secured the *Viking* for the night and went up to dinner. The evening was usually spent with friends in Pel-Hall, listening to music, playing cards or ping-pong, or walking to East Rock on a cloudless night. We sat there, looked out over the ocean, and the light sound of surf far below echoed faint a distant storm. Stars marched up from the sea to take their places in the night, and I would remember long ago a camp in Damariscotta and a crackling bonfire on a clear night and someone asking, "Where do stars come from?"

Friendships were made fast then lost at summer's end. Back in school, I found myself filled with so many stories ready to be told to my landlocked friends, but each story vanished as I tried to share it. I had gone on a journey, they had stayed behind. They would not hear of it, my wasting time telling them how great it had been. Many years would pass before I could share my stories with anyone.

In the 1960s many of Portsmouth's historic buildings were spared the wrecker's ball during the reign of urban renewal that swept the country. Dorothy Vaughn snapped the city out of its sleep. She became the first of many to publicly warn the people of Portsmouth to stop the wholesale destruction of the town's old neighborhoods, or risk losing the symbols of their past. Strawbery Banke Museum and the waterfront of Portsmouth are the gift's of Vaughn's conscience.

Generations: note grandfather is the only one who still focuses on the thrill of kite flying (soccer ball middle-left is suspended in mid-air) (photo by author)

Part of this renewal plan had included connecting downtown with an eventual interstate highway system that would pass just to the north of town. The row of old warehouses on Ceres and Market Streets, standing tired and for the most part empty, leaning shoulder to shoulder against one another, was a pitiful sight. The plans of the highway engineers included tearing down these warehouses to make room for the extension that would end near the new federal building on Daniel Street. We can only imagine what flavor and feel the old port area would have today if the work had been completed. Today, the extension sits on the shoulder of the old waterfront, waiting.

Shortly after the plan was abandoned, Dick Morton, in retirement from the hotel business, quietly bought most of the unwanted buildings along the waterfront. He spent much of his time puttering around his buildings. Morton and his handful of men devised ways efficiently to gut the buildings, then construct attractive efficiency apartments on the upper floors and store fronts on the street level.

One of the first new business tenants was the Blue Strawbery Restaurant on Ceres Street. Vanguard chef, Jim Haller and his partners, driven by their own dreams, could not have picked a more unlikely spot for their restaurant. The waterfront of Portsmouth? It was dark. It was dingy. It was dirty. But it still had a certain character. Their restaurant had character, also, and today it remains one of New England's premier establishments. The Blue Strawbery inspired a flood of wonderful restaurant openings throughout Portsmouth, causing critics from Boston and New York to draw a comparison with San Francisco.

Soon Theater-by-the-Sea became a neighbor of the Blue Strawbery. Actors and directors of exceptional talent came to Portsmouth while waiting for their call to Broadway. They thrived, not on the money they were making in their little waterfront theater, but on being there, on being a part of something that was important to them and the small dedicated group of theatergoers of Portsmouth. Their theater was cozy with low bare-timbered ceilings and brick interior. Seats crawled and pressed up against a wall while the stage stood tight against the other. The floor above had been cut away to accommodate the lighting and crew. John Kimball was the leader through those lean years, and he barely knew from season to season if the funds would be there to keep the theater going.

I saw John in Samuel Beckett's *Waiting For Godot*; it was simply a performance and production the likes of which comes once in a lifetime, when everything clicked in that magical moment, not because it was the best acting anyone would ever see, but because it was the best of what the world had to offer at a time in our town, a time when the rest of the world didn't much care.

When these players finally looked up from their work, they saw the world had indeed taken notice, and a deliberate consciousness overwhelmed them and they slowly woke one by one from their dream. A moment in time one thought would last forever slipped through their fingers like a fist full of sand and there was nothing to be done. From that time forward the magic of that little theater was lost by the hand of its own success.

As the waterfront was revived with much of the same spirit as inspired merchants of an earlier time, we'll always remember the men and women who led the revival of the 1960s. Men and women such as Dorothy Vaughn, Rosamond Thaxter, Jim Haller, Dick Morton, John Kimball, who without feasibility studies behind them did what had to be done.

The old waterfront has taken on a new commercial flavor much

Miss Rosamond Thaxter, granddaughter of poet Celia Thaxter, sitting at Celia's desk (Star Island Corporation Private Collection)

different from its origins centuries ago. Now the Blue Strawbery is joined by many other fine restaurants as well as unique shops. On a warm summer night Ceres Street is filled with people leisurely strolling up and down its narrow way. Theater-by-the-Sea moved to a new and larger theater pit in an old brewery warehouse downriver from the St. John's Episcopal Church where, sadly, it would fail. But today the performing arts are well represented by Prescott Park Arts Festival, Ceres Street Jazz Festival, and several new theaters including Portsmouth Academy of Performing Arts (P.A.P.A.) Theater where TBS was located on Bow Street, Pontine Movement Theatre, and New England Repertory Theatre Company.

Today, the people of the Piscataqua River basin are faced with new economic challenges which threaten the quality of life they have enjoyed for years. The Strategic Air Command's Pease Air Force Base has closed, high-tech industry once buoyed by defense spending has fallen into decline, and the Portsmouth Naval Shipyard, whether or not it closes its doors to 6,300 workers, has an uncertain future serving as the region's economic foundation.

Industrial shipping on the Piscataqua today helps maintain its standing as the eighth most active port on the east coast, with an average of 300,000 tons of general cargo imports monthly. However, as was true in the nineteenth century, exports continue to represent a small percentage of port activity, yet as the Boston transportation hub reaches out to satellite cities for relief from its overcrowded infrastructure, the port may play a greater role in overseas shipping in the future.

The port's longstanding tradition as a commercial fishing center is also threatened. Since the times of David Thomson in the 1620s the cod grounds off the coast have been fished by each succeeding generation. Today, though several hundred thousand pounds of fish are being landed at the New Hampshire State Fish Pier on Pierce Island every year, the stock of ground fish is dangerously low. Lack of early conservation measures is forcing the federal government to step in and do what it feels is best for the historic fishing grounds and their survival.

Many generations have passed since the people of this region relied solely on themselves to determine their future. There is a need now, as much as anytime in the past, for people of vision and dreams and courage to once again guide and lead the region back to a prominent position in the New England community.

The spirit of self-reliance and determination, and the strength for self-discipline that was present in so many of our ancestors, live today in those people from the region who strive to succeed and help make this a better world. Examples have been given use in the lives of 1928 Olympian Ernest Bayer, an oarsman, and his wife, Ernestine Bayer, who helped establish the Philadelphia Girls Rowing Club 1938 and now live in Stratham. Their daughter, Tina, carried on in the tradition and was a world-class rower herself. And recently we can find this spirit to excel in the international long-distance running star, Lynn Jennings of Newmarket and Olympic-medalist Jenny Thompson of Dover.

My own family business's growth of the 1980s caused my father to reevaluate his own life and realize the time was coming when he should retire. Dad was approaching twenty-five years in the company and at sixty-nine the new way of doing business was slowly leaving him behind. We saw in his eyes that his focus had changed. He was looking ahead again, back to his beloved coast of Maine.

Dad retired from our day-to-day operation after the 1986 season. That fall he and Mom moved into their family cottage overlooking Casco Bay on Little John Island. They were finally in the home of their dreams. Not once did he ever look back and long for what had been. Every new change in his life had made him excited for the future, happy to begin a new day. He did work for us as a relief captain now and then.

That next summer he once again sailed downeast, this time in his forty-foot cutter *Aladdin*. More times than not, he would enjoy a sail alone. He never needed company, but it did make the sail a bit nicer to have someone there with him.

In April of 1990 I had planned to join Dad on a trip from Portsmouth to his mooring off Little John Island. At the last minute my plans changed. Dad showed up anyway, early that morning. He looked at the weather and said, why not. As I watched him head down the Piscataqua River, little did I know I would never see him at the helm of his boat ever again.

Throughout that summer, Robin and I were counting the days until our first child would be born. By the time Eliza came on 16 September, Dad seemed fully recovered from two accidents he had had just weeks earlier, one while sailing and the other when he rolled his car down a steep embankment. Following the delivery, Mom and Dad came to the hospital and spent time with their latest grandchild, number eight.

Captain Arnold Whittaker at the helm of his cutter *Aladdin*, in retirement (photo by Jean Whittaker)

Two and a half weeks later on 3 October, while sitting in his favorite chair in their cozy home on Little John Island, after a good day's work out in the yard, Dad suddenly told Mom, "I feel like I'm going to die," as he closed his eyes and passed away.

He left this world with no regrets, nor deep burning dreams undone. He left a legacy of two lifetimes to the people and places he touched, making both better. He was blessed with a vision and soul to make it reality. From that first day of school, when he had told his mother that he didn't need to go to school, to his last days of life on the coast of Maine, he enriched life around him with the warmth of his dreams. May those dreams light the way of his children for generations to come.

REFLECTIONS

Rich is the heritage left to us and our children who live among the Isles and the river Piscataqua, left by dreamers who lived where the lie of the land held their imagination, with its cluster of islands standing sentinel over a river's mouth which led far inland through a lace work of waterways, into a rich and fertile land. The mere nature of the land and handiness of all things needed fueled and inspired these folk to pursue their dreams.

This land had as much to do with creating our history as did the men and women who lived there. The people were artists of a new land. They were the artists and the land their canvas.

From the dreams of Captain Smith and David Thomson flowed the first settlements of New Hampshire; from the dreams of Brock and Tucke came a spirit of self-reliance that runs through the very fiber of America today; from the dreams of shipwrights such as Hatch, Badger, Raynes, and those of the Portsmouth Navy Shipyard came the most magnificent ships ever to sail the world; from the dreams of Portsmouth mobs came the thirst for freedom, and from John Paul Jones came the birth of a nation and its navy; from the dreams of Thomas Laighton came an era of summer resorts and the art of repose; from his daughter, Celia, came a sense of longing which beckoned visionaries to her realm; from the dreams of Thomas Elliott came an oasis for spiritual fulfillment. The dreams continue today: those of Dorothy Vaughn to save the symbols of our heritage; those of Jim Haller and John Kimball for a new and ever brighter cultural life in Portsmouth; and the dreams of John Kingsbury who continues to enlighten new generations to the road of salvation for our natural world.

For better or for worse historians have passed lightly over this land. It does not fit neatly into a packaged portrayal of our country's history. Few have taken time to look for, or draw the line that led from this region into the heartland of America, to every corner of our country. The men and women of this land never intended to make a statement to the world, they did not come to make history, at least they were not conscious of doing so. They did not come to make a political, religious, or social statement. Their aim was simple in nature. They wished to provide for those they loved and those people around them a better way of life. Without extraneous thought, they were compelled by their dreams to leave the world a better place than they had found. Some were less fortunate than others in fulfilling their dreams and goals which at times proved ill-begotten. Some had for just a brief moment something that was good and would prove to be good for many generations to come, but times changed and it slipped from their grasp. Still they rose to the highest calling to which one can aspire and we are thankful. They came, worked, and died for a better life.

We never know how high we are
Till we are called to rise
And then, if we are true to plan
Our statures touch the skies.[2]

From the land, the bird rose into the westerly breeze and rode the wind back to its partner, watching over their new spring hatch on the knobs of rocks that long ago became islands in the sea. Together they fretted over their chicks, fed them, and tucked new bedding into the nest. The bird looked up over to the distant land and saw where the mountain rose from the low plain and the river opened to the sea. He looked across the islands and saw sailboats drift along on the breeze. He saw the lighthouse, no one was there. All seemed just right as he looked down at their nest. In time the wind freshened as it backed to the south. Feeling safe, the bird lifted up on the wind and soared effortlessly over the islands, and his spirit was filled with freedom until the sun slipped from the sky and he returned to his partner on the last light of day. The bird settled in for the night, listening to the darkness, for "The sea has many voices,"[3] and he was, forever, watchful of the dangers.

Day's end (photo by Geo. A. Sylvester)

APPENDIX I

A chronology of boats and service to Appledore and Star Island from 1848 to 1993:

1848	Schooner *Springbird*: sails from Newburyport.
1849	*Springbird*: moved to Portsmouth.
1859	*Springbird*: wrecked beyond salvage.
1859	Schooner *Sibyl*: sistership to the famed schooner *America*.
1862	Schooner *Lone Star*: used for twenty years primarily for freight.
1866	SS *Pioneer*: first steam-powered vessel on Appledore.
1869	SS *Appledore*: capacity of 150 passengers, with speed of 10kn.
1873	SS *Major*: renamed *Oceanic*; served again in 1886.
1878ca	SS *Pinnefore*: 45-foot utility vessel and good in seas.
1883	SS *Viking*: 300 passenger capacity.
1898	Naphtha launch *Sam Adams*: island boat, replaced *Pinnefore*.
1901	SS *Merryconeag*: served two seasons.
1903	SS *Rockland*: owned by the Boston & Bangor Steamship Co.
1904	SS *Mineola*: served two seasons.
1906	SS *Munnatawket*: built in 1890.
1907	SS *Mary Archer*: built in Rockland, Maine.
1908	SS *Forest City*.
1909	SS *Munnatawket*: served again until 1911.
1910	SS *Sightseer*: owned by Piscataqua River Towing Co.
1912	SS *Juliette*: served through 1915, three daily trips.
1916	SS *Sightseer*: returned to service this season.
1917–18	SS *Sightseer*: served as a tow boat in World War I.
1919	SS *Sightseer*: resumes service until 1941. Last steamboat to serve the Isles of Shoals' ferry service.
1930ca	SS *Twilight*: Oscar Laighton's personal launch.
1941	SS *Sightseer*: goes into government service during World War II.
1941–5	Ferry service to the Isles of Shoals suspended.

1946	M/V *Kiboko*: first postwar ferry to serve the Shoals, first diesel-powered ferry on island run.
1962	M/V *Viking*: Viking of Yarmouth, Inc. formed as new company in charge of ferry service. Capacity of 100 passengers, 10kn speed.
1968	Captain Whittaker installed radar in *Viking*. First time in history of island ferry service that radar was used.
1969	M/V *Viking Star*: replaced *Viking*. Capacity 100 passengers, 10kn speed.
1969	M/V *Viking*: used to develop first modern-day regular Isles of Shoals boat tours without stopping at Star Island.
1969	*Viking* dock moved to New Hampshire Port Authority.
1974	M/V *Viking Queen*: 109 foot. Capacity of 385 passengers, 10kn speed.
1979	M/V *Viking Queen*: takes passengers to Great Bay and up the Piscataqua, for inland river cruises during fall foliage season, establishing the first regular trips beyond Dover Point since World War II.
1978–9	*Viking Queen*: winters in Key West, Florida.
1980	M/V *Viking Sun*: capacity of 540 passengers, 11kn speed.
1982–3	*Viking Sun*: winters in St. Thomas, USVI.
1986	M/V *Oceanic*: first fiberglass boat on island run. Largest passenger vessel on Cocheco River since World War II. Capacity of 148 passengers, 15kn speed.
1986	Bob and Robin Whittaker form Isles of Shoals Steamship Company. Captain Arnold Whittaker retires at end of season from full-time operation of ferry service.
1987	M/V *Thomas Laighton*: capacity of 350 passengers, 10kn speed.
1990	*Oceanic*: renews lighthouse cruise of 1800s from Portsmouth, giving close views of five lighthouses: Fort Point Light, Whaleback Light, Nubble Light, Boone Island Light, and White Island Light.

During the 1980s two new boat operations were started and provided non-stop tours of the Isles of Shoals and Portsmouth harbor area: New Hampshire Seacoast Cruises out of Rye harbor, and Portsmouth Harbor Cruises on Ceres Street dock in Portsmouth.

APPENDIX II

Guests' entries in Captain Bob Whittaker's ship's log on M/V *Thomas Laighton:*

In 1987 during a summer cruise a woman came to the pilothouse after I had finished with my narration. Her eyes were full with tears. She quickly relieved my concerns when she said they were tears of overwhelming joy. She went on to explain that two years earlier she had set out from Minneapolis, Minnesota, in search of her family roots. Her journey had taken her through countless volumes of town records, and renewed aquaintances with lost relatives. Piece by piece, she assembled the puzzle, until her personal odyssey brought her to Portsmouth and the Isles of Shoals, where the final piece was put into place. She saw Appledore Island where her ancestors became a part of Appledore village and our American heritage in the 1660s.

At the time, I too, had recently learned that I was descended from Richard Warren and William Brewster of the *Mayflower*, and shared personally in her excitement.

The following list is a sampling of the many entries representing people who wrote of their family heritage in my log book. I have noted, when possible, the town and state in which they lived at the time. I take no responsibility for the accuracy of the entries:

1988 to 1993

___Direct descendants of Captain Samuel Haley 1600s–1700s. Portsmouth, NH, Park Ridge NJ

___Descendants of Thomas Laighton's son Cedric: Cedric's grandson, Hanover, NH; Cedric's great grandson, Washington, DC; Cedric's great great grandson's, ages 7 & 10.

___"Fred McGill – not a native of the Shoals but one who has lived there for parts of 59 years out of 66 since first visit in 1922. I will come back!" winters Fla.

___A Grandmother of Portsmouth, NH was born on Star Island in 1858. Her dad rowed 9 miles from Star Island to Rye to get a Doctor Parsons. Her father brought him back for the delivery. . . . A 7th generation descendant of Major Andrew McClary for whom Ft. McClary is named. [I believe this to be the same Dr. Parsons who performed the autopsies on Karen and Anethe Christensen, sisters-in-law who were brutally murdered on Smuttynose Island in March of 1873—RHW.]

___10th descendant of Phillip Babb who was appointed by the Governor of Mass. as constable of the Isles of Shoals in 1652. He collected taxes and kept the peace. Also he owned a trading post & tavern on Appledore Island. He supplied ships with provisions for their trip to Europe. Massachussets

___. . . – 88 yrs old. grandson of Celia Thaxter

___Muchmore – early name on the Isles before 1700, descendants left before 1800 and went west and south, the present Oklahoma Muchmore contingent:
Ponca City, Okla, Oklahoma City (now in Vermont)

___Andrew Haraden – 5th grandfather. Beheader of the pirate John Philips on the Isles of Shoales. re: stole new schooner *Squirrel* (1630–1636). Gloucester, Ma.

___Great grand daughter of Thomas Leehee who settled on Lungin' Island and raised a family of nine. Molly Lee "Leehee" Clifford a grandmother inspired by Celia Thaxter to become a writer- books -plays & poems. Owner of the famous axe [head] weilded by Louis Wagoner in commiting the murders. [On Smuttynose Island in 1873]. Dover, NH.

___Miles Standish was a 6th great grand father. Rockland, Me.

___When a youngster, coming to Rockland [Maine] on the Boston boat, the Isles of Shoals light house signalled bed time. Rockland, Me.

___Richard Yeaton great g——grand father, lived on the Isles of Shoals in 1683. He was a selectman and lived and died on the Islands. [I believe this lady is a direct descendant of Hopley Yeaton of New Castle, N.H., who became the first commissioned officer in what is known today as the U.S. Coast Guard in 1791—RHW]. El Toro, Ca.

___Maternal grandmother's ancestors landed in Isles of Shoales in 1624. Wilcomb and Robie families then settled in Chester, NH.

___Great great—-grandson of Captain Danforth who commanded a ship in revolutionary war. Related to Danforth of anchors & compass. North Berwick, Me.

___Ephrain and Martha Dormans(sp?) were the last official residents of Gosport, great grandparents. Portsmouth, NH.
___Visited home of ancestors, on the island. They were here early-mid 1600s. Muchmores were fishermen and seafarers on the island. Left the islands for mainland during Revolution. Eliot, Me., Omaha. Neb., San Antonio, Tx, etc.
___Great grand child and great-great grand children of Samuel Rand, stone mason who built the stone chapel on Star Island in 1800. Glastonbury, Conn.
___Descendant of H. Yeaton Comdr of U. S. Coast Guard. Hopley Yeaton is now buried at the Coast Guard Academy, Groton, Conn. Portsmouth, NH.
___Descendant of the John Paul Jones family, from John Paul's brother. Other ancestors from Col. Holman who arrived from England in 1639. Eliot, Me.
___Portsmouth Naval Ship Yard architect for over thirty years. Participated in designing several of the diesel submarines built at the shipyard, *TANG, SALMON, SAILFISH, ALBACORE*-. Participated in triple launching of WW II subs in late 1943. Rye, NH.
___1926–28 on Star Island while father lectured at a summer conference. Oscar Laighton rowed person over to Appledore in his dinghy. Long Beach, Ca.
___Family came from the Isles and were among those evacuated during the revolution. The house in which this person's father was born, now located in York, ME, was one of many floated to the mainland during the revolution. Danville, Indiana.
___So far as this person knew Rev. John Tucke was the only religious ancestor. The rest were pirates. New Castle, NH.
___Twelvth generation descendant of Alexander Shapleigh. The immigrant, shipbuilder & exporter from Kingsweare, England, who traveled from his estate, "Kittery Quay", in Kingsweare to settle Kittery/Kittery Point Maine. The Shapleigh Family Association was organized and incorporated in 1909 as a non-profit geneological association for the descendants of Alexander & is still active today. Wells, Me.
___Descended from Leonard Weeks, Greenland (NH), John and William Clark of Clark Island & the Leightons [*sic*]. Denver, Co.
___Leonard Pomeroy one of the merchants who came to the coast of

New Hampshire with David Thompson. Exeter, NH.

___Wormwood supposedly a pirate seaman who settled Isles of Shoals with two brothers in 1622. Old Forge, Adirondacks.

___Descendant of Thora Ingebretsen subject of the poem *THORA* by Celia Thaxter. The Ingebretsens were cod-fishermen; the Laightons gave them a cottage on Appledore. There is frequent reference to them in Celia's letters, also in Cedric Laighton letters. On the day after the murder at Smuttynose Maren Hontvet yelled to the Ingebretsens and they were the first people at the scene of the crime. They knew & testified against Louis Wagner. Jorgen Edward Ingebretsen probably suffered a mental breakdown as a consequence of the murders [see *Sandpiper* by Rozi Thaxter]. Seven Springs, Stowe, Vt.

___"Prudence C. Randall of Lunging Island, brought up at the Shoals since 1926 when dad, the Reverend Frank B. Crandall obtained island from Frank Ferguson, Malcolm's father. It has been a colorful existence growing up at the Isles of Shoals. Blackbeard's Treasure is still on Lunging." Prudie Randall, Danvers, Ma.

___"Nate Hubbard, ex-pelican 1970–72, great-great grandson of Celia Thaxter, with wife Stephanie out to Star Island for the reunion. We're trying to find a way to move from Hollywood and its 10 million cars back east to my 'roots maybe we'll do something with Aunt Roz's Champernowne Farm in KP [Celia's home in Kittery Point]." Nate Hubbard, Hollywood.

___"On holiday from Gosport, England, had great pleasure to meet captain crew and dog [Whitt]! And to take us to Gosport Harbor in the Shoals islands. Thanks again for a pleasurable trip." Gosport, England.

___They met at Portsmouth Navy Shipyard, he was on submarine, married June of 1946. A descendant of Commodore E. Preble of USS *Constitution*, husband helped commission the USS *Sea Devil* 5/24/44. Served on 3 patrols. Littleton, Co.

___In the 1940's & 50's bombed the rocks off the Isles of Shoals [Duck Island]. Flew out of N. A. S. Squantum & N. A. S. So. Weymouth, in corsairs & hellcats. Hampton Falls, NH.

___"Lived year round on Star Island 1946–1962. The best years of my life. Engineer and caretaker. Met Arnold and Bob Whittaker in [spring] 1962. Gave them breakfast." Bob Wharem, New Hampshire.

___On the *Brooklyn* when the call came in that the *Squalus* was down. Anchored above the sub, soon after the diving bell went down and took off the men.

___"Born in Portsmouth, Hampshire, England . . . visiting [a local family] to see Portsmouth, New Hampshire. [Seeing the] sea - loving people on this trip to the Shoal Islands is the highlight of our fortnights holiday. Thank you for a wonderful trip. Maybe we shall be back again one day.' Portsmouth, England.

___In 1942, was assigned to Portsmouth Harbor Surf Station [Wood Island], now abandoned. Had about 30–35 men on duty - rescue and surveillance of small craft, perceived basic seamanship knowledge, then assigned to Greenland patrol.

On Whaleback Light Station in '42, there were two men assigned, civilians, in the old lighthouse service. They rowed on to Frisbee's store at Pepperell Cove for supplies. No power boats! Incredibly, they didn't speak a word to each other! Knew their duties so didn't need to talk! This person was assigned TD (temperary duty on Whaleback) for a week & the keeper didn't say a word, just pointed & grunted! A lost part of history - the light house service. Tulsa, Okla.

___Grandson of John Hontvet & Marin Hontvet from Smuttynose, Isles of Shoals. Worcester, Ma.

___Great grandson of John & Marin Hontvet. Glenolden, Pa. Great-great grand daughter of John & Marin Hontvet. Marin was soul servivor of Smuttynose murders.

___Grandfather was born on Star Island, and went to school in what is now the chapel. Boylston, Ma.

___Three Seeley brothers came to these Isles in 1622. This person's mother was a direct descendant. General Cilley of the Revolutionary War changed name to present spelling. Brookfield, Wisc.

___Descendant of Miss Underhill's family. She was the Star Island school teacher washed away on Star Island in 1848. Ambler, Pa.

___"I'm visiting America from Gosport Hants England. In comparing, the two towns are quite similar [Ports. England and Ports. NH] except the distance from Gosport to Portsmouth back home is a lot smaller. Also back home there are a lot more naval ships stationed. Both towns are very friendly and people are always helpful. Gosport, Hants England.

___A tenth great grand father, Edward Smale, signed the first of three petitions for incorporation of Appledore in 1653. Another ancester, Benjamin Remick, designed the sloop-of-war *Ranger*, of which John Paul Jones was captain. Litchfield, Me.

___A descendant from Anthony Brackett who first settled at Strawbery banke in 1630. Greenland, NH.
___John Bickford — settled in Dover Point, NH in 1623. Essex Junction, VT.
___A descendant of Pocahontas. N. Weare, NH.
___A direct descendant of Rev. Robert Jordon who served as minister on the Isles of Shoals in 1640.

NOTES

Chapter 1 Life Returns

1. Ola E. Winslow, *Portsmouth: The Life of a Town* (New York: Macmillan, 1966), p.2.
2. Title of book by John P. Adams, *Drowned Valley* (Durham, N.H.: University Press of New England, 1976), p.14.
3. Early fishermen referred to these islands as *Sholes* for either the abundance of schooling or *Sholing* fish; or, as I believe, they were referring to the nine ledges that surround the isles that rise like pinnacles from the ocean bottom. At certain tide levels and sea conditions water breaks over these ledges, and from a distance the foam frothing over them appears to be schools, or *sholes* of fish. First recorded reference using the Isles of Shoals name was by Levitt in 1623.

Chapter 2 The People from the Sea

1. Archeologists have found native American sites throughout the Canadian Maritimes and northern New England dating back 6,000 to 8,000 years. In those sites they found fish bones of offshore species, such as swordfish.
2. Lyman V. Rutledge, *Ten Miles Out* (Boston, Mass.: Isle of Shoals Unitarian Assoc., 1964), p.71.
3. Ola E. Winslow, *Portsmouth: The Life of a Town* (New York: Macmillan, 1966), pp.7–8.
4. ibid., p.9.
5. ibid., p.10.
6. ibid., p.16.
7. Ralph E. Thompson and R. Mathew, *The First Yankee* (Salem, Oreg.: privately printed, 1979), p.22.
8. Also on board were two native Americans, Maneddo and his servant Sassacomoit.
9. As cited in Thompson and Mathew, op.cit., pp.20–1.
10. ibid.
11. ibid., p.27.
12. They were sighting the Camden Hills of Maine; today the island is still called Georges and lies at the eastern end of Muscongus Bay.

13. As cited in Thompson and Mathew, op.cit., pp.29, 32.
14. ibid., pp.31–2.
15. ibid., p.35.
16. ibid., p.46.
17. ibid.
18. ibid.
19. Rutledge, op.cit., pp.2, 12.
20. Winslow, op.cit., p.21.
21. Rutledge, op.cit., p.13.
22. John S. Jenness, *The Isles of Shoals* (Cambridge, Mass.: Riverside Press, 1875), p.69.
23. ibid., p.27.
24. Thompson and Mathew, op.cit., p.68.
25. ibid.
26. Jenness, op.cit., p.86.
27. ibid., p. 36.

Chapter 3 David Thomson and His Dream

1. Ralph E. Thompson and R. Mathew, *The First Yankee* (Salem, Oreg.: privately printed, 1979), p.57.
2. ibid., p.73.
3. This was made without a land treaty with the natives.
4. John S. Jenness, *The Isles of Shoals* (Cambridge, Mass.: Riverside Press, 1875), p.54.
5. ibid.
6. "The more scientifically inclined believed that variation might hold the secret of determining longitude; that it might change in some regular and ultimately predictable manner with latitude. Nothing might seem more reasonable than this, too. And what a tidy scientific solution it was! Such ideas persisted until about 1620, and, meanwhile, the course indicated by the compass remained subject to doubt." Douglas Phillips-Burt, *A History of Seamanship* (Garden City, N.Y.: Doubleday, 1971), p.191.
7. Thompson and Mathew, op.cit., p.89.
8. ibid., p.98.
9. ibid., p.95.
10. ibid., pp.99–100.
11. ibid., p.102.
12. ibid., p.116; and Winslow, *Portsmouth: The Life of a Town* (New York: Macmillan, 1966), p.26.

13. Thompson and Mathew, op.cit., p.117.
14. ibid., p.123.
15. ibid.
16. ibid., p.128.
17. ibid., p.129.
18. ibid., p.109.
19. ibid., p.126.

Chapter 4 New England Lost and Gained

1. The highest recorded wind in the world was measured at 231mph on Mt. Washington, N.H., 12 April 1934.
2. Lyman V. Rutledge, *The Isles of Shoals in Lore and Legend* (Boston, Mass.: Star Island Corporation, 1965), p.21.
3. John S. Jenness, *The Isles of Shoals* (Cambridge, Mass.: Riverside Press, 1875), p.97.
4. ibid., pp.135–6.
5. ibid., p.134.
6. ibid., pp.135–6.
7. Rutledge, op.cit., p.19.
8. See Appendix II for entries made in captain's log by descendants of these early settlers.
9. Rutledge, op.cit., p.18.
10. Maurice Ashley, *The Battle of Naseby, and the Fall of King Charles I* (Stroud, England: Alan Sutton, 1992), p.148.
11. Rutledge, op.cit., p.29.
12. Jean A. Sargent and Ina B. Mansur, *Babb Families of New England* (Laurel, Md.: privately printed, 1987), p.378.

Chapter 5 Stability and Self-Reliance

1. A Reverend Moody, in 1822 did his best to instill temperance among the people of the Isles of Shoals, but gave up after only a few weeks. In the time he served the Shoals community, forty-seven men "in less than three months [consumed] more than six hundred gallons of rum . . . or about five gills per day." John S. Jenness, *The Isles of Shoals* (Cambridge, Mass.: Riverside Press, 1875), p.159.
2. *Portsmouth 350*, p.27.
3. Raymond A. Brighton, *They Came to Fish* (Dover, N.H. Randall/Winebaum Enterprises, 1979), vol. 1, p 159.
4. *Dedication of A Memorial*, p.20.

5. ibid., p.22.
6. ibid.
7. ibid., p. 23.
8. ibid., p. 25.
9. ibid., p.7.
10. Lyman V. Rutledge, *The Isles of Shoals in Lore and Legend* (Boston, Mass.: Star Island Corporation, 1965), p.46.

Chapter 6 Pirates and Ghosts

1. Robert C. Ritchie, *Captain Kidd and the War Against the Pirates* (Cambridge, Mass.: Harvard University Press, 1986), p.155.
2. Lyman V. Rutledge, *The Isles of Shoals in Lore and Legend* (Boston, Mass.: Star Island Corporation, 1965), p.30.
3. ibid., p.31.
4. Samuel Adams Drake, *Nooks and Corners of the New England Coast* (New York: Harper, 1875), pp.178–9.
5. Ritchie, op.cit., p.178.
6. ibid., p.182.
7. ibid.
8. Drake, op.cit., p.179.
9. Rutledge, op.cit., pp.34–6.
10. Sam Haley, Jr., in 1820 uncovered four bars of silver while gathering flat stones for a wall. He realized $4,000 from the sale of the bars and was able to afford the construction of the still visible breakwater between Malaga and Smuttynose.
11. Rutledge, op. cit., pp.32–3.
12. Drake, op.cit., p.177.
13. Rutledge, op.cit., p.32.

Chapter 7 Seeds of Revolt

1. James Street, *The Revolutionary War* (New York: Dial Press, 1954), p.35.
2. *Portsmouth 350*, p.50.
3. The other two men were Israel Putnam and William Prescot; see Ola E. Winslow, *Portsmouth: The Life of a Town* (New York: Macmillan, 1966), p.88.
4. *N.H. Provincial Papers*, vol. 7, p.709.
5. *Portsmouth 350*, p. 46.
6. Raymond A. Brighton, *They Came to Fish* (Portsmouth: Randall/ Winebaum Enterprises, 1979)

Chapter 8 John Paul Jones Comes to Portsmouth

1. James Otis, *The Life of John Paul Jones* (New York: A.L. Burt, 1900), p.25.
2. The Portsmouth Naval Shipyard Museum curator Jim Dolph has found evidence that indicates the *Ranger* might have been built in Portsmouth at Ringe Wharf rather than at Badger's Island in Kittery.
3. Robert Rogers parted company with the rebels, led a unit of Tory militia during the Revoultion and eventually moved back to England.
4. Otis, op.cit., p.2.
5. ibid., p.5.
6. ibid., p.27.
7. ibid., p.64.
8. Raymond A. Brighton, *They Came to Fish* (Dover, N.H.: Randall/Winebaum Enterprises, 1979), vol. I, p.70.
9. ibid.
10. Will Durant and Ariel Durant, *The Age of Napoleon* (New York: Simon & Schuster, 1975), p.10.
11. Otis, op.cit., p.83.
12. ibid., p.164.
13. ibid., p.266.
14. ibid., p.130.

Chapter 9 A New Nation

1. Elwin L. Page, *George Washington in New Hampshire* (Portsmouth, N.H.: Peter E. Randall, 1932), p.55.
2. ibid., p.72.
3. ibid., p.73.

Chapter 10 Public and Private Shipyards

1. Barbara W. Tuchman, *The First Salute* (New York: Alfred A. Knopf, 1988), p.118.
2. U.S. Navy, *Cradle of American Shipbuilding*, p.14.
3. ibid.
4. The Cold War created an inflation in funding during relatively peaceful times.
5. U.S. Navy, op.cit., p. 33.
6. Raymond A. Brighton, *Port of Portsmouth Ships and the Cotton Trade* (Portsmouth, N.H.: Peter E. Randall, 1986), p.7.

7. ibid., p.14.
8. ibid., p.20.
9. ibid., p.11.
10. See Appendix II.
11. Brighton, op.cit., p.145.
12. Raymond A. Brighton, *Tallships of the Piscataqua, 1830–1877* (Portsmouth, N.H.: Peter E. Randall, 1989), p.348, quote from the *Portsmouth Chronicle.*
13. ibid.

Chapter 11 Thomas Laighton and the Grand Resort Era

1. Lyman V. Rutledge, *The Isles of Shoals in Lore and Legend* (Boston, Mass.: Star Island Corporation, 1965), pp.67–8.
2. Rosamond Thaxter, *Sandpiper* (Portsmouth, N.H.: Peter E. Randall, 1963), p.7.
3. Oscar Laighton, *Ninety Years at the Isles of Shoals* (Boston, Mass.: Star Island Corporation, 1971), p.15.
4. Thaxter, op.cit., p.9.
5. Rutledge, op.cit., pp.63–4.
6. Laighton, op.cit., pp.44–5.
7. ibid., p.30.
8. Thaxter, op.cit., p.50.
9. ibid., p.61.
10. Rutledge, op.cit., pp.87–8.
11. Laighton, op.cit., p.30.
12. Thaxter, op.cit., p.39.
13. Rutledge, op.cit., p.81.
14. ibid., p.95.
15. ibid., p.1.
16. ibid., p.100.
17. ibid.
18. ibid.
19. ibid., p.101.
20. ibid., p.100.
21. ibid., p.101.

Chapter 12 The Age of Elegance

1. See Appendix I for ferryboat chronology.
2. On 14 March 1876 the last town meeting of Gosport was held on Star Island. The islands on the New Hampshire side of the Shoals from that day forward became incorporated into the town of Rye, New Hampshire.
3. The alleged murders by Louis Wagner still leave many questions to be answered 120 years after their occurrence. It is suspected by many that the true story has yet to be told.
4. A number of years earlier, Oscar had purchased the schooner, a sister ship of *America* taking *Springbird*'s place. The bigger *Sybil* had proven to be faster, and far more comfortable than any other vessel in the area competing for the right to ferry the Shoals people. Steam ferries, in service on the river since the 1830s, provided excursions to the Shoals but, for an unexplained reason, the Laightons did not have one in regular service until the 1860s. Most likely it was a simple question of economics and demand.
5. Lyman V. Rutledge, *The Isles of Shoals in Lore and Legend* (Boston, Mass.: Star Island Corporation, 1965), p.117.
6. ibid., p.100.
7. ibid.
8. ibid., p.117.
9. Rosamond Thaxter, *Sandpiper* (Portsmouth, N.H.: Peter E. Randall, 1963), pp.236–7.
10. ibid., pp.240–1.
11. Rutledge, op.cit., p.140.
12. ibid., p.148.
13. Oscar Laighton *Ninety Years at the Isles of Shoals* (Boston, Mass.: Star Island Corporation, 1971), p.145.
14. ibid., pp.145–6.
15. ibid.
16. Fredrick T. McGill, Jr., and Virginia F. McGill, *Something Like a Star* (Boston, Mass.: Star Island Corporation, 1989), p.5.
17. Rutledge, op.cit., p.141.
18. ibid., p.141.
19. ibid., p.142.
20. McGill and McGill, op.cit., p.51.

Chapter 13 Yankee Clippers on the Piscataqua

1. Louis L'Amour, *The Warrior's Path* (New York: Bantam Books, 1980), p.130.
2. *Sea History* 64, winter 1992/3, pp.12–19. Today, one can go by boat across New York harbor to the Witte scrapyard on the Arthur Kill in Staten Island, and see an actual steamboat graveyard. *Steamboat Bill*, 199, Fall 1991, p.217.
3. Raymond A. Brighton, *Tallships of the Piscataqua, 1830–1877* (Portsmouth, N.H.: Peter E. Randall, 1989).
4. ibid., p.352.

Chapter 14 Dynamite, Prisons, and Life Between the Wars

1. John P. Adams, *Drowned Valley, the Piscataqua River Basin* (Hanover, N.H.: University Press of New England, 1976), p.14.
2. Fifty tons is equivalent to fifty 2,000 lb bombs used by the air force during the war with Iraq.
3. Adams, op.cit., p.16.
4. Ibid., p.14.
5. Peter E. Randall, *There Are No Victors Here* (Portsmouth, N.H.: Peter E. Randall, 1985), p.92.
6. Adams, op.cit., p.11.
7. ibid., p.4.
8. Remarks by Colonel W.E. Domina, USMC, 21 January 1971.
9. ibid.
10. ibid.
11. Adams, op.cit., pp.250–5.
12. ibid., pp. 257ff.

Chapter 15 Portsmouth and the Submarine

1. Richard E. Winslow, *Portsmouth-built* (Portsmouth, N.H.: Peter E. Randall, 1985), p.24.
2. ibid., p.25.
3. In 1915, this building was also used by a German contractor to inflate their blimps or dirigibles. The building was large enough for both the blimp and the *L-8*.
4. Winslow, op.cit., pp.28–9.
5. ibid., p.41.
6. ibid., p.45.

7. ibid., p.51.
8. ibid., p.100.
9. ibid., p.65.
10. Nat A. Barrows, *Blow All Ballast!* (New York: Dodd, Mead, 1940), pp.49–51.
11. *A History of Portsmouth Naval Shipyard*, p.58.
12. This is a direct quotation from an unknown passenger aboard the *Thomas Laighton*, 1990.
13. Winslow, op.cit., p.105.
14. ibid., p.109.
15. *A History of PSNY*, p.59.
16. Winslow, op.cit., p.93.
17. John T. Mason, Jr., *The Atlantic War Remembered* (Annapolis, Md.: Naval Institute Press, 1990), p.137.
18. Winslow, op.cit., p.134.
19. ibid., p.138.
20. ibid., p.148.
21. ibid., p.150.
22. ibid., p.158.
23. ibid., p.161. When USS *Thresher* passed by the Isles of Shoals on her last trip, my Dad was alone on Star Island and watched her sail to the horizon. He was possibly the last non-affiliated civilian ever to see the submarine before her tragic loss.
24. ibid., p.163.
25. ibid., pp.172–3.
26. Winslow, op. cit., p. 165.

Chapter 16 The Conference Years and a Natural History Saved

1. Frederick T. McGill, Jr. and Virginia F. McGill, *Something Like a Star* (Boston, Mass.: Star Island Corportaion, 1989), pp.199–201.
2. Lyman V. Rutledge, *Ten Miles Out* (Boston, Mass.: Isles of Shoals Unitarian Assoc., 1964), p.31.
3. SML today is the largest undergraduate marine science field study center in North America, enrolling over 3,500 students since it began.
4. Rutledge, op.cit., p.33.
5. John M. Kingsbury, *Oil and Water* (Ithaca, N.Y.: Shoals Marine Laboratory, 1975), p.11.
6. ibid., p.26.

Chapter 17 Generations

1. Frederick T. McGill, Jr. and Virginia F. McGill, *Something Like a Star* (Boston, Mass.: Star Island Corporation, 1989), p.78.
2. Emily Dickinson, *No. 1176*, st. 1.
3. T.S. Eliot, "The Dry Salvages", *Four Quartets*, I, 24.

BIBLIOGRAPHY

Adams, John P. *Drowned Valley*. Hanover, N.H.: University Press of New England, 1976.

Adams, John P. *The Piscataqua River Gundalow*. Durham, N.H.: private printing, 1982.

Ashley, Maurice. *The Battle of Naseby, and the Fall of King Charles I*. Stroud, England: Alan Sutton, 1992.

Bardwell, John D. *The Diary of the Portsmouth, Kittery and York Electric Railroad*. Portsmouth, N.H.: Peter E. Randall, 1986.

Barrows, Nat A. *Blow All Ballast!* New York: Dodd, Mead, 1940.

Brewster, Charles W. *Rambles about Portsmouth*, first series. Somersworth, N.H.: New Hampshire Publishing Company, 1971. From 1873 edn.

Brighton, Raymond A. *They came to Fish*. Dover, N.H.: Randall/Winebaum Enterprises, 1979.

Brighton, Raymond A. *Tallships of the Piscataqua, 1830–1877*. Portsmouth, N.H.: Peter E. Randall, 1989.

Brighton, Raymond A. *Port of Portsmouth Ships and the Cotton Trade*. Portsmouth, N.H.: Peter E. Randall, 1986.

Brighton, Raymond A. *Clippers of the Port of Portsmouth, and the Men Who Built Them*. Portsmouth, N.H.: Peter E. Randall, 1985.

Brighton, Raymond A. *The Checkered Career of Tobias Lear*. Portsmouth, N.H.: Peter E. Randall, 1985.

Brighton, Raymond A. *The Prescott Story*. Portsmouth, N.H.: Peter E. Randall, 1982.

Candee, Richard M. *Atlantic Heights, A World War I Shipbuilder's Community*. Portsmouth, N.H.: Peter E. Randall, 1985.

Chapelle, Howard I. *The History of American Sailing Ships*. New York: W. W. Norton, 1935.

Clark, Charles E. *The Eastern Frontier, 1610–1763*. Hanover, NH: University Press of New England, 1983.

Chapelle, Howard I. *The History of the American Sailing Navy*. New York: W.W. Norton, 1949.

Coffin, Robert P. *Kennebec, Cradle of Americans*. Camden, Maine: Down East Enterprises, 1965. From 1937 edn.

Drake, Samuel Adams. *Nooks and Corners of the New England Coast*. New York: Harper, 1875.

Durant, Will and Durant, Ariel. *The Age of Napoleon*. New York: Simon & Schuster, 1975.

Ellsberg, Commander Edward. *Captain Paul*. New York: Dodd, Mead, 1941.

F., A. and L., R., ed. *Letters of Celia Thaxter*, ed. by her friends. Boston, Mass.: Houghton, Mifflin, 1895.

Garvin, James L. *Historic Portsmouth*, early photographs from the collections of Strawbery Banke, Inc. Somersworth, N.H.: New Hampshire Publishing Company, 1974.

Hammond, Otis Grant. *Reverend John Tucke, 1702–1773*. New Hampshire Historical Society, 1914.

Jenness, John S. *The Isles of Shoals*. Cambridge, Mass.: Riverside Press, 1875.

Kingsbury, John M. *Here's How We'll Do it*. Ithaca, N.Y.: Bullbrier Press, 1991.

Laighton, Oscar. *Ninety Years at the Isles of Shoals*. Boston, Mass.: Star Island Corporation, 1971.

Mason, John T., Jr., *The Atlantic War Remembered*. Annapolis, Md.: Naval Institute Press, 1990.

McGill, Frederick T., Jr., and McGill, Virginia F. *Something Like a Star*. Boston, Mass.: Star Island Corporation, 1989.

McGill, Fredrick T., Jr., *Letters to Celia*. Boston, Mass.: Star Island Corporation, 1972.

Openo, Woodard D. *Tugboats on the Piscataqua, A Brief History of Towing on One of America's Toughest Rivers*. Portsmouth, N.H.: Peter E. Randall, 1992.

Oppel, Frank, ed. *Tales of the New England Coast*. Secaucus, N.J.: Book Sales, Inc., 1985.

Otis, James. *The Life of John Paul Jones*. New York: A. L. Burt, 1900.

Page, Elwin L. *George Washington in New Hampshire*. Portsmouth, N.H.: Peter E. Randall, 1932.

Phillips-Birt, Douglas. *A History of Seamanship*. Garden City, N.Y.: Doubleday, 1971.

Randall, Peter E. *There Are No Victors Here, A Local Perspective on the Treaty of Portsmouth*. Portsmouth, N.H.: Peter E. Randall, 1985.

Randall, Peter E. *Portsmouth and the Piscataqua*. Camden, Maine: Down East Books, 1982.

Randall, Peter E. *All Creations and the Isles of Shoals*. Camden, Maine: Down East Books, 1980.

Ritchie, Robert C. *Captain Kidd, and the War against the Pirates*. Cambridge, Mass.: Harvard University Press, 1986.

Rogers, Fred Blackburn. *Montgomery and The Portsmouth*. Portsmouth, N.H.: Peter E. Randall, 1990.

Rutledge, Lyman V. *Ten Miles Out*. Boston, Mass.: Isles of Shoals Unitarian Assoc., 1964.

Rutledge, Lyman V. *The Isles of Shoals in Lore and Legend*. Boston, Mass.: Star Island Corporation, 1965.

Sargent, Jean A. and Mansur, Ina B. *Babb Families of New England*. Laurel, Md: privately printed, 1987.

Scott, Jack Denton. *The Gulls of Smuttynose Island*. New York: G. P. Putnam, 1977.

Smith, Yvonne Brault. *John Haley Bellamy, Carver of Eagles*. Portsmouth, N.H.: Peter E. Randall, 1982.

Stackpole, Everett S. *History of New Hampshire, vol. I*. New York: American Historical Society, 1916.

Street, James. *The Revolutionary War*. New York: Dial Press, 1954.

Thaxter, Celia. *Among the Isles of Shoals*. Hyannis, Mass.: Wake-Brook House, 1873.

Thaxter, Celia. *An Island Garden*. Bowie, Md.: Heritage Books, 1978, 1894.

Thaxter, Celia. *The Heavenly Guest*, ed. O. Laighton. Andover, Mass.: Smith & Coutts, 1935.

Thaxter, Rosamond. *Sandpiper, The Life and Letters of Celia Thaxter*. Portsmouth, N.H.: Peter E. Randall, 1963.

Thompson, Ralph E. and Mathew, R. *The First Yankee*. Salem, Oreg.: privately printed, 1979. Reprinted by the Thompson Island Educational Center, Boston.

Tuchman, Barbara W. *The First Salute*. New York: Alfred A. Knopf, 1988.

Vallier, Jane E. *Poet on Demand, The Life, Letters and Works of Celia Thaxter*. Camden, Maine: Down East Books, 1982.

Whitehouse, Robert A. and Beaudoin, Cathleen C. *Port of Dover, Two Centuries of Shipping on the Cocheco*. Portsmouth, N.H.: Peter E. Randall, 1988.

Winslow, Ola E. *Portsmouth: The Life of a Town*. New York: Macmillan, 1966.

Winslow, Richard E., III. *Portsmouth-Built: Submarines of the Portsmouth Naval Shipyard*. Portsmouth, N.H.: Peter E. Randall, 1985.

Winslow, Richard E., III. *The Piscataqua Gundalow: Workhorse for a Tidal Basin Empire*. Portsmouth, N.H.: Peter E. Randall, 1983.

Winslow, Richard E., III. *"Wealth and Honor," Portsmouth During the Golden Age of Privateering, 1775–1815*. Portsmouth, N.H.: Peter E. Randall, 1988.

OTHER READINGS

Books

A Stern and Lovely Scene, A Visual History of the Isles of Shoals. Durham, N.H.: University Art Galleries, University of New Hampshire Press, 1978.

Harper's New Monthly Magazine, vol. 44, June to November 1874. New York: Harper Brothers, 1874.

Strawbery Banke, Portsmouth, New Hampshire, Official Guidebook. Printed for Strawbery Banke, Inc., 1982.

Dissertations

Domina, Colonel W.E. "Remarks" before Piscataqua History Club. Portsmouth, N.H., 21 January 1971.

Magazines

Atlantic Monthly, 35, "A Memorable Murder," by Celia Thaxter, May 1875.

Sea History, #64. National Maritime Historical Society, winter 1992-3.

Steamboat Bill, #199, fall 1991.

Booklets

Bonfanti, Leo. *Biographies and Legends of the New England Indians*, vol. 1. Wakefield, Mass.: Pride Publications, 1968.

Borror, Arthur C. *Breeding Birds of the Isles of Shoals*. Ithaca, N.Y.: Shoals Marine Laboratory, 1980.

Cahill, Robert Ellis. *New England's Pirates and Lost Treasures.* Peabody, Mass.: Chandler-Smith, 1987.

Cahill, Robert Ellis. *New England's Riotous Revolution.* Peabody, Mass.: Chandler-Smith, 1987.

Fowler-Billings, Katherine. *Geology of the Isles of Shoals.* Concord, N.H.: State of New Hampshire Department of Resources and Economic Development, 1977.

Howard, Richard A. *Flowers of Star Island, The Isles of Shoals.* Jamaica Plains, Mass.: Arnold Arboretum, 1968.

Kingsbury, John M. *Oil and Water, The New Hampshire Story.* Ithaca, N.Y.: Shoals Marine Laboratory, 1975.

Portsmouth 350, 1623–1973, Commemorative volume. Committee Chairman: Betty Nelson. Portsmouth, N.H.: Ranger, 1973.

Rutledge, Lyman V. *Moonlight Murder at Smuttynose.* Boston, Mass.: Star King Press, 1958.

U.S. Navy, *Cradle of American Shipbuilding,* Portsmouth Naval Shipyard. Library of Congress LC78–600146.

Wilson, Forbes K. *Observations on Two Great Storms,* 1978. York, Maine: privately printed, 1978.

Newspapers

Portsmouth Chronicle

Porsmouth Herald

Portsmouth Journal

INDEX

Numbers in italic indicate illustrations

THE PORTRAICTUER OF CAPTAYNE IOHN SMITH ADMIRALL OF NEW ENGLAND
These are the Lines that shew thy Face; but those
That shew thy Grace and Glory, brighter bee:
Thy Faire-Discoueries and Fowle-Overthrowes
Of Salvages, much Civilliz'd by thee
Best shew thy Spirit; and to it Glory Wyn;
So, thou art Brasse without, but Golde within
If so; in Brasse (too soft Smiths Acts to beare)
I fix thy Fame, to make Brasse Steele out weare.
Thine, as thou art Virtues
John Davies. Heref:
The most remarqueable
by the high and mighty
Ipswich
Snadoun hill
Boston
Hull
Poynt Davies
Schooters
Sandwich
Dartmouth
SouthHampton
P. Wynthorp
Cape ANNA
Barstable
Bristow
Salem
Talbotts Bay
Fawmouth
Charles Towne
Frauncis Ile
The River CHARLES
Charlton
Claiborne Ils.
P. Saltonstale
London
Oxford
Poynt Sutliff
Poynt Gorge
Cape JAMES
NEW Plimouth
P. Standish

D
HONY SOIT QVI MAL Y PENSE
Aborden
Gunnells Ils
Lowmonds
Norwich
St John Towne
The River forth
Fines Ils
Pembrocks Bay
Martins Ile
Gervards Ils
Hoghton Ils
Barty Ils
Willowby Ils
Paynes Ils
A Scale of Leagues
2
4
6
8
10
44 1/2
44
43 1/2
42